SAINTS, SLAVES, AND BLACKS

Contributions to the Study of Religion
Series Editor: Henry W. Bowden

Private Churches and Public Money: Church-Government
Fiscal Relations
Paul J. Weber and Dennis A. Gilbert

A Cultural History of Religion in America
James G. Moseley

Religious Mythology and the Art of War: Comparative
Religious Symbolisms of Military Violence
James A. Aho

SAINTS, SLAVES, AND BLACKS

The Changing Place of Black People Within Mormonism

NEWELL G. BRINGHURST

Contributions to the Study of Religion, Number 4

Greenwood Press
Westport, Connecticut • London, England

Library of Congress Cataloging in Publication Data

Bringhurst, Newell G.
    Saints, slaves, and Blacks.

    (Contributions to the study of religion, ISSN 0196-
7053; no.4)
    Bibliography: p.
    Includes index.
    1. Church and race relations—Mormon Church—History.
2. Afro-American Mormons.   3.   Melchizedek Priesthood
(Mormon Church)   I. Title.   II. Series.
BX8643.A35B74   261.8'34896073   81-1093
ISBN 0-313-22752-7 (lib. bdg.)   AACR2

Library of Congress Catalog Card Number: 81-1093
ISBN: 0-313-22752-7
ISSN: 0196-7053

First published in 1981

Greenwood Press
A division of Congressional Information Service, Inc.
88 Post Road West, Westport, Connecticut 06881

Printed in the United States of America

10 9 8 7 6 5 4 3 2 1

To the two most important
women in my life
my wife
Mary Ann
and
my daughter
Laura

Contents

Tables

Foreword

Mormonism emerged in the nineteenth century as one of the few religious expressions in American culture with no antecedents anywhere else. It quickly spread to Europe and elsewhere, but the new faith owed little to those churches and confessions that were originally brought to North America from other continents. Yet, like all religious expressions, Mormonism reflected the historical conditions in which it arose and took distinctive shape. Alongside their restorationist hopes, perfectionist aspirations, and millennialist dreams, faithful Mormons embodied social attitudes common to the culture that nurtured them. One of these subsidiary viewpoints was prejudice toward black people, and this volume provides detailed analysis of that attitude over the course of approximately 150 years.

Professor Bringhurst provides us with a case study of how cultural influences are often absorbed by religious groups and then become perpetuated as part of the sacred tradition. Using Mormon racial discrimination as a specific example, he shows how an early social attitude can be codified as part of religious behavior itself and then survive long after the demise of conditions that initially generated it. Bringhurst carefully elucidates how early Mormon doctrine correlated ideas of sin, depravity, and dark-skinned peoples. He shows why men saw ordination to the priesthood and women saw marriage to men ordained to the priesthood as crucial elements in the salvation process. Then with a depth and breadth that surpasses other works in this field, Bringhurst explains why blacks, stemming from a race defined by doctrine to be inferior, could not participate fully in the most sacred aspects of Mormon liturgy. To be sure, the Church of Jesus Christ of Latter-day Saints was a social minority itself, and siege mentality might have contributed to its exclusionist tactics. But its fundamental doctrine about perpetual growth through eternity fed fears of racial intermarriage. Once established, those attitudes condoned a century of segregation by giving it sacramental importance. It was not until 1978 that new doctrine opened up avenues for racial parity within the church.

How do early prejudices and long-standing discriminatory practices change? While holding to transcendental affirmations on one level, religions reflect their social origins, and they mirror later paradigmatic changes as well. In this volume Professor Bringhurst furnishes a valuable chronicle of how one religious institution has responded to culture change. He argues that denial of the priesthood to blacks does not go unerringly back to Joseph Smith, the prophet and founder of Mormonism. He shows further that there was room in Smith's revelations to make reversal of the policy of exclusion possible. Still, the most important factors have been Mormon social and institutional growth in an American society that became increasingly concerned about justice for blacks in this century. A vigorous foreign missions program has made church leaders aware of converts around the world too; people of every racial hue now accept Mormon tenets. This pluralism in a microcosm contributed materially to the life of a church whose ideas have always benefited from promptings in its larger cultural setting. Bringhurst's basic achievement is to reconstruct a history of important racial attitudes in the Church of Jesus Christ of Latter-day Saints, offering a test case for similar studies of ideological change in other American denominations.

Henry Bowden

Preface

This study had its genesis in the sociogeographic environment of my youth and in the atmosphere of turbulence and confrontation which prevailed during the 1960s. Growing up in Utah, the headquarters of the Church of Jesus Christ of Latter-day Saints (Mormons), I was intrigued and somewhat perplexed by the now-defunct church practice that excluded blacks from the Mormon priesthood—a lay-oriented organization composed of virtually all male members of the church over twelve years of age. My interest in this issue intensified as the Mormons came under increased fire from activist groups and individuals during the late 1960s. On one occasion the Utah National Guard (of which I was a member) was called out in response to civil rights protestors demonstrating in front of the Latter-day Saints church headquarters in Salt Lake City.

I decided to examine Mormon-black relations in terms of their historical origins and development. This seemed like a timely topic in light of continuing protests against the Mormon church and its practice of black priesthood denial, which reached a fever pitch by the late 1960s and early 1970s. Black athletes of various universities refused to participate in sports contests with Mormon-owned and operated Brigham Young University. A number of universities, including Stanford, San Jose State, and the University of Washington even went so far as to terminate all future athletic competition with Brigham Young University. It was during this period of tension that my study took shape.

Suddenly and unexpectedly in June 1978, Latter-day Saint officials announced the repeal of their exclusionary practice of black priesthood denial. In the light of this dramatic change, I reexamined some of my previous assumptions revising, somewhat, my study by considering not only the evolution of Mormon antiblack attitudes and practices, which predominated throughout the course of Latter-day Saint history, but also those positive Mormon concepts of Christian universalism, which existed from Mormonism's earliest days. These universalistic concepts ultimately paved the way for the repeal of black priesthood denial and have been a primary impetus for the current extraordinary appeal of Mormonism in nonwhite parts of the world, including black Africa.

Acknowledgments

Over the ten-year period from 1970 to 1980, during which this study slowly assumed its final form, I received invaluable help from a large number of individuals and several institutions. Without this help, this study would not have been possible.

Larry Nielson, of El Toro, California, a personal friend and fellow scholar concerned about the status of blacks within his church, encouraged me to probe the controversial history of Mormon-black relations. W. Turrentine Jackson, Daniel Calhoun, and Roland Marchand of the University of California, Davis, further encouraged me and gave of their time and knowledge. Vera Loomis and her staff in Interlibrary Loan at the University of California, Davis, aided me in securing a large number of monographs and early Latter-day Saint newspapers and periodicals, thus saving me the time and expense of extensive travel.

I am deeply indebted to the staff of the Historical Department of the Church of Jesus Christ of Latter-day Saints for allowing me access to the diaries and correspondence of a number of important early Latter-day Saints. James Kimball, William G. Hartley, Ronald K. Esplin, Leonard J. Arrington, Davis Bitton, Jeffery O. Johnson, and Ronald Walker were particularly helpful in bringing to my attention certain documents and information contained in the LDS Church Archives. Noal Barton of the LDS Church Genealogical Society also provided valuable information on a number of early Mormon blacks.

Special thanks goes to Lester E. Bush, Jr., of Gaithersburg, Maryland, whose own ground-breaking work on the Mormon-black issue provided a basic framework and a high standard against which to measure my own work. In addition, over the past four years Dr. Bush has unselfishly shared with me his own research materials. Finally, he read three preliminary drafts of my study and offered numerous suggestions that helped me to avoid a number of embarrassing errors.

Other scholars have read all or part of my work, providing additional information, offering suggestions, and giving me the benefit of their knowledge. These include Mario S. DePillis and Leone Stein of the University of Massachusetts; Sterling M. McMurrin, Ronald G. Coleman, Larry Gerlach, and Everett L. Cooley of the University of Utah; Marvin Hill, Thomas G. Alexander, and James B. Allen of Brigham Young University; Klaus Hansen, of Queens College, Ontario, Canada; the late Fawn Brodie, University of California, Los Angeles; Jan Shipps, Indiana University-Purdue University, Indianapolis; Gail Casterline and Linda Evans of the Chicago Historical Society; Stanford Layton and Jay Haymond of the Utah State Historical Society; Armand Mauss, Washington State University; William D. Russell, Graceland College; H. Michael Marquardt of Sandy, Utah; Wesley P. Walters, of Marissa, Illinois; Merton Dillon, Ohio State University; F. Ross Peterson, Utah State University; Donald J. Pisani, Texas A & M University, Lawrence B. Lee, San Jose State University; and Reja-E Busailah of Indiana University at Kokomo.

I express appreciation to my former colleagues and the staff at Indiana University at Kokomo who encouraged me in this project. Special thanks goes to Karla Runyon and Rita Martin for their invaluable help in typing the manuscript. Indiana University provided financial support through a Grant-in-Aid during the summer of 1978 and a Summer Faculty Fellowship in 1979, which facilitated my research and writing.

Finally this study was greatly aided by the support of my immediate family. My father and brother and their wives gave of their hospitality in providing lodging during the summers of 1977, 1978, and 1979, as I completed my research in Salt Lake City. Most important, I cannot adequately express my deep appreciation to my wife Mary Ann and daughter, Laura, to whom this book is dedicated. Their help and encouragement facilitated this project. Mary Ann aided me in my basic research and has served as an invaluable critic and advisor during the ten long years it took to finish this study. All this help notwithstanding, I alone assume full responsibility for this work.

Introduction

In June 1978, the Church of Jesus Christ of Latter-day Saints (Mormons) abandoned its controversial practice of denying black males offices within its lay priesthood—an organization consisting of virtually all male Mormons, ages twelve and over. According to the official church announcement, this decision was arrived at following long deliberations with church leaders "supplicating the Lord for divine guidance." To many observers this change was long overdue. While virtually all major American religious denominations had, for some time, eschewed race as a criteria for determining the position of their individual members, the Mormons had tenaciously upheld black priesthood denial despite intense criticism.

This tenacity dramatizes a fundamental fact—the deep historical roots of Mormon black priesthood denial as part of a larger network of Latter-day Saint racist attitudes and practices. By Mormon racism, I mean those ideas and practices promoted by Latter-day Saint spokesmen affirming the basic racial inferiority of all nonwhites, while upholding white racial superiority. These ideas, which were evident in the earliest Mormon writings, intensified gradually, evolving into actions specifically directed against black people. These, in turn, were codified as Mormon dogma during the nineteenth century.

This book has as its main theme changing Mormon attitudes and practices toward black people as they evolved during the period from 1820 to 1980. It traces the initial articulation of ideas emphasizing nonwhite racial inferiority as outlined in Joseph Smith's writings, particularly his

Book of Mormon, published in 1830, and his *Pearl of Great Price,* completed in 1842 (but not published as a book until 1851). By the late 1840s, Smith's ideas, as well as those of other Mormon leaders, evolved into actual practices directed against black people. These practices included black priesthood denial and prohibitions on black participation in certain sacred temple ordinances. Such ideas and practices remained in force for over 100 years. It was not until the post-World War II period that Latter-day Saint leaders began to move away from their ideas of black racial inferiority; this paved the way for the abandonment of black priesthood denial in June 1978.

The emergence of Mormon theories and practices directed against blacks took place within the context of a nineteenth-century American society agitated by the issues of slavery, race, and abolition. Like other Americans, the Mormons were forced to confront these issues despite their efforts to divorce themselves from these and all other secular issues that would interfere with their attempts to isolate themselves as they prepared for the millennium and Second Coming. In response to pressures both within and outside Mormonism, the church adopted attitudes that were both antislavery and antiabolitionist. Although the Saints generally rejected slavery for themselves and disapproved of its existence among slaveholding southerners, they were hostile toward those who actively campaigned to end it. In fact, Mormon opposition to abolition became dogma when the church incorporated an antiabolitionist statement into their *Doctrine and Covenants*—a set of Joseph Smith's writings canonized as church scripture in 1835. A Mormon antiabolitionist stand was prompted by the external pressures imposed by an American society that generally rejected both the tactics and aims of the abolitionists. Mormon dislike for abolition was also encouraged by an acceptance of those racist concepts so prevalent in nineteenth-century America. Joseph Smith and other Mormon leaders found these concepts particularly acceptable in light of their lower-middle-class socioeconomic origins. By the same token, church racist beliefs were reinforced by a Mormon willingness to uphold their antiabolitionist position throughout the antebellum period. In fact, Mormon racist concepts and practices became so strong that they survived into the post-Civil War period, despite the abolition of slavery. These ideas and practices conformed to the prevailing racial attitudes and practices of a larger American society that condoned racial segregation and upheld the subordinate status of blacks during the late nineteenth and early twentieth centuries. The Mormons practiced their own form of racial segregation by avoiding all missionary contact with blacks both within the United States and abroad, even as they expanded such activities among various other racial-ethnic groups. Not until recently, following the emergence of Mormonism as a major American and indeed as a worldwide religion, have Latter-day Saint leaders adjusted their racial ideas and doctrines to conform to those of a contemporary society more enlightened about race and the status of dark-skinned peoples.

The changes in Mormon attitudes and practices toward black people fills a unique chapter in American religious history. Like many other religious denominations, the Mormons shared those racist ideas prevalent in American society during the nineteenth and early twentieth centuries. The Mormons incorporated these attitudes and practices into the super-structure of their ideology and doctrine as it was being developed by Joseph Smith and other church leaders during Mormonism's formative years. The Mormons, in codifying racist concepts as doctrine, stood in contrast to most major American religious denominations, such as the Methodists, Baptists, and Presbyterians, whose theology had evolved to the point that doctrinal codification was unnecessary. The Mormons also differed from certain indigenous religious groups such as the Camp-bellites (Disciples of Christ), the Millerites (Seventh-day Adventists), Christian Scientists, and Jehovah's Witnesses who, unlike the Saints, avoided race as a central theme in their doctrinal writings. As a result, when the movement for black rights gathered force by the mid-twentieth century, many denominations were able to endorse it, whereas Latter-day Saint leaders stubbornly clung to certain racist ideas and practices that they perceived as part of Mormon dogma. Therefore, the June 1978 announcement admitting blacks to the Mormon priesthood came as a surprise, particularly to critical non-Mormon observers, both white and black.

SAINTS, SLAVES, AND BLACKS

1 | Initial Latter-day Saint Racist and Antislavery Attitudes, 1820-1830

> And he . . . caused . . . a sore cursing . . . to come upon them because of their iniquity . . . the Lord God did cause a skin of blackness to come upon them.
>
> *Book of Mormon,* 2 Nephi 5:21

> It is against the law of our brethren . . . that there should be any slaves among them.
>
> *Book of Mormon,* Alma 27:9

Fourteen-year-old Joseph Smith, like so many other residents of the "Burned-over District" of New York State, was caught up in the religious excitement of the Second Great Awakening during the early 1820s.[1] Young Smith, according to his own recollections, was concerned about the salvation of his soul and confused as to the correct source of religious authority among the various local denominations competing for his allegiance. In search of answers to these problems Smith, on a spring day in 1820, retired to pray in a grove near the family farm house at Palmyra, New York. The alleged result of Smith's fervent praying was the visit of two supernatural personages—God the Father and his son Jesus Christ. According to Smith, these two divine visitors assured the young farmboy that his sins were forgiven and told him that none of the existing denominations represented the correct source of divine authority. Finally, Smith was told to await further instructions concerning this matter. Three years later, he was allegedly visited by another supernatural being—this

time an angel by the name of Moroni, who revealed to Smith the existence
of a set of gold plates located in a hillside near his home. Under divine
guidance, Smith took possession of the plates in 1827. These plates, according to Mormon belief, contained the sacred writings of an ancient American civilization. With the aid of a set of seer stones, known as the Urim
and Thummin, Smith allegedly "translated" these ancient writings into
the *Book of Mormon,* a task completed in 1830. In that same year this
book was published and canonized as holy scripture by Smith's followers
after the establishment of the Mormon church in 1830.[2]

Joseph Smith's book detailed the rise and fall of an ancient American
civilization descended from a group of Israelites who migrated from the
Holy Land to the New World about 600 B.C. Initially led by a man named
Nephi, these "Nephites," as they came to be known, built up a flourishing
civilization on the North and South American continents, which lasted
until A.D. 400.

Smith's account of these ancient Americans incorporated racist concepts
of nonwhite racial inferiority as contrasted with white racial superiority.
Mormon racism was particularly evident in those *Book of Mormon* passages
outlining the conflicts and divisions plaguing the Nephite nation. These
people, under the wise leadership of Nephi, built up a complex, urban
society as God's chosen people. But Nephi's two brothers Laman and
Lemuel challenged Nephi's authority. In a brief skirmish, the two dis-
obedient brothers were defeated. Undaunted, they led a group of dissident
Nephites into the wilderness, where they became a nomadic people.[3] These
rebels rejected correct Nephite religious principles and so were "cut off
from the presence of the Lord."[4] Moreover, Laman, Lemuel, and their
followers were cursed with a "skin of blackness" by "the Lord God."[5]
Thereafter they were known as Lamanites, "a dark, and loathsome, and
filthy people full of idleness and all manner of abomination."[6] Smith also
described another group of dissidents who clashed with the Nephites, the
Amlicites. As a sign of their rebellion, they painted red marks on their
foreheads. In time the Amlicites apparently became a dark-skinned people
like the Lamanites.[7] A third group, the Zoramites, as the Lamanites and
Amlicites, opposed the Nephites and lived apart from them. They eventually became a dark-skinned people and were absorbed by the Lamanite nation.[8] These three nations, along with other tribes and individuals who
from time to time dissented from the Nephites, were collectively known

as Lamanites.[9] On various occasions these dark-skinned opponents attacked and fought against the righteous Nephites. The Nephites usually prevailed over their evil, dark-skinned foes.

In time, however, even the light-skinned, civilized Nephites became unrighteous. A portion of these Nephites mixed with the Lamanites, "becoming wicked, wild and ferocious, yea, even becoming Lamanites," presumably acquiring a dark skin emblematic of their wickedness and evil.[10] The rest of the Nephite nation also became unrighteous and were ultimately wiped out in a series of bloody wars fought among themselves and with their dark-skinned neighbors. Smith maintained that a significant portion of the degenerate, dark-skinned Lamanites survived this warfare, becoming in time,

> a dark, filthy, and a loathsome people, beyond the description of that which ever hath been amongst us, yea, even that which hath been among the Lamanites and this because of their unbelief and idolatry.[11]

According to Mormon theology, the present-day Indians are considered the descendants of these dark-skinned survivors.[12]

Joseph Smith's racist ideas appear to have been the product of an alienated boyhood, in which he was exposed to the unsettled conditions of a lower-middle-class environment.[13] The Smith family in the years prior to Joseph's birth in 1805 and during his formative years led a "nomadic existence." By the time Joseph Jr. was eleven, the Smiths had lived in nine different communities.[14] These numerous moves resulted from the efforts of Joseph Smith, Sr., to provide for his family. After repeatedly failing to eke out a living as a farmer in various parts of New England and failing as a merchant, the elder Smith in 1816 moved his family to Palmyra, New York. Here, he again turned to farming and was somewhat more successful. But even in Palmyra members of the Smith family, including young Joseph, had to work outside the home to supplement the family's meager income. This situation seems to have created anxiety in the minds of young Joseph and his mother Lucy Mack about the family's social status. This anxiety was further intensified by the social ostracism experienced by the Smith family at the hands of their more affluent neighbors. The Smiths were looked down upon because of their lower-middle-class status and were thus isolated socially.[15] In addition, the family was internally divided by conflicting religious views. Lucy Mack, along with two sons and one daughter, joined the Presbyterian Church. Other family members held back, including young Joseph and his father. The elder Smith, in fact, clung tenaciously to his mystical Universalist beliefs.[16] These family difficulties and conflicts bothered young Joseph and helped to make him "an alienated youth the product of an alienated family."[17] Smith's alienation was further exacerbated by the religious fervor of the Second Great Awakening in which a number of denominations competed for Smith's allegiance.[18]

It was this confusion and conflict that apparently caused Smith to seek divine guidance and to write the *Book of Mormon*, completed in 1830. According to Smith, this work contained answers to those questions that had troubled him during the early 1820s, along with the correct religious principles to be followed by his Mormon community of true believers.

Smith's book also outlined several concepts emphasizing his role as a religious leader. Thus, Smith claimed to be a member of the "chosen race" by virtue of his "descent" from the ancient Tribe of Joseph—one of the Chosen Tribes of Israel. He also claimed powers as a "Prophet, Seer, and Revelator."[19] By assuming such religious authority, Smith was able to cope with anxieties and self-doubts resulting from his lower-middle-class socioeconomic background.

The *Book of Mormon* also reflected the racial attitudes of a larger nineteenth-century American society that discriminated against non-white groups. Contemporary Americans were particularly interested in the Indians, the primary group considered in Smith's book. Although the Indian issue had involved white Americans since colonial times, it took on new meaning during the 1820s. For the first time, the federal government dealt with the "Indian problem" in a comprehensive fashion, establishing the Bureau of Indian Affairs, which implemented Andrew Jackson's vigorous Indian removal policy during the late 1820s. Interest in the Indian was particularly evident in Joseph Smith's upstate New York environment. Tales describing the ancestors of the contemporary Indian were especially popular, in part because of the close proximity of numerous Indian burial grounds.[20] Residents were fascinated by stories concerning the racial-ethnic origins of the American Indian. A number of authors, the most prominent being Ethan Smith, suggested that the Indians were descended from the Israelites—a concept embraced by Joseph Smith in the *Book of Mormon.*[21]

Through his book, Smith also mirrored contemporary American anxieties over the impending millennium. Nineteenth-century Americans expected an apocalyptic struggle between the forces of good and evil as a prelude to the millennium and Second Coming.[22] In his book, Joseph Smith painted this millennialistic struggle in contrasting racial images of black and white.[23] The Lamanites, Amlicites, and Zoramites as dark-skinned "eschatological enemies" stood in sharp contrast to the righteous light-skinned Nephites. The latter group served as an example of those who were awaiting the millennium. The wicked Lamanites, on the other hand, symbolized the corrupt society to be avoided in preparing for the millennium. As the path of this millennium was long, narrow, and hazardous, the curse of a dark skin, like that placed upon the Lamanites, Amlicites, and Zoramites, stood as a potent millennialistic warning for those who might waver. Those Nephites who misbehaved were threatened with the curse of a dark skin. Such people would retrogress racially—becoming even darker than the Lamanites—if they persisted in their wicked ways.[24] Others who fought against God's chosen people were also threatened with a "mark" or a "dark skin."[25] Finally, Joseph Smith issued the ultimate millennialistic threat: that those who rejected the true faith, as had the Nephites, could be exterminated if they persisted in their unrighteous behavior.[26] The millennialistic symbol was inescapable. Evil as represented by a dark skin stood as the racial counterimage to be avoided by God's chosen people as they prepared for the millennium.[27]

Yet, despite its millennialistic racist concepts, Joseph Smith's work held out hope for its dark-skinned counterfigures. The process of racial degeneration could be reversed, given the right conditions. The curse of a dark skin and savage behavior was lifted from those Lamanites who accepted the true faith and allowed themselves to be inspired by the righteous example of the fair-skinned Nephites.[28] Joseph Smith promised contemporary American Indians that if they became "civilized" and adopted the true faith they would lose "their scales of darkness" and become "a white and delightsome people."[29]

Moreover, the *Book of Mormon*, like the New Testament, promoted universal Christian salvation for all mankind, without regard to race, color, or bondage. The atonement of Christ was "infinite for all mankind," with Christ making himself manifest "unto every nation, kindred, tongue and people."[30] In one of its most famous passages, the *Book of Mormon* declared that the Lord "denieth none that came unto him, black and white, bond and free, male and female, and he remembereth the heathen: and all are alike unto God, both Jew and Gentile."[31] According to Mormon scripture the Nephites made a special effort to preach to all, "both old and young, both bond and free, both male and female."[32] Alma, a Nephite missionary and one of the principal heroes in this work, tried to carry the true gospel "unto every soul."[33] Other Nephite missionaries preached among the dark Lamanites explaining that "All men are privileged . . . and none are forbidden from receiving the True Gospel."[34]

Even though *Book of Mormon* racial concepts occupied a special place in Latter-day Saint thought because of the book's scriptural status, these concepts were not unique to Mormonism. Thus, environmentalism—that is, the belief that a particular social situation and/or a certain geographic setting promoted the evolution of particular races and ethnic groups— was widely held by racial theorists during the early nineteenth century.[35] As Joseph Smith, other thinkers believed that racial changes took place within a relatively short chronological span.[36] Smith's suggestion that certain fair-complexioned peoples had retrogressed into a wild, savage, idolatrous, dark-skinned state mirrored a widespread belief that all contemporary, primitive, dark-skinned peoples had degenerated from ancestors who had previously enjoyed an "advanced culture."[37] His optimistic belief that the process of racial degeneration could be reversed echoed the theories of non-Mormon writers who maintained that contemporary dark-skinned peoples had the capacity to regain the "original perfection" of a light skin, and a "civilized" state that they had once possessed.[38] Finally, Smith's descriptions of a golden age, when all peoples were "exceedingly fair and delightsome" with no "Lamanites nor any manner of ites . . . " reflected a general racial belief that all mankind, given identical, "optimum" cultural-geographic conditions, might overcome all distinctions of race and become one white universal race.[39] This dovetailed with a general American millennialistic belief, and to some extent an earlier Enlightenment optimism, that all mankind had the capacity to "return" to a pristine, pure white racial state like that occupied by the inhabitants of the Garden of Eden prior to the fall of Adam.[40]

In addition to, and somewhat in contrast to its emphasis on nonwhite racial inferiority, Joseph Smith's book expressed antislavery attitudes. Smith's willingness to address the slavery issue reflected general American concern over this question during the 1820s. Thoughtful Americans like Thomas Jefferson labeled the controversy over slavery during the Missouri crisis as a "fire bell in the night."[41] Throughout the 1820s efforts by the American Colonization Society to abolish slavery through compensated emancipation and the colonization of freed blacks abroad attracted notoriety.[42] In Virginia and South Carolina slavery contributed to underlying social tensions evident during the 1820s. These tensions came to the surface in Nat Turner's 1831 rebellion and in the nullification crisis of 1831-32.[43]

In Joseph Smith's home state of New York there was lively debate over slavery and the status of free blacks. Even though a statute had been adopted in 1799 providing for the gradual manumission of all New York slaves born after this date, black servitude continued to exist and remained an issue for the next thirty years.[44] The status of New York's free blacks also generated controversy. In 1821 and again in 1824, the state constitution was amended to limit black participation in the electoral process.[45] The expression of intense anti-black sentiments in Rockland County before 1830, the emergence after this date of strong antislavery feeling in the "Burned-over District," and prominent antiabolitionist feelings in Utica and New York City indicate great interest by New Yorkers in slavery and the status of blacks during the 1820s.[46]

In this environment, the *Book of Mormon* registered its opposition to slavery. It was "against [Nephite] law . . . " to hold slaves.[47] Thus in contrast to Old Testament peoples, the Nephites refused to enslave those less favored than themselves, namely, the dark Lamanites. "Neither do we desire to bring anyone to the yoke of bondage."[48] In fact, the idolatrous Lamanites were the ones who practiced slavery and made repeated efforts to enslave the "civilized" Nephites.[49] Lamanite slaveholding was cited as additional proof of this people's ferocious and wicked nature.[50] At the same time Nephite resistance to these dark-skinned slaveholders was described as a struggle for freedom from "bondage" and "slavery."[51] While such antislavery attitudes stood in sharp contrast to those Old Testament teachings that approved or at least tolerated slaveholding among certain "chosen peoples," they conformed to the prevailing antislavery attitudes in Joseph Smith's upstate New York environment during the 1820s.[52]

As for the role and place of blacks generally, Joseph Smith's book did not directly address this issue but seemed to allude to it. Smith's use of the term "black" interchangeably with "red" to describe various dark-skinned peoples indicates a possible dislike of contemporary blacks.[53] At one point Smith discussed the unrighteous behavior of Cain, a Biblical counterfigure, labeled both by certain Latter-day Saints and by some non-Mormon Americans as the direct ancestor of black people.[54] In addition, Joseph Smith's interest in blacks was apparently reflected in his *Book of Mormon* description of a people known as the Jaredites.[55] According to Smith this people migrated to the Western Hemisphere and built up a civilization, but like the Nephites they died out because of their unrighteousness. The rise and fall of this nation occurred before the later arrival of the first Nephites. Whereas Joseph Smith carefully described the Hebraic ethnic background of Nephi and those who had arrived later, he was vague in describing the racial origins of the Jaredites. He did, however, point out that the Jaredites had originally lived in a region near the Tower of Babel and later in the Valley of Nimrod.[56] These areas were identified in at least one later Mormon account as regions inhabited by ancestors of the contemporary black.[57]

The *Book of Mormon* became an important medium for the expression of Latter-day Saint racist concepts emphasizing inherent nonwhite racial inferiority. It also contained the genesis of Mormon antislavery thinking.[58] Though the racial ideas contained in the work reflected those held by other Americans during the early nineteenth century, they were particularly important to Joseph Smith's followers, as the *Book of Mormon* was canonized as holy scripture after the formation of the Mormon church in 1830. These early Mormons found this scriptural affirmation of inherent nonwhite inferiority easy to accept in a Jacksonian American society that routinely discriminated against Indians, blacks, and other nonwhites. Such racist views were appealing to those Saints who, like Joseph Smith, came from a lower-middle-class socioeconomic background.[59] A number of Mormonism's early leaders, in the words of one historian, "were poor farmers or artisans ... down on their luck at the time of [their] conversion" to Mormonism.[60] The initial presentation of Mormon racist beliefs through the *Book of Mormon* thus provided a scriptural basis for the later development of those racial concepts specifically directed against black people.[61] These theories would emerge after 1830 as Mormonism's focus shifted westward from New

York to Ohio, a state then deeply divided over the issue of abolition, and ultimately into Missouri, a slave state. Joseph Smith would articulate these later racial theories as the Latter-day Saints assumed an antiabolitionist position during the turbulent decade of the 1830s.

NOTES

1. The circumstances surrounding Joseph Smith's alleged early visions and indeed all of his youthful activities have generated a great deal of historical controversy. For two rather different accounts, see Fawn M. Brodie, *No Man Knows My History,* 2d. ed. (New York, 1971), pp. 1-82; and Donna Hill, *Joseph Smith: The First Mormon* (New York, 1977), pp. 32-97.

2. Brodie, *No Man Knows My History,* pp. 34-61; Hill, *Joseph Smith,* pp. 70-89.

3. *Book of Mormon,* Alma 22:28.

4. Ibid., 2 Nephi 5:20.

5. Ibid., 2 Nephi 5:21-24.

6. Ibid., 1 Nephi 12:23.

7. Ibid., Alma 3:13-19.

8. Ibid., Alma 31:2.

9. Ibid., Alma 43:13, 47:35; Helaman 11:24.

10. Ibid., Helaman 3:16, 11:24.

11. Ibid., Mormon 5:15.

12. Ibid., 1 Nephi 12:23.

13. For a discussion of the relationship between Mormon lower-middle-class social origins and the tendencies to accept racist ideas, see Appendix B of this study.

14. Pearson H. Corbett, *Hyram Smith Patriarch* (Salt Lake City, Utah, 1963), p. 9.

15. Hill, *Joseph Smith,* pp. 32, 42, 45-46.

16. Ibid., p. 48.

17. Robert B. Flanders, "To Transform History: Early Mormon Culture and the Concept of Space and Time," *Church History* 40 (1971): 110.

18. See Whitney R. Cross, *The Burned-Over District* (Ithaca, New York, 1950) for the best description of the religious enthusiasm affecting this region.

19. *Book of Mormon,* 2 Nephi 3:11.

20. Brodie, *No Man Knows My History,* pp. 34-37.

21. Klaus J. Hansen, "The Millennium, the West, and Race in the Antebellum American Mind," *Western Historical Quarterly* 3 (October 1972): 380.

22. For two discussions of American millennialism during the nine-teenth century see Ernest Lee Tuveson, *Redeemer Nation* (Chicago, 1968); and Ernest R. Santeen, *The Roots of Fundamentalism: British and American Millennialism* (Chicago, 1971).

23. See Hansen, "The Millennium, the West, and Race," for a good discussion of the close relationship between race and millennialism.

24. *Book of Mormon,* Jacob 3:8.

25. Ibid., Alma 3:16.

26. Ibid., Jacob 3:3. The Indians apparently also received a promise that America would be "the land of their inheritance" and that "the Lord God will not suffer that the Gentiles [whites] will utterly destroy the mixture of thy seed, which are among thy brethren." See 1 Nephi 13:30.

27. Hansen, "The Millennium, the West, and Race," p. 379.

28. *Book of Mormon,* Alma 24:17-18; 3 Nephi 3:15-16.

29. Ibid., 2 Nephi 30:6.

30. Ibid., 2 Nephi 9:5-22, 25:16, 26:13.

31. Ibid., 2 Nephi 26:25, 26:33.

32. Ibid., Alma 1:30.

33. Ibid., Alma 5:49, 29:2.

34. Ibid., Alma 17:8, 23:4-18; Helaman 5:18-19, 48-52; 3 Nephi 2:12-16; 2 Nephi 26:28.

35. Marvin Harris, *The Rise of Anthropological Theory* (New York, 1968), pp. 25-26, 58; William Stanton, *The Leopard's Spots* (Chicago, 1960), pp. 9-11.

36. Harris, *Rise of Anthropological Theory,* p. 86. According to Harris, some American racial theorists believed that racial change could take place within a single lifetime.

37. Ibid., p. 54; Hansen, "The Millennium, the West, and Race," p. 381.

38. Harris, *Rise of Anthropological Theory,* p. 84.

39. *Book of Mormon,* 4 Nephi 1:10-20. Besides being of one universal race, all the people "had all things common among them; therefore there are not rich and poor, bond and free, but they were all made free, and partakers of heavenly gifts." (4 Nephi 3). Compare this with Thomas F. Gossett, *Race: The History of an Idea in America* (Dallas, 1963), p. 243; George M. Fredrickson, *The Black Image in the White Mind* (New York, 1971), p. 43.

40. Tuveson, *Redeemer Nation,* pp. 53, 78.

41. Glover Moore, *The Missouri Controversy, 1819-1821* (Lexington, Kentucky, 1953). See also Richard H. Brown, "The Missouri Crisis: Slavery and the Politics of Jacksonianism," *South Atlantic Quarterly* 65 (Winter 1966): 55-72.

42. P. J. Staudenraus, *The African Colonization Movement 1816-65* (New York, 1961), pp. 1-142.

43. Stephen B. Oates, *The Fires of Jubilee* (New York, 1975): William W. Freeling, *Prelude to Civil War* (New York, 1965).

44. Edgar J. McManus, *A History of Negro Slavery in New York* (Syracuse, New York, 1966), pp. 174-79; Lee Benson, *The Concept of Jacksonian Democracy: New York as a Test Case* (Princeton, New Jersey, 1961), p. 303.

45. McManus, *History of Negro Slavery,* p. 187; Benson, *Concept of Jacksonian Democracy,* pp. 8, 10, 303, 315, 318.

46. Benson, *Concept of Jacksonian Democracy,* pp. 301-3; Whitney R. Cross, *The Burned-Over District,* pp. 76, 81; McManus, *History of Negro Slavery,* p. 186; Leonard L. Richards, *Gentlemen of Property and Standing: Anti-Abolition Mobs in Jacksonian America* (New York, 1970).

47. *Book of Mormon,* Alma 27:9; Mosiah 2:13.

48. Ibid., Alma 44:2. See also Mosiah 2:13; Alma 27:9. It is interesting to compare such *Book of Mormon* prohibitions with those portions of the Old Testament condoning the holding of slaves by God's chosen people and the rules to be followed in such slaveholding. See Genesis 14:14, 24:34, 30:43; Exodus 20:17, 21:2-32; Leviticus 25:39-55; 2 Samuel 8:2, 6, 14; 1 Chronicles 18:2, 6, 13; Proverbs 29-30.

49. *Book of Mormon,* Mosiah 7:15; Alma 43:29.

50. Ibid., Alma 50:22.

51. Ibid., Alma 43:45-49, 48:10-11, 53:17.

52. Cross, *The Burned-Over District,* 217-26.

53. Compare *Book of Mormon,* 2 Nephi 5:21, with Alma 3:13. However, this same work also uses the terms "dark" or "darkness" on four occasions: 1 Nephi 12:23; Jacob 3:9; Alma 3:6; Mormon 5:15; and the term "filthiness" three times: Jacob 3:5, 9, 10 to describe these same people.

54. *Book of Mormon,* Helaman 6:27; Ether 8:15. According to Winthrop Jordan, *White Over Black: American Attitudes Toward the Negro, 1550-1812* (Chapel Hill, North Carolina, 1968), a few Americans during the colonial and early national period attempted to link Cain to contemporary blacks. But such efforts were not so prominent as attempts to link the contemporary blacks to Ham, the son of Noah. See Jordan, pp. 242, 416, as compared with pp. 17-18, 35-37, 41-43, 200-201.

55. This discussion was a digression from the main text. The *Book of Mormon* narrative was primarily concerned with the activities of the Nephites and Lamanites. See Ether 1-5.

56. Ibid., Ether 1:3, 5, 33, 2:1.

57. In fact, suggestions of a link between Jaredites and the contemporary black man through their common descent from the biblical figure Ham were made in 1843 by Joseph Smith and Parley P. Pratt. See Chapter 5.

58. At the same time, however, the *Book of Mormon* also contained a number of passages that could be construed as recognizing a master-servant relationship. These often look upon bondage as a punishment for wicked behavior. See Jacob 5:15-75; Mosiah 7:15, 20, 22, 11:21, 23, 29:18; Alma 50:22, 61:12.

59. See Appendix B.

60. Marvin S. Hill, "Quest for Refuge: An Hypothesis as to the Social Origins and Nature of the Mormon Political Kingdom," *Journal of Mormon History* 2 (1975): 13 n.57.

61. In fact, in June 1830 the Reverend Diedrich Willers, a minister for the German Reformed Church, perceived a relationship between the *Book of Mormon* and negative attitudes toward black people. Willers believed the *Book of Mormon* to be an account of "the origins of [contemporary] Blacks. . . ." Although Willers was obviously incorrect in pinpointing blacks as the book's main racial target, he was correct in anticipating the future Mormon willingness to embrace a body of racist scriptural ideas specifically directed against blacks. See D. Michael Quinn, ed. and trans., "The First Months of Mormonism: A Contemporary View by Rev. Diedrich Willers," *New York History* 54 (July 1973): 317-32.

2 | The Origins of Mormon Antiabolitionism, 1830-1839

> We do not believe it right to interfere with bond-servants . . .
> to meddle with or influence them in the least to cause them
> to be dissatisfied with their situations in this life. . . .
> *Doctrine and Covenants,* 134:12 (August 1835)

Joseph Smith and other Mormon leaders in Kirtland, Ohio, were upset by the 1836 visit of an abolitionist to their community. Arriving in April of that year, James W. Alvord, an organizer for the American Anti-Slavery Society, established a Kirtland chapter of eighty-six members. Smith and other Mormons reacted against this development, particularly when outside newspaper reports appeared describing Alvord's Kirtland success. The *Philanthropist,* a Cincinnati-based abolitionist publication, announced that Kirtland residents received Alvord and "his doctrines of liberty . . . kindly."[1] Moreover, these reports contrasted Alvord's Kirtland greeting with his reception in nearby non-Mormon communities when angry antiabolitionist mobs showered him with stones, snowballs, and rotten apples.[2]

Though Joseph Smith and other Mormon leaders expressed relief that no mob violence greeted Alvord during his Kirtland visit, they worried about his success because of the parallels that outsiders might draw between themselves and the abolitionists.[3] It was true that most Mormons did not like slavery and subscribed to the antislavery concepts of the *Book of Mormon,* but they did not publicize these views during the 1830s, in large part

because of their awareness of the violence inflicted upon avowed abolitionists like Alvord. Antiabolitionist violence, so prevalent during the 1830s,
was not simply the spontaneous outburst of lower-class rabble but was
often organized or at least encouraged by community leaders or "Gentlemen of Property and Standing."[4] Thus, Mormon leaders, already sensitive
to the hostility and violence generated by their unusual religion, eschewed
abolitionism and at the same time avoided speaking out against slavery.

In this spirit, Mormon leaders affirmed their opposition to abolitionism following Alvord's visit. Joseph Smith led the way in a front-page
editorial published in the official Church periodical, the *Messenger and
Advocate.* Smith declared, "we have no right to interfere with the slaves,
contrary to the mind and will of their masters." As for Alvord's Kirtland
activities, Smith noted that "very few" Mormons were involved and that
Alvord had presented his arguments to "nearly naked walls."[5] Smith's
views were echoed by other Church spokesmen, who declared that the
Mormons "stand aloof from abolitionist societies."[6]

While Mormon antiabolitionism emerged as the dominant Church
reaction to the slavery issue in the mid-1830s, it was *not* Mormonism's
initial attitude, which was one of detachment. During the early 1830s,
Latter-day Saint spokesmen through their official Church newspaper,
the *Evening and Morning Star*, based in Independence, Missouri, tried to
avoid the slave issue altogether. The *Star,* edited by William Wines Phelps,
a recent convert from upstate New York, ignored Nat Turner's Rebellion
and the burgeoning abolitionist movement.[7] When the *Star* broached the
topic of slavery, it did so gingerly, reprinting noncontroversial articles
from other periodicals. Typical attitudes discussed Spanish slave vessels,
a cholera epidemic among some West Indian slaves, and the colonization
of blacks in Liberia.[8]

At least two reasons can be suggested for this attitude. First, Phelps,
despite his own basic dislike for slavery, chose to remain silent in order
to avoid offending his proslavery, non-Mormon Missouri neighbors.[9]
Second, the *Star's* format and editorial style were not suited for the
extensive discussion of black slavery or, indeed, for any other noneccle-
siastical issue. The *Star* was primarily a vehicle for disseminating doctrines
and instructions to church members both within and outside Jackson
County. It also served as a channel of communication between the two
principal Mormon centers of Kirtland, Ohio, and Independence, Missouri.[10] Since it appeared only once a month, the *Star* set aside only a

limited amount of space for non-Mormon secular stories, including those about slavery and abolition.

A Latter-day Saint desire to remain aloof from slavery and abolition revealed itself in the Mormon response to Joseph Smith's "Revelation and Prophecy on War." At the same time, the prophecy itself reflected increased Mormon anxiety over the growing slave controversy. Joseph Smith purportedly received this prophecy at Kirtland on December 25, 1832, during the South Carolina nullification crisis. The revelation predicted that numerous wars would "shortly come to pass, beginning at the rebellion of South Carolina." In time, prophesied Smith, "the Southern States shall be divided against the Northern States" and war would spread to "all nations."[11] Black slaves would be involved in these apocalyptic events. "And it shall come to pass, after many days, slaves shall rise up against their masters, who shall be marshaled and disciplined for War."[12]

This prophecy was destined to become one of the best-known of all Mormon revelations, yet initially Smith and other Mormon leaders gave it only limited exposure. Thus although Smith publicly declared that "not many years shall pass away before the United States shall present such a scene of *bloodshed* as has not a parallel in the history of our nation," he did not specifically quote his own revelation.[13] Likewise, editor Phelps anticipated a "Rebellion" or "dissolution of South Carolina from the Union" as one of the "Signs of the Time." Yet, like Smith, he avoided the Mormon prophecy.[14] In general this revelation received limited exposure throughout the 1830s.[15] In fact, Smith's prophecy was not even published and made available to the general church membership until 1851, seven years after Smith's death.[16] Therefore, even though the prophecy itself indicates underlying Mormon anxieties over the slavery issue during the 1830s, its limited publicity demonstrates Mormonism's basic desire to remain aloof from this vexing question.[17]

However, by the summer of 1833, Mormon efforts to stay separate from the slavery issue were undermined by a dramatic increase of Latter-day Saint migrants entering Missouri.[18] This massive influx, coming primarily from nonslaveholding areas in the East and Midwest, caused editor Phelps to depart from his aloof position. Phelps, anticipating the possible migration of free blacks as part of this influx, published an article entitled "Free People of Color." This article, appearing in the July 1833 *Star*, outlined the procedures necessary for "Free People of Color" to migrate to Missouri. It was accompanied by a companion article in which Phelps tried to clarify

his own position on the issues of slavery and race. This second article tried
to assure non-Mormon Missourians that the Saints "had nothing to say . . .
as to slaves." Nevertheless, he stirred up a hornets' nest when he betrayed
his basic antislavery feelings. Phelps imprudently observed that "in connection with the wonderful events of this age much is doing towards abolishing slavery and colonizing the blacks in Africa."[19]

Phelps' antislavery declaration was too much for non-Mormon Missourians, already sensitive about the ever-increasing influx of nonslaveholding
Mormons into their state. These two *Star* articles helped to trigger violence
against Phelps and his fellow Saints. On July 15, the non-Mormon residents
of Jackson County circulated a "Secret Constitution" outlining the alleged
misconduct of the Saints. This document accused the Saints, among other
things, of "tampering with our slaves, and endeavoring to sow dissentions
and raise seditions amongst them." The Mormons were also assailed for
"inviting free negroes and mulattoes" into Missouri. The angry non-Mormons
then called upon the Saints to leave Jackson County immediately.[20] In the
wake of this uproar, Phelps attempted to redeem himself by issuing a *Star*
"Extra" on July 16. In this "Extra," printed in the form of a handbill and
distributed throughout the county, Phelps reversed his position with regard
to "Free People of Color." He declared that he did not want free blacks in
Missouri or even in the Mormon Church. As for slavery, the Mormon editor,
for some unexplained reason, stuck by his earlier description of abolition
and colonization as "wonderful events." He then editorialized:

> We often lament the situation of our sister states in the South, and
> we fear, lest, as has been the case, the blacks should rise and spill
> innocent blood: for they are ignorant and little may lead them to
> disturb the peace of society.[21]

Needless to say, Phelps' "Extra" did not arrest the deteriorating Mormon
situation in Jackson County. In fact, the Mormon editor's statements,
coupled with other non-Mormon grievances, activated mob violence
against the Saints.[22] The office of the *Star*, which also served as a home
for the Phelps family, was destroyed and its contents scattered in the
street. Phelps and his fellow Saints fled the county and were granted temporary asylum in Clay County, just to the north of Jackson.[23]

After the Mormon expulsion from Jackson County, W. W. Phelps was
relieved of his position as editor of the *Evening and Morning Star* and replaced by Oliver Cowdery, Second Elder and intimate advisor to Joseph

Smith. The journal itself resumed publication at Kirtland, Ohio, in late 1833. As for the slavery issue, the *Star* departed from its earlier detached antislavery position and assumed a definite antiabolitionist stance. As early as January 1834, the *Star* described individuals who would influence the slaves to rebellion as "beneath even the slave himself and unworthy of the privileges of a free government."[24] Even W. W. Phelps, the former *Star* editor, now limited to the role of submitting monthly reports from Clay County, denounced the "false prophets" who directed the "abolition of slavery societies."[25] By August 1835, the church as a whole embraced antiabolitionism as an "official" policy. A "General Assembly" of the church approved the following resolution:

> We believe it just to preach the gospel to the nations of the earth
> and warn the righteous to save themselves from the corruption of
> the world; but we do not believe it right to interfere with bond-
> servants neither preach the gospel to, nor baptize them, contrary
> to the will and wish of their masters, nor to meddle with or in-
> fluence them in the least to be dissatisfied with their situations
> in this life thereby jeopardizing the lives of men. Such interference
> we believe to be unlawful and dangerous to the peace of every
> government allowing human beings to be held in servitude.[26]

This declaration, first printed in the *Latter Day Saints Messenger and Advocate,* which replaced the *Star* as the church's major organ, became church law by virtue of its incorporation into the newly published *Doctrine and Covenants.* This latter work was primarily made up of the revelations of Joseph Smith. It was published in September 1835 and accepted in that same year by the church membership as Holy Scripture on a par with the Bible and *Book of Mormon.*[27]

The Saints also expressed antiabolitionist sentiments through their secular publications. In October 1835, the *Northern Times,* a weekly political publication set up by several prominent church leaders, echoed the antiabolitionist position enshrined in the *Doctrine and Covenants* just two months before.[28] This periodical declared, "We are opposed to abolition, and whatever is calculated to disturb the peace and harmony of our Constitution and Country. Abolition does hardly belong to law or religion, politics or gospel, according to our idea on the subject."[29]

One month later, in November 1835, Joseph Smith reaffirmed the earlier "official" Mormon antiabolitionist position through a letter addressed "To the Elders of the Church." This epistle cautioned missionaries to avoid going "unto . . . slaves or servants" unless granted permission by the master.[30] In conclusion, it admonished "Servants" to "obey in all things your masters, according to the flesh, not with eye service, as men-pleasers, but in singleness of heart, fearing God."[31]

From November 1835 until April 1836, there was a lull in Mormon antiabolitionist statements.[32] In the spring of 1836, Latter-day Saint antiabolitionist activity resumed. Joseph Smith led the way in a letter to Editor Oliver Cowdery, printed on the front page of the *Messenger and Advocate*. Smith denounced northern abolitionists and dissociated the church from their activities.[33] He rejected abolitionist suggestions that slavery was an "evil." Smith gave scriptural legitimacy to his antiabolitionist arguments by quoting from both the Old and the New Testaments. The Mormon leader concluded by referring to the previously issued "belief of the Church concerning masters and servants" as contained in the *Doctrine and Covenants.*[34]

Other Mormons followed the lead of their prophet in denouncing abolitionism. Oliver Cowdery, through editorials in both the April and May issues of the *Messenger and Advocate,* condemned the "corrupting" and "dangerous" activities of the abolitionists. He held up the specter of slave rebellion, black pauperism, and miscegenation. Two other church spokesmen attacked abolitionism through the pages of the *Messenger and Advocate* during this same period.[35]

Mormon opposition to abolitionism was primarily motivated by a Latter-day Saint desire to avoid any and all identification with the abolitionist movement. This desire stemmed, in large part, from Mormonism's presence in Kirtland, Ohio, on the Western Reserve. This region was a hotbed of abolitionism during the 1830s. Oberlin College, located near Kirtland, was the center for abolitionist actions throughout the Ohio Valley.[36] Such abolitionist activity made Ohio the focal point of more antiabolitionist violence than any other state in the Union.[37]

Because of their close proximity to such violence, the Ohio-based Saints were particularly anxious to avoid the abolitionists. They worried about the parallels that non-Mormons might draw between themselves and the abolitionists. At least two articles appearing in non-Mormon newspapers described the similarities between the two movements.[38] The formation of parallel missionary organizations by both the Mormons and the abolitionists possibly caused further Mormon anxieties. The Saints in 1835 estab-

lished "Seventies . . . to preach the gospel of Mormonism." This was followed by the American Anti-Slavery Society's formation of its own "Seventy," a group of antislavery missionaries. Thus, the Ohio Mormons had one
more reason to emphasize their differences with the abolitionists.[39]

Outside of Ohio, the Mormons were also anxious to avoid identification with the unpopular abolitionists as they carried the message of Mormonism throughout the Northeast and Midwest during the 1830s. The
Mormons were well aware of the antiabolitionist riots that rocked these
areas during the 1830s.[40] In this regard, Heber C. Kimball expressed alarm
at the violence directed against an abolitionist in Concord, New Hampshire.
He concluded that "Abolitionism in that county . . . was . . . very unpopular."[41] The missionary-minded Saints striving for respectability in these
regions did not want to be identified with the detested and unpopular
abolitionists.[42]

The Mormons, in avoiding and condemning the abolitionists, were like
other northern-based church groups during the 1830s. The official Mormon
antiabolitionist resolution of August 1835 was similar to the declarations of
other northern-based church groups. The Methodists in their 1836 national
convention adopted a resolution asserting that their members had "no right,
wish or intention to interfere with the civil and political relation as it exists
between master and slave in the slave-holding states of this Union."[43] In a
similar fashion, the Baptists, Presbyterians, and Catholics, in national meetings of their respective churches, avoided the issue of slavery and abolition.[44]
Even the Quakers, who had earlier pushed for the gradual elimination of
slavery, withdrew from active participation in all antislavery movements
and condemned abolition in general.[45] Several interdenominational organizations, including the Bible, Home Missionary, and Tract Societies, also rejected involvement in the abolitionist movement.[46]

The Mormons in Ohio and in other nonslaveholding regions were not
the only Saints afraid of being identified with the abolitionists. Missouri-
based Mormons felt a special need to oppose the abolitionists because Missouri was a slave state.[47] The Saints wanted to prevent a repetition of the
misunderstandings that had led to the Mormon expulsion from Jackson
County in 1833. At that time non-Mormon Missourians had accused the
Saints of "tampering with" black slaves and attempting to "corrupt" and
"instigate them to bloodsheds [*sic*] ."[48] These Missourians gave at least
one specific example they believed to be such a case. This involved an
alleged conversation between a Mormon and a black slave belonging to a

Presbyterian minister in which the former suggested that the latter might
not be satisfied with his condition.[49] Such allegations, in the words of one
distressed Saint, went "the rounds in the public prints."[50] Non-Mormon
charges that the Saints had stirred up "a seditious feeling" and "urged the
slaves to be unfaithful" appeared in newspapers as far away as Vermont,
Washington, D.C., and even in Joseph Smith's former home of Palmyra,
New York.[51] Mormon antiabolitionist statements after 1833 can be seen
as an attempt to refute such charges.[52]

By 1836, the Missouri-based Saints had an additional reason for dis-
associating themselves from the abolitionists. Those Saints who had fled
to Clay County, Missouri, following their expulsion from Jackson County
were charged by their new neighbors as being:

> non-slaveholders, and opposed to slavery; which in this peculiar
> period when abolition has reared its deformed and hagard [*sic*]
> visage in our land, is well calculated to excite deep and abiding
> prejudice in any community where slavery is tolerated and prac-
> ticed.[53]

In June 1836 local citizens asked the Saints to leave Clay County. Residents of the county suggested that the Saints relocate in Wisconsin, a
nonslaveholding territory.[54] The besieged Mormons attempted to refute
these charges at a special meeting that same month. They reiterated the
"official" church antiabolition position of August 1835. They also reaffirmed their support for the April 1836 antiabolitionist statements of
Joseph Smith, Oliver Cowdery, and others.[55] Finally they adopted a resolution in which they expressed their opposition to "the abolitionists" and
affirmed the "right" of the Missourians "to hold slaves."[56] Nevertheless,
all this antiabolitionist activity did little to relieve the situation of the
Clay County Saints. They were forced to migrate north, to Caldwell and
Daviess Counties on the upper Missouri plains.

Adding to their own difficulties, the Missouri-based Mormons found
local residents generally agitated over the issues of slavery and abolition.
The 1832 visit of Theodore Weld to St. Louis, accompanied by the formation of the American Anti-Slavery Society, caused "excitement" throughout the state.[57] By 1835, Missouri citizens feared that abolitionists from
Illinois would flood their state with literature and cause unrest among their
slaves. Members of the American Colonization Society were forced to leave

Hannibal that same year, for distributing literature promoting their cause.[58] Also in 1835, the abolitionist doctrines taught at Marion College, a Presbyterian institution in Palmyra, Missouri, stimulated a wave of antiabolitionist activity.[59] The antislavery activities of Elijah Lovejoy in St. Louis generated controversy, culminating in the destruction of his press and his expulsion from the state in July 1836.[60] Missourians pushed for legislation outlawing the dissemination of antislavery literature. They also called for a law to punish any person found guilty of inciting the slaves to insurrection either through writing or speech.[61]

Outside of Missouri, Mormons in other slaveholding regions were also anxious to avoid identification with the abolitionists. The Latter-day Saints wanted to make their religion acceptable in the slaveholding South. The church as a northern-based organization was anxious to prevent possible southern misunderstanding concerning its views on slavery and abolitionism as Mormon missionaries moved into this region.[62] Joseph Smith's November 1835 epistle had special relevance for southern-based missionaries. In his antiabolitionist letter of April 1836, Smith wrote, "In one respect I am prompted to this course in consequence of many Elders having gone into the Southern States, besides there being now many in that county who have already embraced the fulness of the Gospel. . . ."[63] In this same letter the Mormon leader admonished his northern-based followers that the hand of fellowship should not be withdrawn from the southerner simply because he "will not renounce slavery."[64] In a *Messenger and Advocate* editorial, Oliver Cowdery expected the Saints' antiabolitionist position to alleviate the "deep anxiety felt by our southern brethren [*sic*] on" the slave issue. He hoped that Mormon missionaries "laboring in the South" would present the Mormon position "in a fair light."[65]

Mormon antiabolitionism was also encouraged by two secondary factors. The first involved a Mormon repugnance for basic abolitionist goals, despite the Saints' own dislike of slavery. The Mormons rejected the abolitionist goals of immediate, uncompensated emancipation for all black slaves. In addition, the abolitionist desire to absorb these emancipated blacks into the mainstream of American society upset those Latter-day Saints obsessed about racial intermixture.[66] In contrast to these abolitionist goals, W. W. Phelps and other Mormons favored gradual compensated emancipation and colonization of the freed blacks abroad.

Besides shunning the goals of the abolitionists, the Mormons rejected abolition for a second reason. This involved a Mormon acceptance of a pre-millennialistic philosophy that was at variance with the reform-minded goals of the abolitionists. As pre-millenialists, the Mormons believed the Second Coming to be imminent.[67] The Saints, therefore, saw no need to rid society of its various evils, including slavery, through reform prior to that occurrence. At this time Latter-day Saints felt that reform and perfection, including the abolition of slavery, could not be brought about prior to the millennium.

The Mormons were not alone in expressing such antiabolitionist feelings within a millennialistic framework. William Miller, the founder of the Adventist movement and Joseph Smith's principal millennialistic rival, denounced the abolitionists as "fire-skulled, visionary, fanatical, treasonable, suicidal, demoralizing, [and] hotheaded. . . ."[68] Other millennialistic groups, like the Shakers and the Perfectionists, avoided active involvement in the abolitionist movement despite their dislikes for slavery.[69]

Mormon antiabolitionism, therefore, reached a peak during the years 1835-36 primarily because of a Mormon desire to avoid any and all identification with the abolitionist movement. To a lesser extent the Mormons lashed out at the abolitionists because of their dislike of proposed abolitionist means for abolishing the Peculiar Institution and because abolitionism was at a variance with the pre-millennialistic philosophy embraced by the Saints.

From 1837 until 1839, the Saints expressed their antiabolitionism in a more subdued fashion. Church spokesmen remained basically antiabolitionist, but they made fewer and less strident statements. Joseph Smith waited for seven months, until July 1838, before he responded to the rather pointed question, "Are the Mormons Abolitionists?" In his dilatory reply, Smith answered, "No . . . we do not believe in setting the Negroes free."[70] Other church leaders also affirmed Mormon antiabolitionism during the late 1830s, yet they did so less frequently and with less shrillness than earlier.[71]

A decline in antiabolitionist statements might, at first glance, seem incongruous in light of Mormonism's shifting geographic focus. In late 1837 and early 1838 Joseph Smith and his followers completely abandoned Kirtland, Ohio. They moved the church headquarters to Far West, Missouri, in Caldwell County, where a number of Saints had previously settled. One might logically assume that church leaders would be anxious to play up their antiabolitionist position following their move to this slave state. However, this was not the case. The Saints maintained their restrained posture even during a series of bloody conflicts with their non-Mormon Missouri neighbors, which culminated in their forced exodus from the state during the winter of 1838-39.

The decline in church antiabolitionist expressions, even in the face of Missouri anti-Mormon hostility, can be explained in several ways. First, slavery and abolitionism were only fringe issues during the Mormon-non-Mormon conflicts of 1838-39. These hostilities were primarily provoked by the tremendous influx into Missouri of Mormons who were in a militant mood, willing to fight for their status in Missouri.[72] Only one non-Mormon newspaper out of the dozens commenting on this struggle tried to link the Saints to the abolitionists.[73] The limited importance assigned the issues of slavery and abolition during this conflict stood in sharp contrast to the attention given these issues during the earlier Mormon-non-Mormon conflicts of 1833 and 1836. Second, by the late 1830s, the Saints did not find it necessary to actively assert their antiabolitionism, because of its common knowledge among Mormon and non-Mormon alike. Finally, a decline in Mormon antiabolition activity reflected the emergence of a more tranquil mood in American society generally over the issues of slavery and abolition by the late 1830s.[74]

While Mormon antiabolitionism represented the dominant Mormon reaction toward the slave issue during the 1830s, certain Mormons continued to express dislike for slavery. In a December 1833 revelation Joseph Smith proclaimed "it is not right that any man should be in bondage one to another."[75] Two months later, the *Evening and Morning Star* condemned an incident in which several Missouri slaveowners had sent their black slaves to "insult and abuse" some young Mormon ladies. The *Star* questioned the right of such men to hold slaves.[76] In October 1834, W. W. Phelps once more revealed his basic antislavery feelings in boasting that the Missouri-based Saints did not have to depend on slave labor. In that same month two southern-based Mormon missionaries, David W. Patten and Warren Parrish, lamented the "power of tyranny that exists in the slave states."[77] As late as 1838 Oliver Cowdery, writing from Missouri, expressed in private his basic antislavery feelings. "I have been long enough in slaveholding states to know that they never will, neither can they compete with free states in point of society, enterprise and intelligence."[78] Despite such anti-slavery sentiments, Mormon antiabolitionism predominated during the 1830s. The ability of the Saints to express concurrently *both* antislavery and antiabolitionist sentiments, with an emphasis on the latter, was perhaps best dramatized in a statement made by the besieged Missouri Saints in August 1836. "We have no part for or against slavery, but are opposed to the abolitionists and consider that men have a right to hold slaves or not according to the law."[79] The Mormons would continue to express anti-abolitionist and antislavery feelings concurrently—generally with an emphasis on one or the other—from the 1830s until 1865, when slavery was finally abolished.

The emergence of Mormon antiabolitionism took place against the backdrop of an American society increasingly agitated over the slavery issue during the 1830s. The Saints were anxious to avoid being identified with the abolitionists who, like the Saints, were a despised and persecuted group. The Saints, moreover, eschewed abolition because they wanted to remain in Missouri and promote their religion in the slaveholding South. Therefore, throughout most of the 1830s, the Mormons lashed out at abolitionists like James W. Alvord and the concepts they represented. These antiabolitionist actions helped to create a Mormon intellectual environment in which Joseph Smith was able to develop a set of racist theories specifically directed against black people. This latter development occurred as Smith and other Mormons tried to cope with the problems created by the few blacks associated with the Mormon movement during the 1830s.

NOTES

1. Cincinnati, *Philanthropist* 22 April 1836.

2. John L. Myers, "Anti-Slavery Activities of Five Lane Seminary Boys in 1835-36," *The Bulletin of the Historical and Philosophical Society of Ohio* 21 (April 1963): 101-2.

3. *Latter Day Saints Messenger and Advocate* (Kirtland, Ohio), April 1836. Along this line Smith explained "I fear that the sound might go out, that 'an Abolitionist' had held forth several times to this community, and that the public feeling was not aroused to create mobs or disturbances, leaving the impression that all he said was concurred in, and received as Gospel, and the word of Salvation." Smith might have also been concerned about

the participation by Mormons in the Kirtland chapter founded by Alvord. It is difficult to determine the number of Mormons among the chapter's eighty-six charter members. I have been unable to secure a complete list of names. One contemporary source gives only the names of seven officers in the local Kirtland society. These include Darius Martindale, president; Samuel Branch, vice president; Samuel Billings, secretary; and Alfred Morley, treasurer. Jeduthun Ladd, Quartus Clarke, and Milton Cole are listed as members of the executive committee (*Philanthropist,* 22 April 1836). Samuel Billings was later listed as a member of the Nauvoo City Police. See "Journal History," December 29, 1843.

4. For the best discussion of northern antiabolitionist activity during the 1830s, see Leonard L. Richards, *Gentlemen of Property and Standing: Anti-Abolition Mobs in Jacksonian America* (New York, 1970).

5. *Latter Day Saints Messenger and Advocate,* April 1836.

6. Ibid., April, May 1836.

7. Although on one occasion the *Star* in June 1832 made a passing reference (without comment) to "the insurrection of negroes in the southern states." For a discussion of William Wines Phelps see Walter Dean Bowen, "The Versatile W. W. Phelps—Mormon Writer, Educator, and Pioneer" (M.A. thesis, Brigham Young University, 1958), 6-28.

8. *Evening and Morning Star* (Independence, Missouri), October 1832, December 1832, May 1833, June 1833.

9. Phelps expressed concern about the antinorthern attitudes of the non-Mormon Missourians in his September 1831 letter to the Canadaigua (New York) *Ontario Phoenix.* According to Phelps these Missourians "with customs, manners, [and] modes of living . . . entirely different from the northerners . . . hate Yankees worse than snakes." Richard Lloyd Anderson, "Jackson County in Early Mormon Descriptions," *Missouri Historical Review* 65 (April 1971): 276.

10. Loy Otis Banks, "The Evening and Morning Star," *Missouri Historical Review* 43 (1949): 324-25.

11. *Doctrine and Covenants,* 87:1, 3.

12. Ibid., 87:4.

13. Joseph Smith, Jr., to N. E. Sextus, 7 January 1833, Joseph Smith, Jr., Letterbooks, LDS, Church Historical Department, Salt Lake City, Utah. Italics in original.

14. *Evening and Morning Star,* January 1833. This was the case despite the fact that Phelps apparently recorded this revelation in a bound manuscript volume ("Book B") sometime after 12 June 1833 while in Independence. It also appears that Phelps made at least two other manuscript copies of this same revelation during the 1830s. See Earl E. Olson, "The Chronology of the Ohio Revelations," *B.Y.U. Studies* 11 (Summer 1971): 333, 335, 338.

15. Although two churchmen, Orson Pratt and Wilford Woodruff, later claimed that they publicized this revelation during the 1830s. See *Journal of Discourses* (Liverpool, 1854-1886) Orson Pratt, 12, 11 August 1867; 13, 10 April 1870; 17, 29 February 1875; 18, 26 August 1867; 25 February 1877; *Journal of Discourses,* Wilford Woodruff, 14, 1 January 1871.

16. This revelation, unlike most of the other revelations given by Joseph Smith, was not initially published in the early editions of the *Doctrine and Covenants,* but instead was compiled and presented in the *Pearl of Great Price,* in 1851, along with the "lost" biblical books of Moses and Abraham (to be discussed in Chapter 3). This was the case despite the fact that his prophecy was included along with Smith's other pronouncements in a bound manuscript volume, the "Kirtland Revelations," compiled by Fredrick G. Williams, an early church scribe. See Olson, "Chronology of Ohio Revelations," pp. 333-34.

17. In 1860 Brigham Young explained that "It was not wisdom to publish it [the "revelation and Prophecy on War"] to the world, and it remained in the private *escritoire,*" *Journal of Discourses,* Brigham Young, 8, 20 May 1860.

18. The extraordinary growth of Mormonism in Jackson County is evident from an examination of the population statistics of the period from May 1832 to July 1833:

MONTH	*MORMON POPULATION IN COUNTY*
May 1832	300
November 1832	800
March 1833	1,000
July 1833	1,200

These figures are significant if considered in light of the fact that the total population of Jackson County in 1832 was only 5,071. Figures compiled from Fawn M. Brodie, *No Man Knows My History,* 2d ed. (New York, 1977), pp. 120-21; and S. George Ellsworth, "A History of Mormon Missions in the United States and Canada" (Ph.D. diss., University of California, 1951), p. 133.

19. *Evening and Morning Star,* July 1833.

20. As quoted in the *Evening and Morning Star,* December 1833.

21. *Evening and Morning Star,* "Extra," 20 July 1833. In his reference to past and possible future slave rebellions, Phelps was possibly thinking of Nat Turner's Rebellion and/or Joseph Smith's "Revelation and Prophecy on War."

22. At least two authors have argued that issues other than slavery and race were more crucial in generating non-Mormon Missouri hostility against

the Saints culminating in the Latter-day Saint expulsion from Jackson County in 1833. See Richard L. Bushman, "Mormon Persecutions in Missouri, 1833," *B.Y.U. Studies* 3 (Autumn 1960): 11-20; Warren A. Jennings, "Factors in the Destruction of the Mormon Press in Missouri, 1833," *Utah Historical Quarterly* 35 (Winter 1967): 57-76.

23. Jennings, "Factors in the Destruction of the Mormon Press in Missouri, 1833," pp. 69-72.

24. *Evening and Morning Star,* January 1834.

25. *Latter Day Saints Messenger and Advocate,* April 1835.

26. Ibid., August 1835.

27. This antiabolitionist resolution was not a "revelation" but was part of a section entitled "A Declaration of Belief Regarding Governments and Laws in General" near the end of the early editions of the *Doctrine and Covenants.* Eventually this declaration was incorporated in section 134:12 of this work, where it remains today.

28. This publication was initially edited by Fredrick G. Williams, a church scribe and counselor to Joseph Smith in the First Presidency. For a brief biographical sketch of Williams, see Fredrick G. Williams, "Fredrick Granger Williams of the First Presidency of the Church," *B.Y.U. Studies* 12 (Spring 1972): 243-61. Oliver Cowdery eventually succeeded Williams as editor.

29. *Northern Times* (Kirtland, Ohio), 9 October 1835.

30. *Latter Day Saints Messenger and Advocate,* November 1835. If the master refused to allow the missionary to preach, "the responsibility be upon the head of the master of that house and the consequences thereof; and the guilt of that house is no longer upon thy skirts. Thou art free; therefore, shake off the dust of thy feet, and go thy way."

31. Colossians 3:22.

32. Although Oliver Cowdery, as editor of the *Northern Times,* expressed his concern over the abolitionist—antiabolitionist question on at least two occasions in February 1836 and wrote editorials to that effect. See Leonard J. Arrington, "Oliver Cowdery's Kirtland, Ohio 'Sketch Book,'" *B.Y.U. Studies* 12 (Summer 1972): 421-22, entries for February 2 and 4, 1836.

33. *Latter Day Saints Messenger and Advocate,* April 1836.

34. Ibid.; Genesis 9:25-26; Ephesians 6:5-9; I Timothy 6:1-5. By quoting Genesis, an attempt was made to link the black man's alleged descent from Ham and Canaan with his present condition of servitude. Various aspects of Mormon racial theories and attitudes toward the black man will be discussed in Chapter 3.

35. *Latter Day Saints Messenger and Advocate,* April and May 1836.

36. The importance of Oberlin and the Western Reserve in the northern antislavery crusade is discussed in Gilbert Hobbs Barnes, *The Anti-*

Slavery Impulse 1830-1844 (New York, 1964); Dwight L. Dumond, *The Anti Slavery Origins of the Civil War* (Ann Arbor, Michigan, 1939); and W. G. Burroughs, "Oberlin's Part in the Slavery Conflict," *Ohio Archaeological and Historical Quarterly* 20 (1911): 269-83. It is worth noting that Lorenzo Snow, who was to become an apostle and president of the church, was a student at Oberlin College before joining the Latter-day Saint movement in June 1836. Ivan J. Barrett, *Joseph Smith and the Restoration: A History of the Church to 1846,* 2d ed. (Provo, Utah, 1973), pp. 327-28.

37. Edward Coleman Reilley, "The Early Slavery Controversy in the Western Reserve" (Ph.D. diss., Western Reserve University, 1940), p. 160.

38. *New York Courier,* n.d., reprinted in the *Latter Day Saints Messenger and Advocate,* June 1835; and the *Philadelphia Courier,* 2 August 1834, reprinted in the *Messenger and Advocate,* December 1835. The Saints were probably also aware and concerned about the religious-millennialistic appeals by the local (Geauga County) antislavery society, which attacked those religious groups or "professing Christians who pray for the universal spread of the gospel and the speedy commencement of the millennium, while they at the same time oppose the abolition of slavery, exhibit a striking instance of the inconsistency of the human character." *Painesville (Ohio) Republican* 28 September 1837.

39. Barnes, *The Anti-Slavery Impulse,* pp. 104-5, and *Doctrine and Covenants,* 107:25. In the formation of the "Seventy" and "Seventies" both the abolitionists and Mormons were apparently influenced by the example of Jesus in the New Testament, who appointed and ordained seventy missionaries to go out and preach the Gospel. See Luke 10:1-20.

40. See Richards, *Gentlemen of Property and Standing;* and Lorman Ratner, *Powder Keg: Northern Opposition to the Anti-Slavery Movement, 1831-1840* (New York, 1968).

41. Journal of Heber C. Kimball, 3 September 1835, reprinted in Orson F. Whitney's *Life of Heber C. Kimball* (Salt Lake City, Utah, 1888), p. 96.

42. For a discussion of Mormon difficulties in trying to secure respectability within American society generally, see David Brion Davis, "Some Themes in Counter-subversion: An Analysis of Anti-Masonic, Anti-Catholic, and Anti-Mormon Literature," *The Mississippi Valley Historical Review* 47 (September 1960): 205-24.

43. Donald G. Mathews, *Slavery and Methodism* (Princeton, New Jersey, 1965), p. 142.

44. Mary Burnham Putnam, *The Baptists and Slavery, 1840-1845* (Ann Arbor, Michigan, 1913), p. 11; C. Bruce Staiger, "Abolitionism and the Presbyterian Schism of 1837-38," *Mississippi Valley Historical Review* 36

(1949-50): 395-401; Madeline Hook Rice, *American Catholic Opinion in the Slavery Controversy* (New York, 1944).

45. Thomas E. Drake, *Quakers and Slavery in America* (New Haven, Conn., 1950), pp. 132-33, 144-45.

46. Clifford S. Griffin, *Their Brothers' Keeper* (New Brunswick, New Jersey, 1960), pp. 177-78, 181-82.

47. The importance of Missouri in the formation of Mormon anti-abolition has been noted by several writers. See for example Stephen G. Taggart, *Mormonism's Negro Policy: Social and Historical Origins* (Salt Lake City, 1970); and Dennis L. Lythgoe, "Negro Slavery and Mormon Doctrine," *Western Humanities Review* 21 (1967): 327-38.

48. As quoted in the *Evening and Morning Star,* December 1833. Also quotation of Isaac McCoy as contained in Warren Jennings, "Isaac McCoy and the Mormons," *Missouri Historical Review* 61.

49. *Evening and Morning Star,* January 1834.

50. Ibid.

51. *Illinois Advocate and State Register,* 23 November 1833; *Vermont Intelligencer,* 24 August 1833; Palmyra (N.Y.) *Wayne Sentinel,* 23 August 1833. Also the *Maysville (Kentucky) Eagle,* as reprinted in the Washington (D.C.) *Daily National Intelligencer* 23 July 1834.

52. In addition, the Saints were possibly influenced by talk of returning and "redeeming" their "Zion" in Independence. According to one source, the date set for such a return was 11 September 1836. See Joseph Smith, *History of the Church,* 2d ed. (Salt Lake City, 1978)2: 145

53. Reprinted in the *Latter Day Saints Messenger and Advocate,* August 1836.

54. Ibid.

55. Ibid. It is interesting to note that the Clay County Saints in quoting from the August 1835 statement took a harder line than that intended by the original declaration: "We do not believe it right to interfere with bond servants nor preach the gospel to, nor meddle with, or influence them in the least to cause them to be dissatisfied with their situation in this life." By omitting the phrase "nor baptize them contrary to the will or wish of their master," they seemed to close the possibility of baptizing black slaves (at least for the time being in Clay County). Cf. *Doctrine and Covenants,* 134:12.

56. *Latter Day Saints Messenger and Advocate,* August 1836.

57. Benjamin G. Merkel, "The Abolition Aspects of Missouri's Anti-Slavery Controversy 1819-1865," *Missouri Historical Review* 44 (1948-50): 236-37.

58. W. Sherman Savage, "The Contest over Slavery between Illinois and Missouri," *Journal of Negro History* 28 (July 1943): 313, 315.

59. Merkel, "Abolition Aspects," pp. 242-44.

60. Ibid., pp. 239-46.

61. Savage, "The Contest over Slavery," pp. 373-75; Merkel, "Abolition Aspects," p. 246.

62. S. George Ellsworth, "A History of Mormon Missions in the United States and Canada, 1830-1860" (Ph.D. diss., University of California, 1951), p. 29; Jan Shipps, "Second Class Saints," *Colorado Quarterly* 11 (1962): 183-88. La Mar C. Berrett, "History of the Southern States Mission, 1831-1861" (M.A. thesis, Brigham Young University, 1960).

63. *Latter Day Saints Messenger and Advocate,* April 1836. See also similar statements made in November 1835 and May 1836.

64. Ibid., April 1836.

65. Ibid.

66. See, for example, Oliver Cowdery's antiabolitionist statement of April 1836 in the *Latter Day Saints Messenger and Advocate,* April, 1836: "And insensible to feeling must be the heart, and low indeed must be the mind, that would consent for a moment, to see his fair daughter, his sister, or perhaps, his bosom companion, in the embrace of a NEGRO!"

67. Mormon pre-millennialistic expectations were reflected in various church writings during the 1830s, see, for example, *Doctrine and Covenants,* 18:28, 42, 33:6, 45:49, 68, 69, 71, 58:45. See also the *Evening and Morning Star,* particularly the issues for December 1832 and March 1833.

68. As quoted in Francis D. Nichol, *The Midnight Cry* (Washington, D.C., 1944), p. 58. According to Whitney Cross, *The Burned-Over District,* Ithaca, New York, 1950), pp. 318-19, William Miller reacted negatively to abolitionism as well as other reform movements because he was afraid that such activities would distract the faithful from their primary task of preparing for the end of the world.

69. Edward Deming Andrews, *The People Called Shakers* (New York, 1953), pp. 214, 232-33; David M. Ludlum, *Social Ferment in Vermont 1791-1850* (New York, 1939), pp. 247-48.

70. *Elders Journal* (Kirtland, Ohio: Far West, Missouri), November 1837, July 1838. This question was first posed in the November 1837 issue of the Journal but not answered until July 1838. The reason for the delay was that this periodical, which replaced the *Messenger and Advocate* as the official church journal, was initially issued in Ohio but had its publication interrupted by serious division within the church in late 1837. The *Journal* resumed publication in Missouri in July 1838.

71. Sydney Rigdon, *Oration Delivered by Mr. S. Rigdon, on the 4th of July, 1838, at Far West Caldwell County, Missouri* (Far West, Missouri, 1838), p. 8; Parley P. Pratt, *Mormonism Unveiled* (New York, 1838), p. 39.

72. For a thorough discussion of this conflict and its causes, see Leland H. Gentry, "A History of the Latter-day Saints in Northern Missouri from 1836 to 1839" (Ph.D. diss., Brigham Young University, 1965). See also F. Mark McKiernan, "Mormonism on the Defensive: Far West," in F. Mark McKiernan, Alma R. Blair, and Paul M. Edwards, eds., *The Restoration Movement: Essays in Mormon History* Lawrence, Kansas, 1973), pp. 121-40.

73. *Missouri Republican,* August 25, 1838. Even here it was done in a conjectural and indirect manner. This periodical described the Mormons as "most of whom we believe are abolitionist" and talked about expelling "Mormons, abolitionists and disorderly persons" from the county.

74. Richards, *Gentlemen of Property and Standing,* pp. 155-65.

75. *Doctrine and Covenants.* Although this statement condemned bondage in general, it is not completely clear whether it was specifically addressed to black slavery or human bondage in general. While this statement is made within the context of a discussion of the rights and privileges guaranteed under the Constitution, there are suggestions that Smith was primarily concerned with economic rather than human bondage. See *Doctrine and Covenants,* 104:16-18, 83-84. A second revelation dated six months earlier in which Smith affirms that the American Constitution upheld the "principle of freedom . . . rights and privileges" for "all mankind" might also be construed as an antislavery statement. *Doctrine and Covenants,* 98:5.

76. *Evening and Morning Star,* February 1834.

77. *Latter Day Saints Messenger and Advocate,* November 1834.

78. Oliver Cowdery to Warren A. and Lynn Cowdery, 2 June 1838, as reprinted in Stanley R. Gunn, *Oliver Cowdery: Second Elder and Scribe* Salt Lake City, Utah, 1962), pp. 182-83.

79. *Latter Day Saints Messenger and Advocate,* August 1836.

3 | *Black Mormons and Mormon Racist Theories, 1830-1839*

There was blackness[that] came upon all the children of
Canaan, that they were despised among all people.

Pearl of Great Price, Moses, 7:8

[He] was cursed . . . as pertaining to the Priesthood . . . being
of that lineage by which he could not have the right of Priesthood. . . .

Pearl of Great Price, Abraham, 1:26-27

In July 1835, a year before the unwelcome visit of James W.
Alvord, Joseph Smith and his Kirtland followers received another non-
Mormon visitor, one Michael H. Chandler. In contrast to Alvord, Chandler
did not come to preach the doctrine of abolition. Instead, Chandler came
as a salesman of Egyptian artifacts. He hoped to sell Smith some ancient
mummies and papyrus scrolls that he had inherited from his uncle. He felt
that Smith might be interested in these items because of stories he had
heard about Smith's earlier "discovery" of the gold plates and translation
of their "reformed Egyptian" characters into the *Book of Mormon.* Chandler was right. Smith purchased his Egyptian artifacts.[1]

Smith took a special interest in his new purchase, particularly the papyrus
rolls. He pronounced one of these rolls the ancient writings of the biblical
prophet Abraham. Over the next several years, Smith utilized this document in "transcribing" his Book of Abraham, a scriptural work presented
as one of the lost books of the Old Testament.[2] Basically it related the

experiences of the prophet Abraham during his sojourn in Egypt. In telling this story, it outlined a number of important doctrinal precepts that were eventually incorporated into the superstructure of Mormon theology. These included the concepts of a premortal existence, that is, the idea that the human spirit existed in an earlier state prior to being born into this world, and a belief in a plurality of Gods.[3]

The book of Abraham also presented a number of racist concepts emphasizing the inherent racial inferiority of certain dark-skinned peoples. This book, therefore, was somewhat analogous to the *Book of Mormon*. However, it did not focus on the Indians, but instead examined certain peoples believed to be ancestors of contemporary blacks. The Book of Abraham cast two groups in an unfavorable racial-cultural light—the Chaldeans and the Egyptians. According to the book, both of these groups were descendants of Ham, the alleged ancestor of all contemporary blacks.[4]

The development of Mormon racist concepts specifically directed against the ancestors of contemporary blacks reflected an increased Latter-day Saint preoccupation over the place of blacks in Mormonism during the 1830s. Initially, however, the status of blacks did not differ from that of any other ethnic group. As objects for probable Mormon salvation, black people fell within the purview of Mormon universalism. The *Book of Mormon* proclaimed a basic desire to preach the Gospel among all peoples, blacks as well as whites. "All men are privileged the one like unto the other and none are forbidden."[5] Joseph Smith expressed this same universalism through the *Doctrine and Covenants.* According to Smith, the voice of the Lord was "unto all men . . . " and he was "no respecter of persons."[6] As for the gospel, it was "free unto all" regardless of "Nation, kindred, [or] tongue."[7] "All those who humble themselves before God" would "be received by baptism into his Church," including the "heathen nations."[8] The Mormon Prophet instructed missionaries to go "into all the world" and preach the gospel "unto every creature . . . both old and young, both bond and free."[9] Finally, the Mormon gathering to Zion would include the righteous from "every nation under heaven" brought together "from the ends of the earth."[10]

Other Mormon spokesmen expressed these same universalistic desires. Parley Parker Pratt was one of the most prominent exponents of Mormon universalism. Pratt, an important missionary, a prolific pamphleteer, and an interpreter of church doctrine, expressed his desire to preach the gospel "to all people, kindred, tongues, and nations without any exceptions."[11] Through poetry he outlined the "mission of the Twelve" to all nations, including those on "India's and Afric's [*sic*] sultry plains . . . where darkness, death and sorrow reign."[12]

Those universalistic sentiments were also expressed in the Mormon periodicals published during this period. W. W. Phelps wrote in the *Evening and Morning Star* that the Lord had "some choice souls among every nation, kindred, [and] tongue" who must "hear his voice and be gathered to Zion."[13] He anticipated that Mormon missionaries would preach throughout the world with "some [sent] to Africa."[14] Scriptural instructions in the *Messenger and Advocate* ordered the Mormons to go "into all the world and preach the Gospel to every creature."[15] "All the families of the earth, would be "blessed . . . whether they are the descendants of Shem, Ham, or Japheth."[16] The *Messenger and Advocate* traced this universalism through the history of the True Gospel and proclaimed that its

> order was the same; it produced the same effect among all people, whether they were Scythian, Barbarian, bond or free, Jew or Gentile, Greek or Roman, it mattered not what they were; for in this respect, there was neither Greek nor Jew, bond nor free, male nor female; but they were all one in Christ Jesus, and the same blessings belonged to all, and the same fruits followed all, and the order was the same, whether it was in Africa, Asia, or Europe.[17]

This universalism appeared in the first Mormon hymnal, published in 1835. The Saints were exhorted to spread the Gospel "throughout Europe, and Asia's dark regions, to China's far shores, and to Afric's [*sic*] black legions."[18]

These universalistic sentiments were reflected in the actual relations between blacks and the Ohio Saints. According to one contemporary non-Mormon observer, the Mormons in Ohio recognized "the natural equality of [all] mankind without excepting the native Indians or the African race."[19] The Saints seemed to anticipate the presence of black people in their Kirtland Temple, completed in 1836. The temple's initial rules of conduct were addressed to "old or young, rich or poor, male or female, bond or free, black or white, believer or unbeliever."[20]

In this atmosphere, at least two blacks joined the early church in Ohio and left their marks on Mormonism. One of these was "Black Pete." A controversial figure, Pete, through his activities as a self-styled "revelator," attracted notoriety in the contemporary non-Mormon press.[21] Unfortunately, little is known about his background. According to one account, Pete migrated to Ohio from Pennsylvania, where he had been born of slave parents.[22] After his arrival in Ohio, Pete joined the Mormon movement in late 1830 or early 1831. This "man of colour" was "a chief man . . . sometimes seized with strange vagaries and odd conceits."[23] On at least one occasion Pete fancied he could "fly" and

> took it into his head to try his wings; he accordingly chose the elevated bank of Lake Erie as a starting-place, and, spreading his pinions, he lit on a treetop some fifty feet below, sustaining no other damage than the demolition of his faith in wings without feathers.[24]

There is some confusion over Pete's other Mormon activities. According to one reminiscence, Pete "wanted to marry a white woman," but Joseph Smith could not get any "revelations" for him to do so.[25] Another account has Pete active at the time when Joseph Smith and other church authorities were not in Kirtland. Whatever the case, the Mormon Prophet brought forth a February 1831 revelation condemning false revelators such as Black Pete. The Mormon Prophet proclaimed that only authorized individuals could "receive revelations."[26] As a result Black Pete was apparently "tried for [his] fellowship" and "cut off" from the church.[27]

A second black man, Elijah Abel, joined the Latter-day Saint movement at a somewhat later date. Abel was a most important individual because of his unique status as one of the very few blacks to hold the Mormon priesthood during the nineteenth century. Little, however, is known about his background and activities up to the mid-1830s. Abel was born in 1810 in Maryland. Later, for some unknown reason, he migrated to Kirtland, Ohio. Here he embraced Mormon teachings and was baptised into the church in September 1832.[28]

Following his Mormon conversion, Abel assumed an active role in Church affairs. By 1836, Abel was ordained an elder in the Mormon priesthood.[29] This ordination, according to at least one account, was performed by Joseph Smith.[30] Abel moved up through the Mormon priesthood and in December 1836 advanced to the priesthood rank of Seventy.[31] Abel, moreover, by virtue of his priesthood status was certified by Ohio state authorities as a duly-licensed "minister of the Gospel."[32] Thus Abel had the authority to perform certain church ordinances, including marriages. In addition, Abel, like other members of the church, received a patriarchal blessing. This sacred ordinance was inspired by the ancient blessings conferred by the heads of certain chosen families in the Old Testament. He received his blessing at the hands of Joseph Smith, Sr., father of the Mormon Prophet. This blessing recognized Abel as a member of the Mormon "family" of true believers and told him that as an "ordained Elder" he was "annointed to secure thee against the power of the destroyer." But, at the same time, this blessing seemed to set Abel apart from his white Mormon counterparts by alluding to his blackness. However, the blessing promised Abel that he would "be made *equal* to thy brethren, and thy Soul be *white* in eternity and thy robes glittering."[33]

Despite his unique status, Abel, like so many of his fellow Saints, served as a church missionary during the late 1830s. The field of Abel's missionary labors included New York State and Canada. Abel was described by one admirer as a "powerful preacher" and a "servant of the most high God." However, Abel's missionary activities also generated controversy. According to one account, the non-Mormon residents of St. Lawrence County, New York, accused Abel of murdering a woman and five children. "Handbills were pasted up in every direction . . . and a great reward was offered for him." He was apparently successful in refuting these charges and left the community "unmolested."[34] However, Abel ran into further difficulties. His teachings and behavior came under attack from his fellow missionary Saints. These Mormons took issue with Abel's idea "that there would be Stakes of Zion in all the world, that an elder was a High Priest and he had as much authority as any H.P." He was also accused of "threatening to knock down" a fellow elder. Abel rationalized this behavior, declaring that the "elders in Kirtland make nothing of knocking down one another." Even though his questionable behavior was scrutinized by the top church leadership—including Joseph and Hyrum Smith, Sidney Rigdon, as well as the Quorum of Seventies—no disciplinary action was taken against the black priesthood-holder.[35]

Despite the notoriety generated by Black Pete and Elijah Abel, the number of black Mormons in Ohio remained very small. In fact, according to Apostle Parley P. Pratt, there were fewer than "one dozen free negroes or mulattoes" in the entire Mormon movement as of 1839.[36] Within Ohio itself, that state's antiblack laws undoubtedly diminished the feasibility of any large-scale black gathering. Ohio statutes, enacted in 1804 and 1807, limited the migration of free blacks into the state and required the posting of a $500 bond for each and every black person who did so.[37] During the 1830s, moreover, state authorities tightened up these statutes to stem the continuing migration of blacks into the state.[38] These legal constraints, combined with economic difficulties within the Mormon movement during this period, made any large black Mormon gathering to Ohio utterly impractical. In addition, any large migration of blacks to Kirtland would probably hurt the Mormon cause. Black people, along with antislavery zealots, were prime objects of northern antiabolitionist mob violence during the 1830s. The Saints, therefore, apparently avoided converting free blacks to Mormonism.

The Ohio-based Saints were not alone in confronting the issue of blacks and their status within Mormonism. The Mormons in Missouri were also involved with this issue. As in Ohio, Latter-day Saint universalism initially prevailed. Mormon preaching in Missouri was directed toward representatives "of all of the families of the earth; Shem, Ham, and Japheth."[39] Parley P. Pratt reflected this same universalism in his preaching while traveling to Missouri by steamer. When a group of passengers asked him to preach, Pratt agreed only on condition that "all classes black or white, should have the same privilege" of hearing his discourse.[40]

The publication of "Free People of Color" by W. W. Phelps in July 1833 represented the most dramatic expression of Mormon universalism or desire to gather all peoples, including blacks, to their Missouri Zion. At the same time the non-Mormon Missouri response to this article graphically illustrated the complications inherent in this undertaking. Missouri was not the most conducive environment for free blacks, Mormon or otherwise. White citizens of this state had expressed strong hostility toward free blacks ever since Missouri had applied for statehood in 1819-20. At that time Missouri citizens hoped to include a provision in their state constitution prohibiting all free blacks from migrating into the state. The desire for such a clause generated animated controversy. Finally, under the Compromise of 1820, Missouri agreed to allow the migration of free blacks into the state, but only under severe statutory limitations. These laws stipulated that a "free negro or mulatto" could enter the state only if he was an American citizen and had a "certificate of citizenship" attesting to this fact. The failure to produce this certificate upon request could result in a $500 fine.

The Mormons were sensitive to this situation in printing "Free People of Color." This article, accompanied by the text of Missouri antiblack laws, represents a Mormon effort to clarify their position on free blacks with their Missouri neighbors. Phelps also hoped "to prevent any misunderstanding among the [Mormon] churches abroad, respecting free people of color, who may think of coming to the Western boundaries of Missouri as members of the church. . . ." The editor of the *Star* concluded: "So long as we have no special rule in the church, as to people of color, let prudence guide; and while they as well as we, are in the hands of a merciful God, we say: Shun every appearance of evil."[41]

This was not to be. The non-Mormon residents of Jackson County viewed "Free People of Color" in a different light. Unlike the Saints, they did not see it as a document anticipating the *possible* migration of black Mormons into the state. Instead, they perceived it as an open invitation to "negroes and mulattoes from other states to become 'Mormons' and settle among us."[42] Phelps in an "Extra" edition of the *Star* attempted to further "Clarify" his position.

> Having learned with extreme regret, that an article entitled, "Free People of Color," in the last number of the *Star,* had been mis-understood, we felt in duty bound to state in this Extra, that our intention was not only to stop free people of color from emigrating to this state, but to prevent them from being admitted as members of the Church.[43]

The non-Mormon citizens of Jackson County, however, rejected this state-ment as a "weak attempt to quiet our apprehension." By this time, more-over, non-Mormon citizens of Jackson County had a number of other grievances against their Latter-day Saint neighbors that, coupled with their anger over Phelps' twice-stated opinion that "abolition" and colonization" were "wonderful events," caused them to expel the Saints from Jackson County.[44] Therefore, "Free People of Color," instead of paving the way for the migration of Mormon blacks into Missouri, made the situation of the Missouri Saints more difficult.

The difficulties generated by "Free People of Color" coupled with the controversial behavior of Mormon blacks like Black Pete and Elijah Abel took place at a time when the Saints were already agitated over the issues of slavery and abolition. These conditions enabled Joseph Smith to view blacks in an inferior light through his Books of Moses and Abraham, scriptural writings produced during the 1830s. In these works, Smith for the first time enunciated racist concepts specifically directed against certain biblical counterfigures considered the ancestors of contemporary blacks. These concepts were initially presented in the Book of Moses completed in 1833. This work was considered a correction and supplement to the Book of Genesis of the Old Testament.[45] Smith detailed the deeds, or rather misdeeds, of Cain and his wicked descendants, who were identified by some biblical literalists—including at least one prominent Latter-day Saint—as the alleged ancestors of present-day blacks.[46] Cain's murder of Abel was discounted as a spontaneous outburst of anger and described as a carefully planned conspiracy between Cain and Satan.[47] As punishment, Cain was "cursed from the earth" to be "a fugitive and a vagabond."[48] In addition, "the Lord set a mark upon Cain" and he "was shut out from the presence of the Lord."[49] Cain's descendants were also described in an unfavorable light. Lamech, one such descendant, entered into a "covenant with Satan" and killed one of his relatives.[50] For this deed, Lamech was "cursed," along with "his house," by the Lord. He was also "despised and cast out" from "among the [righteous] sons of man."[51] Other descendants of Cain were described as a segregated, dark-skinned people: "And Enoch also beheld the residue of the people which were the sons of Adam; and they were a mixture of all the seed of Adam save it was the seed of Cain, for the seed of Cain were black, and had not place among them."[51]

The Book of Moses also expressed racist concepts in its discussion of the "people of Canaan." This group, like Cain and his descendants, came to be identified with contemporary black people even though they were allegedly descended from Seth, a righteous son of Adam. Initially the "people of Canaan . . . dwelt in the land of Canaan . . . a land of promise" and "righteousness . . . by the sea east."[53] But the people of Canaan became unrighteous. They went into battle against the people of Shum, "a great people," and "utterly" destroyed them. As punishment for this act, the "people of Canaan" were compelled to occupy a land that was "barren and unfruitful."[54] In addition, "a blackness came upon all the children of Canaan, that they were despised among all people."[55] Because of their degraded condition, the people of Canaan were not considered fit subjects for conversion to the true faith. Thus, "all the people, save it were the people of Canaan," were called to repentance. Smith, moreover, seemed to suggest that the "curse" inflicted upon the people of Canaan could "befall . . . all people that fought against God."[56]

Joseph Smith's Book of Moses also concerned itself with the activities of Ham and his son Canaan, already identified by the Saints and other biblical literalists as the ancestors of contemporary black people. At first Smith described Ham as an individual who, along with his father and two brothers, "walked with God."[57] However, following the Deluge, Ham became unrighteous and incurred the wrath of his father Noah by looking upon his "nakedness" while the latter was drunk in his tent. When Noah "awoke from his wine" he cursed not Ham, but Ham's son Canaan to be "a servant of servants . . . unto his brethren."[58] In addition to the curse of servitude, Smith implied that Canaan received a racial curse in which "a veil of darkness" covered him so "that he shall be known among all men."[59]

Racist theories of inherent black inferiority were also evident in Joseph Smith's Book of Abraham "transcribed" from the Egyptian papyrus rolls acquired from Michael H. Chandler in 1835.[60] Like the Book of Moses, this work contained descriptions of the misdeeds of certain alleged ancestors of contemporary blacks. The book of Abraham examined the activities of the Prophet Abraham and his unrighteous "fathers" in the "land of the Chaldeans," people with links to Ham and black biblical counterfigures.[61] More important, Smith's book briefly discussed the activities of Pharaoh and the Egyptian people, identified with the same Hamatic ancestors of black people.[62] Pharaoh was described as "a descendant from the loins of Ham and . . . a partaker of the blood of the Canaanites by birth."[63] This account also elaborated on the racial and ethnic origins of the Egyptian people themselves:

> From this descent of Pharaoh sprang all the Egyptians, and thus the blood of the Canaanites was preserved in the land.
>
> The land of Egypt being first discovered by a woman who was the daughter of Ham, and the daughter of Egyptus, which in Chaldean signifies Egypt, which signifies that which is forbidden.
>
> When this woman discovered the land it was under water, who afterwards settled her sons in it and thus from Ham sprang the curse of the land.[64]

The Book of Abraham, in a number of crucial verses, then discussed the limits of Pharaoh's religious authority. Pharaoh was described as a "righteous man" who "judged his people wisely and justly" and was "blessed" by his "father . . . Noah . . . with the blessings of wisdom." But he was "cursed as pertaining to the priesthood" because he was "of that lineage by which he could not have the right of priesthood."[65]

Joseph Smith and his fellow Saints were not unique in articulating racial theories linking blacks to various biblical antiheroes and less-favored groups. Southern proslavery advocates promoted the concept of a genealogical link between contemporary blacks and certain counterfigures, including Ham and Canaan. This concept was a "favorite theory of the Southerners" during the 1830s.[66] Such theories, moreover, were not limited to the South. A number of northern, non-Mormon churchmen emphasized a literal relationship between Ham, Canaan, and contemporary blacks in their effort to counter the arguments of northern abolitionists.[67] Non-Mormon racial theorists also suggest a literal lineage between contemporary blacks and Cain. These theorists asserted that "the black skin of the Negro" was "the mark of Cain."[68] As for the Hamatic origins of the Egyptians, David Walker supported this idea as early as 1830. In his famous *Appeal*, Walker described the role of "the sons of Africa or of Ham" in building the Egyptian pyramids.[69] Such concepts reflected a "widespread romantic interest in Egyptian culture and civilization prevalent in America during the 1830's."[70]

Besides reflecting a contemporary interest in black racial origins, Mormon racist concepts as articulated in the Books of Moses and Abraham represent a "harder" Mormon line taken against blacks than that earlier assumed toward the Indians in the *Book of Mormon*. In contrast to the earlier work, the Books of Moses and Abraham tended to discount the possibility of racial " improvement," or transformation to a "white and delightsome" state for its dark-skinned subjects. Joseph Smith moved away from his earlier, optimistic belief that a person's "racial deformities," that is, his dark skin and accompanying habits or behavior, could be "improved" by his exposure to righteous or "civilizing" elements.[71] Also differing with his earlier *Book of Mormon* theories, Smith rejected racial intermixture as a method for bringing about racial improvement. Eschewing earlier environmental racial theories, the Books of Moses and Abraham assigned a larger role to heredity and lineage as factors in perpetuating the disadvantageous position of certain dark-skinned counterfigures. In a number of cases these people were not even considered fit objects for salvation.[72] This Old Testament particularism stood in sharp contrast to the Christian universalism expressed just a few years before in the *Book of Mormon.*

Joseph Smith's pessimism concerning racial regeneration and salvation of certain biblical counterfigures reflected an increased sensitivity to America's deepening racial difficulties after 1830. Before this date Smith, along with most Americans, believed that red-skinned or even black-skinned people could be uplifted and regenerated. Ultimately all mankind would become one universal white race. By the critical decade of the 1830s, however, racial regeneration no longer seemed possible. Racial intermixture or miscegenation was certainly out of the question as a means to bring about this regeneration.[73] Mormon writers such as W. W. Phelps seemed to believe that only the strict separation of blacks and whites through compensated emancipation and colonization of the blacks abroad would solve America's race problem. Pessimism concerning the possible racial regeneration of dark-skinned peoples was not limited to Joseph Smith and his followers. Many non-Mormon racial theorists embraced the idea that the racial improvement of dark-skinned peoples was not possible even in a favorable environment because such peoples were inherently inferior.[74]

Not only did Mormon racist ideas represent a "harder" Mormon line toward blacks, but the Saints utilized such ideas against certain white opponents. Throughout the 1830s Joseph Smith and his followers were confronted by divisions within the church and anti-Mormon enemies on the outside. From within, Joseph Smith's claim to Mormon authority was challenged. Certain disillusioned Mormons left the church in protest over the way Smith handled certain spiritual and secular questions. The ranks of the disaffected included such important figures as Martin Harris, Warren Parrish, and the Whitmers, David and John.[75] During this same period Smith and his followers faced non-Mormon hostility. Anti-Mormon mobs in Missouri attacked Latter-day Saint settlements on several occasions throughout the 1830s. Joseph Smith himself felt the full brunt of such anti-Mormon violence. He was tarred and feathered in Ohio. Later, after his migration to Missouri, the Mormon Prophet was jailed and threatened with execution.

These confrontations caused some Saints to look for parallels between their adversaries and the alleged ancestors of contemporary blacks. Oliver Cowdery utilized such ancestors in explaining how the wrath of God fell

on those who opposed His chosen people. He warned that the "Egyptians
... the posterity of Ham" had been swallowed up in the Red Sea for their
opposition to God's chosen people.[76] For a similar offense, the "posterity
of Canaan" felt the "shock" of God's divine punishment when the walls of
Jericho came tumbling down.[77] W. W. Phelps drew the most vivid parallels
between Mormon opponents and the alleged ancestors of contemporary
blacks. He speculated "that God causes the Saints or people that fall away
from his Church to be cursed in time, with a *black skin.*" In support of his
theory, Phelps then asked:

> Was or was not Cain, being marked, obliged to inherit the curse, he
> and his children forever? And if so, as Ham, like other sons of God,
> might break the rule of God, by marrying out of the church, did or
> did he not have a Canaanite wife, whereby some of the *black seed*
> was preserved through the flood, and his son, Canaan, after he had
> laughed at his grandfather's nakedness, heired three curses: one from
> Cain for killing Abel; one from Ham for marrying a black wife, and
> one from Noah for ridiculing what God had respect for? Are or are
> not the Indians a sample of marking with blackness for rebellion
> against God's holy word and holy orders? And can we not observe
> in the countenances of almost all nations . . . a dark, sallow hue, which
> tells the sons of God, without a line of history, that they have fallen
> or changed from the original beauty of grace of father Abraham.[78]

On an immediate level, church spokesmen drew parallels between Mormon
adversaries and contemporary blacks. W. W. Phelps accused anti-Mormon
persecutors of acting more heathenish than "the untaught Hottentots."[79]
The *Elders Journal,* which by the late 1830s became the official church
periodical, used such parallels in denouncing a number of prominent
Saints who left the church. "One thing we have learned, that there are
negroes who were [wear] white skins, as well as those who wear black
ones."[80] This Mormon practice of projecting unfavorable, often black,
racial characteristics on certain opponents would intensify during the
1840s and play a key role in undermining the position of blacks within
Mormonism.

Joseph Smith's articulation of racist concepts specifically directed
against blacks through the Books of Moses and Abraham was of crucial
importance. These concepts presented within a scriptural context paved

the way for the later implementation of black priesthood denial and other practices affirming the subordinate status of Mormon blacks. Smith's racist concepts, particularly those in the Book of Abraham, would in time provide scriptural justification for these practices. Thus, Mormon defenders would refer to those Book of Abraham verses suggesting that blacks as descendants of Ham were "cursed as pertaining to the priesthood." There is, however, little to suggest that the Latter-day Saints implemented black priesthood denial during the 1830s, despite the later assertions of Zebedee Coltrin and Abraham O. Smoot to the contrary.[81] It appears that Joseph Smith and other Mormon leaders continued to accept their black brethren in full fellowship throughout the 1830s despite the controversy generated by individual black members like Black Pete and Elijah Abel.[82]

The articulation of Mormon racist concepts directed against blacks complemented and reenforced the concurrent emergence of strong Latter-day Saint antiabolitionist sentiments. In turn the acceptance of antiabolitionist feelings made it easier for the Saints to embrace such racist concepts. The prevalence of Mormon antiabolitionist views during the 1830s overshadowed basic antislavery feelings. Mormon antipathy for slavery, initially evident in the Book of Mormon, remained in eclipse throughout the 1830s. However, by the 1840s, Mormonism's antislavery impulse would reemerge and become the dominant Mormon response to the slavery issue for the remainder of Joseph Smith's lifetime.

NOTES

1. Donna Hill, *Joseph Smith: The First Mormon* (New York, 1977), pp. 192-94; Fawn M. Brodie, *No Man Knows My History* (New York, 1944), pp. 170-71.

2. There is a controversy concerning the Egyptian papyri origins of this work. Generally, non-Mormon Egyptologists have maintained that Joseph Smith could not have "translated" this work from the papyri allegedly in Smith's possession during the 1830s. On the other hand, Latter-day Saint scholars have retorted that Smith could have translated the Book of Abraham from papyri other than those examined by the Egyptologists. Other Mormon defenders have suggested that the examined papyri have a double meaning. They acknowledge the findings of non-Mormon Egyptologists, which indicates a meaning different from the Book of Abraham, but they maintained

that Joseph Smith in his "translation" came up with a second subtle meaning, which indeed represented the writings of Abraham. This Mormon-Egyptologist conflict over the meaning of the papyri intensified in recent years as the Book of Abraham came to be used as a scriptural justification for Mormon black priesthood denial; see John A. Wilson, Richard A. Parker, Richard P. Howard, et al., "The Joseph Smith Egyptian Papyri: Translations and Interpretations," *Dialogue* 3 (Summer 1968): 67-105; and Klaus Baer, "The Breathing Permit of Hor: A Translation of the Apparent Source of the Book of Abraham," *Dialogue* 3 (Autumn 1968): 109-34.

3. For these concepts see *Pearl of Great Price*, Abraham, 3:22-28, 4:1-31, 5:1-21.

4. In particular see *Pearl of Great Price*, Abraham, 1:1-11, 20-27.

5. *Book of Mormon*, 2 Nephi 26:28.

6. *Doctrine and Covenants*, 1:2, 38:16. See also 1:10.

7. Ibid., 10:51. See also 1:23, 1:34, 112:4.

8. Ibid., 20:37, 45:54.

9. Ibid., 43:20. See also 38:33, 40-41, 39:15, 42:58, 58:47, 63:37, 77:8, 112:1, 16, 21, 28, 114:1, 18:28, 58:64.

10. Ibid., 45:69, 58:9, 45. See also 45:71, 33:6.

11. For an overview of Parley P. Pratt and his activities see his *Autobiography* (Salt Lake City, 1873). For Orson Pratt see T. Edgar Lyon, "Orson Pratt—Early Mormon Leader" (Ph.D. diss., University of Chicago, 1932); Parley P. Pratt, *A Voice of Warning and Instruction to All People* (New York, 1837), pp. 139-40.

12. Parley P. Pratt, *The Millennium and Other Poems* (New York, 1839), pp. 57-58.

13. *Evening and Morning Star* (Independence, Missouri), December 1832, March 1833.

14. Ibid., October 1832.

15. *Latter Day Saints Messenger and Advocate* (Kirtland, Ohio), December 1834. In this they quoted and referred to Luke 25:45, 46, 47; Matthew 28: 19-20.

16. Ibid., February 1835.

17. Ibid., September 1835.

18. Emma Smith, compiler, *A Collection of Sacred Hymns for the Church of Latter Day Saints* (Kirtland, 1835), as quoted in Lester E. Bush, Jr., "Mormonism's Negro Doctrine: An Historical Overview," *Dialogue* 8 (Spring 1973): 17.

19. E. S. Abdy, *Journal of a Residence and Tour in the United States* (London, 1835), 3: 58.

20. Joseph Smith, Jr., *History of the Church*, 2d ed. (Salt Lake City, 1978), 2: 368-69, 14 January 1836.

21. As indicated by articles that appeared in newspapers, not only in Ohio but as far away as New York and Pennsylvania. See *Ashtabula (Ohio) Journal*, 5 February 1831, taken from *Geauga (N.Y.) Gazette* [n.d.]; *Albany Journal*, 16 February 1831, reprinted from *Painesville* (Ohio) *Gazette* [n.d.]; and the *Philadelphia Sun*, 18 August 1831, taken from the *A.M. Intelligencer* [n.p., n.d.].

22. *Naked Truth About Mormonism* (Oakland, Calif.), January 1888. Quotes statement of Henry Carroll, 18 March 1885, concerning Black Pete's background.

23. *Ashtabula Journal*, 5 February 1831 and *Albany Journal*, 16 February 1831.

24. *Philadelphia Sun*, 18 August 1831. Also see *Ashtabula Journal*, 5 February 1831. Later recollections have Pete chasing "a ball that he said he saw flying in the air" or "revelations carried by a black angel." See *Times and Seasons* (Nauvoo, Illinois), 1 April 1842, and *Journal of Discourses* 11, George A. Smith, 15 November 1865.

25. *Naked Truth About Mormonism*, January 1888.

26. *Doctrine and Covenants*, 43:3-6.

27. This according to a later recollection in the *Times and Seasons*, 1 April 1842. However, it is unclear whether "Black Pete" was among those "cut off."

28. Andrew Jenson, *Latter-day Saint Biographical Encyclopedia: A Compilation of Biographical Sketches of Prominent Men and Women in the Church* (Salt Lake City, 1920), 3: 557.

29. Ibid.

30. Eunice Kenney, "My Testimony of the Latter Day Work," manuscript, 1885? (LDS Church Historical Department).

31. "Minutes of the Seventies Journal," kept by Hazen Aldrich, 20 December 1836 (original in LDS Church Historical Department).

32. *Latter Day Saints Messenger and Advocate*, June 1836.

33. It is interesting to note that in this blessing Smith declared "I seal upon thee a father's blessing because thou art an orphan, for thy father hath never done his duty toward thee." "Joseph Smith's Patriarchal Blessing Record," 88, recorded by W. A. Cowdery (original, LDS Church Archives). Copied from Lester E. Bush, "Compilation on the Negro in Mormonism," pp. 16-17 (unpublished manuscript available in LDS Church Archives).

34. Kenney, "My Testimony of the Latter Day Work."

35. "Minutes of the Seventies Journal," 1 June 1839.

36. Parley P. Pratt, *Late Persecutions of the Church of Latter-day Saints* (New York, 1840), p. 28. This statement was an estimate of free blacks only. There are no apparent statements or estimates concerning

the total number of black slaves who were church members or "associated" with the church (through the membership of their masters) during the 1830s. But in light of limited Mormon missionary success in the slaveholding South, this number was probably not very large.

37. Eugene H. Berwanger, *The Frontier Against Slavery* (Urbana, Illinois, 1967), p. 18; Charles I. Hickok, *The Negro in Ohio: 1802-1870* (Cleveland, Ohio, 1896), pp. 41-44.

38. Frank U. Quillin, *The Color Line in Ohio* (Ann Arbor, Mich., 1913), pp. 31-32.

39. Smith, *History of the Church,* 1: 190-91, July 1831.

40. Pratt, *Autobiography,* p. 81.

41. *Evening and Morning Star,* July 1833.

42. As contained in "The Secret Constitution of the Citizens of Jackson County" and "The Manifesto of the Mob." Manuscript copy in LDS Church Archives. Also reprinted in the *Evening and Morning Star,* December 1833.

43. "Extra," *Evening and Morning Star,* 20 July 1833.

44. As outlined in the "propositions of the Mob." First published in the Fayette (Missouri) *Western Monitor*, 9 August 1833, and the *Missouri Republican,* 9 August 1833.

45. This work, as a part of Joseph Smith's larger efforts to revise or "correct" both the Old and New Testaments, was essentially complete by 1833. Certain portions were published in the church newspaper as "The Prophecy of Enoch" and the "Book of Moses." See *Evening and Morning Star,* August 1832, March and April 1833. The complete biblical manuscript was not published until 1867. Then it was published as the *Holy Scriptures* by the Reorganized Church of Jesus Christ of Latter Day Saints. The Utah Mormons, or those Saints who followed Brigham Young west, never published this work because they believed it was "incomplete." See Reed Connell Durham, Jr., "A History of Joseph Smith's Revision of the Bible" (Ph.D. diss., Brigham Young University, 1965), p. 140. See also Robert J. Mathews, *Joseph Smith's Translation of the Bible—A History and Commentary* (Provo, Utah, 1975).

46. A Mormon preoccupation with the activities of Cain was not new. The conspiracy of Cain with Satan and the fact he "was a murderer from the beginning" had been previously noted in the *Book of Mormon,* Helaman 6:27; Ether 8:15. At the same time, however, it must be pointed out that theories linking the contemporary black man to Cain were still tentative among the Saints during the 1830s. One non-Mormon observer, after his visit among the Saints, reported that although they believed that the "descendants of Cain were all now under the curse . . . no one could possibly designate who they were." *Missouri Republican,* 29 April 1837, reprinted

in the *Illinois State Gazette and Jacksonville News,* 24 May 1837. This same observation was later included in Edmund Flagg, *The Far West or a Tour Beyond the Mountains* (New York, 1838), 2: 111.

47. *Pearl of Great Price,* Moses 5:18-33; *Holy Scriptures,* Genesis 5:6-18. It is interesting to compare this detailed account of Cain and his activities with the limited account in the Bible. See Genesis 4:1-11.

48. *Pearl of Great Price,* Moses 5:37; *Holy Scriptures,* Genesis 5:22.

49. *Pearl of Great Price,* Moses 5:40-41; *Holy Scriptures,* Genesis 5:25-26. It should be noted that nothing was said in these writings to suggest directly that the mark was a black skin. According to the standard Bible, Cain "went out from the presence of the Lord" in contrast to being "shut out (Genesis 4:16)."

50. *Pearl of Great Price,* Moses 5:49-50; *Holy Scriptures,* Genesis 5:35-36.

51. *Pearl of Great Price,* Moses 6:52, 54; *Holy Scriptures,* Genesis 5:38, 41. After Lamech, according to this account, "the works of darkness began to prevail among all the sons of man." Moses 5:55; *Holy Scriptures,* Genesis 5:42.

52. *Pearl of Great Price,* Moses 7:22; *Holy Scriptures, Genesis 7:29.*

53. *Pearl of Great Price,* Moses 6:17, 41-42; *Holy Scriptures,* Genesis 6:15, 43-44. Such alleged descent from Seth seems to be supported by at least one scholar, James E. Talmage, who carefully studied these Mormon scriptures and compiled reference notes attesting to this belief in 1902. See Moses 6:41 and Moses 7:61. Because of the close spelling of Cain and Cainan and because both the "people of Cainan" and "seed of Cain" were black, coupled with the fact that the scriptural descriptions of their activities are in close proximity, Moses 7:6-12; Genesis 7:6-14 (people of Cainan) and Moses 7:22; Genesis 7:29 (seed of Cain), there was a tendency, especially in the period after Joseph Smith's death, to link these two peoples together as the descendants of Cain. Further confusion was caused because of the different spellings used in Mormon scripture to denote this people, Cainan (*Holy Scriptures*) and Canaan (Book of Moses) These people have been confused at times with Canaan, the grandson of Noah, and his descendants. Lester E. Bush, Jr., discusses the confusion surrounding and implications for future Latter-day Saint attitudes and practices of alleged black relationships with Cain, Cainan, and Canaan. See his "Mormonism's Negro Doctrine, *Dialogues* (Spring 1973): pp. 35-36, 62. Also see his "Compilation on the Negro in Mormonism," Appendix I (manuscript available in LDS Church Archives).

54. *Pearl of Great Price,* Moses 7:7; *Holy Scriptures,* Genesis, 7:8-9.

55. *Pearl of Great Price,* Moses 7:8; *Holy Scriptures,* Genesis 7:9-10.

56. *Pearl of Great Price,* Moses 7:12, 15; *Holy Scriptures,* Genesis 7:14, 19.

57. *Pearl of Great Price,* Moses 8:27; *Holy Scriptures,* Genesis 8:16. In the standard Bible account only "Noah walked with God," (Genesis 6:9).

58. *Holy Scriptures,* Genesis 9:27-29. This Mormon scriptural account is identical with that in the Bible (Genesis 9:25, 27).

59. *Holy Scriptures,* Genesis, 9:30. This is significantly different from the standard Bible, which does not include the phrase "veil of darkness" (Genesis 9:26).

60. Though the complete text of this work was not finished until 1842, those portions dealing with the Chaldeans and Egyptians including the all important curse " as pertaining to the priesthood . . . " had been written by 1837. See Manuscript #1, containing Abraham 1:1 to 2:18 in the handwriting of W. W. Phelps and Warren Parrish; Manuscript #2, containing Abraham, 1:4 to 2:6 in the handwriting of W. W. Phelps; Manuscript #3, containing Abraham 1:4 to 2:2. All of these were written in 1837. For a discussion of these manuscripts and other Egyptian manuscripts written during the mid-1830s see Hugh Nibley "The Meaning of the Kirtland Egyptian Papers," *B. Y. U. Studies* 11 (Summer 1971): 350-99.

61. These links included a tendency by this people to worship the same "god of Elkenah" as the Pharaoh of Egypt, a descendant of Ham. Also on one occasion a "priest of Elkenah who was also the priest of Pharaoh" sacrificed "three virgins" who were of "royal descent directly from the loins of Ham." Finally Abraham and his seed were promised the "strange land of Canaan" where the "idolatrous nation" of the Canaanites dwelt. See *Pearl of Great Price,* Abraham 1:1, 5-7, 11, 2:6, 18-19.

62. Ibid., Abraham 1:21-27. This digression from the main story of the Book of Abraham was analogous to, and in some ways remarkably similar to, the distinct discussion of the Jaredites contained in the *Book of Mormon.* See Chapter 1 of this study.

63. *Pearl of Great Price,* Abraham 1:21.

64. Ibid., Abraham 1:22-24. Again there is some confusion concerning which "Canaanites" this account is referring to. It could be those people of Cainan (or Canaan) discussed in the Holy Scriptures or "Book of Moses," or it could be to the descendants of Canaan, the son of Ham. The context in which these Egyptians are discussed seem to suggest the latter possibility. This is also suggested in the reference notes of James A. Talmage for this section. See notes for Abraham 1:23 in *Pearl of Great Price.*

65. *Pearl of Great Price,* Abraham 1:25-27.

66. Caroline L. Shanks, "The Biblical Anti-Slavery Argument of the Decade 1830-1840," *Journal of Negro History* 15 (April 1931): 137. Also

see H. Shelton Smith, *In His Image, But . . . : Racism in Southern Religion 1780-1910* (Durham, North Carolina, 1972), pp. 130-31.

67. As suggested by Madeline Hook Rice. See her *American Catholic Opinion in the Slavery Controversy* (New York, 1944), p. 87.

68. Shanks, "The Biblical Anti-Slavery Argument of the Decade 1830-1840," p. 137. Also see Naomi F. Woodbury, "A Legacy of Intolerance: Nineteenth Century Pro-slavery Propaganda and the Mormon Church Today" (Master's thesis, University of California at Los Angeles, 1966).

69. David Walker, *An Appeal to the Colored Citizens of the World*, ed. Charles M. Wiltse (New York, 1965), pp. 19-20.

70. William Stanton, *The Leopard's Spots: Scientific Attitudes Toward Race in America, 1815-59* (Chicago, 1951), p. 47.

71. In the wake of Mormon persecutions, certain Saints appeared to question the commonly accepted criteria of race and technology for determining which peoples were civilized. Oliver Cowdery asked, "Is it color that constitutes a savage, or is it the acts of men that appear disgustful, and awake in our breasts feelings of piety and compassion for them?" *Evening and Morning Star,* February 1834.

72. This was evident in the references made to the "Seed of Cain" and "people of Cainan (or Canaan)" in terms of their exclusion from possible conversion to the true faith, and was graphically illustrated in the ineligibility of Pharaoh for the priesthood because he was of "that lineage" which couldn't hold it even though he was a "righteous man" in other respects.

73. See for example the comments of Oliver Cowdery in the *Evening and Morning Star,* April 1836, and Pratt, *Autobiography,* pp. 235, 241.

74. George M. Fredrickson, *The Black Image in the White Mind* (New York, 1971), pp. 43-47.

75. For a vivid discussion of conflict and factionalism within the church during the 1830s, see Brodie, *No Man Knows My History,* pp. 98-255.

76. *Evening and Morning Star,* March 1834. Through Mormon scripture, Joseph Smith had suggested that contemporary enemies, like their biblical counterparts, would be "smitten" and "cursed." On another occasion the "avenging" of enemies was prescribed "unto the third and fourth generations." See *Doctrine and Covenants,* 24:4-19 and 106:30.

77. *Evening and Morning Star,* January 1833. Priesthood denial was also interjected into Mormon scripture in the wake of the Latter-day Saint difficulties in Missouri during 1838-39. It was declared that those responsible for Mormon suffering would "not have right to the priesthood, nor their posterity." See *Doctrine and Covenants,* 121:21.

78. *Latter Day Saints Messenger and Advocate,* March 1835. Although Phelps' comments were speculative, there are indications that other Mormons

were affixing to their contemporary opponents or enemies, the possibility of undesirable racial characteristics. Joseph Smith, on a figurative level, described the activities of those who persecuted the Saints as "dark and blackening deeds." See *Doctrine and Covenants,* 123:10. In later years President Wilford Woodruff, along with Apostle Orson Hyde and Abraham O. Smoot, recalled how they actually observed apostates and enemies turning black. Hyde, after briefly leaving the church, had allegedly expressed his fear that if he stayed outside the true faith, "the curse of Cain [a black skin] would be upon him." See Matthias F. Cowley, ed., *Wilford Woodruff: History of His Life and Labors as Recorded in His Daily Journals* (Salt Lake City, 1909), pp. 50-53; Marvin S. Hill, "A Historical Study of the Life of Orson Hyde" (M.A. thesis, Brigham Young University, 1955), p. 40; C. Elliott Berlin, "Abraham Owen Smoot, Pioneer Mormon Leader" (M.S. thesis, Brigham Young University, 1955), p. 22. Such accounts, however, must be viewed with caution and a degree of skepticism because they, like the Smoot-Coltrin recollections, were recorded years after the fact.

79. *Latter Day Saints Messenger and Advocate,* October 1835.

80. *Elders Journal* (Far West, Missouri), August 1838.

81. The Smoot-Coltrin recollections recorded in 1879 asserted that Joseph Smith had inaugurated the Mormon practice of black priesthood denial during the 1830s. See L. John Nuttal, Diary, May 31, 1879, p. 170. Typescript copy of original in Special Collection Department of Brigham Young University Library.

82. Although it is very possible that Joseph Smith authorized proscriptions on black priesthood ordination in the slaveholding South, such proscriptions in this region would have conformed to the proscriptions eatablished by other religious denominations. See Carter G. Woodson, *The History of the Negro Church* (Washington, D.C., 1921), pp. 116-17; and his *The Education of the Negro Prior to 1861* (Washington, D.C., 1919), pp. 159-69, 179-90.

4 | *The Climax of Mormonism's Antislavery Impulse, 1839-1852*

Petition also, ye goodly inhabitants of the slave states, your legislators to abolish slavery. . . . Break off the shackles from the poor black man, and hire them to labor like other human beings. . . .

Joseph Smith, 1844

Servitude may and should exist, . . . upon those who are naturally designed to occupy the position of "servant of servants." . . .

Brigham Young, 1852

It was 1844, a presidential election year, and Joseph Smith decided to run for the nation's highest office on a self-styled third-party ticket.[1] Smith adopted a presidential platform outlining his "Views on the Government and Policies of the United States." In this document, Smith enunciated his position on various national issues, including the all-important question of slavery. Smith came out against the Peculiar Institution. He was upset that "Some two or three millions of people are held as slaves, because the spirit in them is covered with a darker skin than ours." He called for the "break down [of] slavery" and removal of "the shackles from the poor black man." This could be done by calling upon southern citizens to petition their legislators to abolish slavery through a program of compensated emancipation. The funds for this program would be obtained through the sale of public lands. Smith was confident that "hospitable and noble" southerners would help rid "so *free* a country" as the United States "of every vestige of slavery."[2]

> Wherefore, were I the president of the United States, by the voice of the virtuous people . . . when that people petitioned to abolish slavery in the slave states, I would use all honorable means to have their prayers granted . . . that the whole nation might be free indeed!

Smith believed that his program could bring about the complete elimination of southern slavery by 1850.[3]

Joseph Smith's campaign proposals for compensated emancipation were addressed not just to his Mormon followers but also to Americans in general. Smith tried to reconcile the differences between the proponents and opponents of Manifest Destiny. The pro-Manifest Destiny forces favored the annexation of Texas and other western territory. Those against Manifest Destiny did not want to see Texas and other potential slavery territory in the Southwest annexed to the United States. Both major political parties were deeply divided internally on this issue. Within the Whig party, "Cotton Whigs" favored expansion, while "Conscience Whigs" opposed it, fearing the expansion of slavery. The Democratic party mirrored a similar split through the rival campaigns for the party's presidential nomination mounted by John C. Calhoun and Martin Van Buren in 1844. Calhoun, the foremost spokesman for the South's Peculiar Institution favored expansion, while ex-President Van Buren assumed a Free-Soil position in opposition to expansion. In addition the Liberty party ran a candidate for president in the 1844 campaign on a strong antislavery-antiannexation platform.[4] Thus Joseph Smith's antislavery-proannexation platform attempted to reconcile these conflicting views. Smith announced that once he was elected president he would annex Texas and proceed to do away with the "evil" of slavery in the following manner, "As soon as Texas was annexed, I would liberate the slaves in two or three States, indemnifying the owners, and send the negroes to Texas, from Texas to Mexico where all colors are alike."[5]

All during his short-lived presidential campaign, Smith continued to hammer away at the Peculiar Institution, denouncing it as a "national evil" that should not be allowed to generate "fleshy capital."[6] Smith denounced Henry Clay, his Whig presidential opponent, for his role in the

Missouri Compromise of 1820, a measure that Smith condemned as "derived for the benefit of slavery."[7] He lamented that America was not an "asylum for the oppressed" as long as the "degraded black slave" was compelled to hold up his manacled hands and cry, "Oh liberty, where are thy charms that sages have told me were so sweet."[8]

Joseph Smith's willingness to campaign for president on a platform calling for the abolition of slavery dramatizes the strong Mormon antislavery feelings prevalent during the 1840s. These feelings emerged following the Mormon expulsion from Missouri and settlement in Nauvoo, Illinois. As early as 1842 Smith, when confronted with the problem of southern converts who had slaves and wanted to migrate to Illinois, a free state, recommended: "I have always advised such [southern converts] to bring their slaves into a free country and set them free."[9] The following year, Smith proposed the abolition of slavery through a program of "national equalization." This program would involve freeing the black slaves and giving them equal rights and privileges and confining them "by strict law to their own species."[10]

Smith's antislavery views were echoed by other church spokesmen. Among the most prominent Mormon foes of the Peculiar Institution was John C. Bennett. A powerful and influential leader, Bennett played a key role in securing a charter for the Mormon city of Nauvoo. The grateful Saints rewarded Bennett by electing him Nauvoo's first mayor. Within the Mormon movement Bennett became an "Assistant President of the Church" and for a year and a half was Joseph Smith's most "intimate friend and advisor."[11] Bennett was asked his views on slavery in a famous exchange with Charles Volney Dyer, a non-Mormon, Chicago-based antislavery advocate.[12] Bennett replied "I [have] ever detested servile bondage. I wish to see the shackles fall from the feet of the oppressed, and the chains of slavery broken."[13] Other prominent Mormons echoed Bennett's sentiments. Sydney Rigdon, a counselor to Joseph Smith, declared "every man should be free" with "the slave liberated from bondage."[14] Several Mormon apostles, including Erastus Snow, denounced the "alarming condition" of involuntary servitude. Apostle Parley P. Pratt in a church tract condemned those who traded "in horses, chariots and SLAVES and SOULS of MEN."[15] Apostle Orson Hyde wanted slavery done "away with."[16]

Mormon antislavery attitudes were not enshrined in the *Doctrine and Covenants* in the manner of earlier antiabolitionist statements, but these

attitudes were widely publicized in church periodicals. The most important
Latter-day Saint publications during the early 1840s were the *Times and
Seasons*, which by 1839 had replaced the *Elders Journal* as the principal
church organ, and the *Nauvoo Neighbor,* a secular newspaper. John Taylor,
a Mormon Apostle and member of the Council of Twelve, edited both of
these Nauvoo publications. Through his role as editor of the *Times and
Seasons* and *Neighbor,* Taylor became a leading defender of the Mormon
faith. He vigorously publicized Mormonism's antislavery position.[17] Taylor
denounced Missouri as a slave state whose "coffers" groaned "with the
spoils of the oppressed."[18] Taylor, like Joseph Smith, assailed Henry Clay
as a "slaveholder" who if elected president would make America the "slavest
and vainest nation on earth."[19] On another occasion the Mormon editor
observed that the South's "traffic in human flesh" made America less than
"an asylum for the oppressed."[20] Poetically, Taylor characterized Africa
as a "meadow of black flowers [used] to beautify white gardens" and
lamented that:

> All the world's an auction;
> All the men and women;
> All the beasts and cattle;
> All that look like human:-
> Are merely goods for sale:
> A little will suffice 'em;
> And little money buys 'em:
> the times are now so frail.[21]

Latter-day Saint dislike for the Peculiar Institution was also evident in
other quarters. Almon M. Babbitt, a Mormon representative in the Illinois
State Legislature, explained that "the Mormons like [so] many others believed that slavery is an evil."[22] The English-based *Latter-day Saints Millennial Star,* which began publication in 1840 for the ever-increasing number of British Saints, registered its "abhorrence" of the "slaveholder who
deprives his fellow-beings of liberty."[23]

Mormon dislike for slavery was motivated by several factors. The most
important was the movement of Mormonism's headquarters from Missouri,
a slaveholding state, to the free state of Illinois. Here the Saints were free
to speak out against the Peculiar Institution without fear of reprisals. In

fact, by the 1840s Illinois citizens, in general, were more inclined to oppose slavery than they had been just a few years before.[24] Illinois antislavery advocates were increasingly active during this period, coordinating their efforts throughout the state.[25] Illinois abolitionists also moved into the political realm, forming the Liberty party, which by 1846 held the balance of power in several northern Illinois counties.[26]

The Mormon presence in this antislavery Illinois environment encouraged the Saints to lash out at Missouri and its Peculiar Institution. The Saints drew parallels between Missouri slavery and the earlier persecutions that they had suffered in that state. They described Missouri as "a land of oppression" where they had been "in bonds."[27] Several Saints, according to one account, were "driven off . . . like a parcel of menial slaves."[28] Joseph Smith even suggested that Missouri citizens were utilizing several orphaned Mormon children left behind as "Mormon slaves."[29] The Missourians were characterized as brutes who routinely "burnt Negroes and butchered Mormons."[30] Slaveholding Missiorians were also denounced for their efforts to extradite Joseph Smith to stand trial on charges growing out of earlier Mormon-Missouri difficulties. These denunciations reached a peak when several Missouri officials seeking Smith entered Illinois disguised as "officers in search of runaway negroes."[31] These Missourians were assailed by the Saints as "nigger drivers" attempting "to steal white men."[32] The Mormons drew parallels between Missouri newspaper notices for "negroes" and Missouri's attempts to enslave the Saints.[33] John Taylor proclaimed that the Saints would "sacrifice their lives [rather] than bow to the yoke of Missouri . . . or be governed by the dictations of the mobcratic nigger drivers of Missouri."[34]

The Mormons were not alone in their dislike of Missouri. Other Illinois citizens attacked this slave state for the way it handled the issues of slavery and abolition. Non-Mormon Illinois residents, like the Saints, were upset at Missourian officials for their arrest, conviction, and imprisonment of three Illinois abolitionists.[35] Likewise, Illinois antislavery advocates condemned Missouri's action against Dr. Richard Eells, an antislavery crusader who aided the escape of Missouri slaves. After one such mission Eells fled into Illinois. When Missouri officials sought his return, the governor of Illinois, under popular pressure, refused the extradition request.[36] Such conflicts between Illinois and Missouri over the latter state's Peculiar Institution continued throughout the 1840s.

In addition to the Mormon move to the free state of Illinois, Latter-day Saint opposition to slavery was encouraged by several secondary factors. One of these was a shift in Mormon millennialistic expectations during the 1840s. Previously, the Saints believed the millennium to be imminent and therefore saw no need to eradicate the various evils of society including slavery, through reform prior to the millennium. The Saints felt that reform and perfection, including the abolition of slavery, could not be brought about prior to Christ's Second Coming. However, by the 1840s, Joseph Smith and other Saints believed the Second Coming to be several decades away.[37] As a result, the Saints had more time to reform society in various ways, including the abolition of slavery.

The Mormons were not alone in expressing their optimistic belief in a reform-oriented, millennialistic philosophy. Non-Mormon religious leaders, including Robert Dale Owen and Alexander Campbell, were passionate believers in reform as a necessary prerequisite for the millennium. Ralph Waldo Emerson and Horace Bushnell also expressed optimistic post-millennialistic beliefs. Emerson emphasized the importance of social reform coupled with scientific advancement, while Bushnell felt that American Christians must be in the vanguard of those reform movements hastening the millennium.[38] Reform through the eradication of slavery would bring America one step closer to this millennialistic utopia.

Mormon millennialistic, antislavery impulses were evident in Latter-day Saint calls for universal freedom for all men. Joseph Smith believed it was God's desire "to ameliorate the condition of every man."[39] On another occasion, the Mormon Prophet announced his support of "UNI-VERSAL LIBERTY" for "*every soul of man—civil, religious, and political.*" Apostle Parley P. Pratt, viewed America in millennialistic-reformist terms as "a land of liberty" where all peoples should be "free from bondage."[41] Various Mormon periodicals called for the breaking "of every yoke" in order to "let the oppressed go free."[42]

A Mormon dislike for slavery was also influenced by the fact that most Mormons were from nonslaveholding areas. Latter-day Saint converts throughout the 1840s came from middle-sized communities in New York and New England, areas of strong antislavery activity. A significant number of new converts also came from the Ohio Valley, another area of strong antislavery sentiment.[43] In addition, after 1837, the Mormons secured a large following in Great Britain, a nation which condemned the Peculiar

Institution. In fact, 4,000 Mormon Englishmen migrated to Nauvoo during the 1840s.[44] By contrast, the Saints drew very few new converts from the slaveholding South.[45]

There was, in fact, little love lost between the Saints and slaveholding southerners. Residents of this region were hostile toward Mormonism as a northern-based movement with distinctive doctrines and teachings.[46] One southern governor "laughed" off Mormonism as a *"religious Ism"* whose "prophets have no honor in our country."[47] In response Joseph Smith told Mormon missionaries to "confine" their activities "to the free states" and not go into any of the "Slave States."[48] Those English Saints migrating to the United States were also discouraged from settling in the South.[49]

While the Saints had their own unique reasons for lashing out against slavery, they were not alone in their views. Other northern-based denominations expressed antislavery feelings. As with the Saints, such attitudes displaced earlier antiabolitionist views. The Presbyterians led the way when part of this denomination assumed an antislavery position during the late 1830s, causing a split within Presbyterianism. By the mid-1840s more Presbyterians came out against slavery, further splitting this denomination.[50] Northern Methodists also attacked slavery, which led to a split between Northern and Southern Methodists.[51] Northern Baptists also experienced a growth of antislavery feeling within their ranks. This resulted in a break with Southern Baptists.[52] Antislavery feeling also increased among smaller denominations in the North, the Catholics and the Quakers.[53] Dislike for slavery was even evident in the nondenominational Home Missionary Society. This precipitated an internal schism, resulting in the formation of the rival antislavery American Mission Association.[54]

Although the Latter-day Saints were like other northern denominations in attacking slavery, they continued to stand apart from abolitionists like William Lloyd Garrison, Theodore Weld, and others. Unlike the American Anti-Slavery Society and the Liberty party, the Mormons presented their antislavery proposals in a low-keyed fashion. In addition, Joseph Smith's program for gradual compensated emancipation and colonization of the liberated blacks abroad stood in sharp contrast to the abolitionists' call for immediate uncompensated emancipation and provision for the liberated blacks in America.

In fact, the Latter-day Saints continued to uphold their earlier anti-abolitionist position, albeit more muted than during the 1830s. In 1842 and again in 1844 Joseph Smith made it clear that the Saints cared "nothing about" nor were "advocates of [immediate] abolition as it now exists"[55] Certain Saints reflected their dislike for abolition by affixing the epithet "abolitionist" to their enemies. Thus, John C. Bennett after his fall from Mormon favor was characterized as "the same abolitionist he always was."[56] Another opponent, Thomas Sharp, editor of the rabidly anti-Mormon *Warsaw Signal* was labeled an "abolitionist . . . nullifier, and . . . second rate man."[57]

Mormon antiabolitionist feelings became particularly pronounced following Joseph Smith's assassination in 1844. In this spirit, the *Times and Seasons* accused the "abolitionists" of "trying to make void the curse of God."[58] Almon Babbitt, the Mormon representative in the Illinois State Legislature, characterized the Saints as "anti-abolitionists . . . in every respect."[59] The Saints moreover continued to uphold their earlier, much publicized *Doctrine and Covenants* antiabolitionist verse of 1835 by retaining it in a second edition of this scriptural work published in 1845.[60]

Mormon antiabolitionist feelings were also reflected in Latter-day Saint attacks on the antislavery actions of several northern denominations. John Taylor, as editor of the *Times and Seasons* and *Nauvoo Neighbor,* was especially active in lashing out at various denominations. He condemned the "sudden ecclasiastical opposition to slavery" among the Methodists, warning that this controversy could lead to "the overthrow of the Methodist and American Union, slavery and peace. . . ."[61] He used stronger language in denouncing the debate and division among the Baptists.

> The inference we draw from such church jars among the sectarian world, is, that the glory which professing clergymen think to obtain for themselves by division of slavery . . . is nothing but vanity and vexation of spirit.[62]

Taylor recommended that "Religion shouldn't be brought into a question wholly national." The slavery issue could be settled only "through the ballot box."[63] As for the Saints, those in the North as well as those in the South would "stick together, and stick to the Union."[64]

Despite such antiabolitionist sentiments, Mormon dislike for slavery was the dominant mood during the early 1840s. Nevertheless, the death of Joseph Smith was an important turning point, the beginning of the decline of Mormonism's own antislavery impulse. This decline became particularly evident during the years 1846 to 1852 as the besieged Latter-day Saints under the leadership of Brigham Young abandoned Nauvoo and migrated west to the Great Basin.

These Great Basin Saints, although still opposed to the Peculiar Institution, were less willing to commit themselves in public. Thus, Brigham Young's observation that the Saints were "adverse" to slavery was confined to his private correspondence.[65] Likewise Apostle Orson Hyde and Wilford Woodruff gave limited exposure to their antislavery feelings. Only in private did these two leaders state that the Mormons "as a people" were "generally . . . opposed to slavery" and would "never . . . sustain" or tolerate it in any regions they occupied.[66] The few Mormons who expressed their antislavery views in public did so in a restrained manner. These critics, in contrast to earlier antislavery Mormons, tended to confine their antislavery feelings to poetry or verse. Apostle Parley P. Pratt proclaimed that in Utah "no chains or fetters bind the limbs of men; no slave exists to tremble, toil or sweat for nought."[67] In a poetic verse at another celebration, Pratt promised all those who migrated to Mormonism's mountain retreat:

Freedom, peace and full salvation
    And the blessings guaranteed—
Liberty to every nation,
    Every tongue, and every creed.[68]

Another Latter-day Saint called for "Liberty and truth . . . to illuminate the whole earth" until the sun "sets for the last time" on the "cottage of the slave."[69] Utilizing biblical analogies, William Clayton, a prominent churchman, explained that "Old Adam," the first man,

had no slave to black his boots, nor
    nigger to attend him.
With his own hands he did his chores, yet
    none would dare offend him.[70]

The Saints were also restrained in using politics as a means of attacking slavery. Thus, these later Saints, in contrast to Joseph Smith's active efforts in 1844, did not take to the political stump in lashing out at slavery. Instead, during the 1848 presidential campaign, apostles George A. Smith and Willard Richards merely suggested that the Latter-day Saints encamped at Council Bluffs, Iowa, might support a candidate who favored Free-Soilism.[71] Once the actual campaign got under way, slavery and Free-Soilism were not even significant issues for the Iowa Saints.[72]

Latter-day Saint leaders, however, were more active in trying to exclude slavery from their western Great Basin settlements. Apostle Willard Richards proclaimed that "Justice demands for us *Free Soil & Free Tariff*."[73] Apostle Daniel H. Wells believed that Mormon adherence to Free-Soil principles could be used to gain political support for Utah statehood.[74] This Mormon goal coincided with President Zachary Taylor's desire to divide the Mexican Cession—including the Mormon-dominated Great Basin—into individual states as soon as possible.[75] Consequently, Taylor, like Young, was willing to accept Free-Soilism as embodied in the Wilmot Proviso as a prerequisite. Taylor sent his personal representative General John Wilson west with a proposal that a single state based on the principles of the Wilmot Proviso be immediately formed out of two western regions: the Mormon-dominated Great Basin and the non-Mormon gold field settlements of the Pacific Coast.[76] Wilson conferred with Brigham Young. The Mormon leader endorsed Taylor's idea provided that the proposed state be divided by 1857 into two states—a Mormon Great Basin state and a non-Mormon West Coast state.[77] The Taylor-Young proposal was embodied in a document known as the Deseret petition. As for slavery, the petition declared that since "a very large majority . . . of the people of the [Great Salt Lake] Valley . . . are opposed" to the Peculiar Institution, they favored a state constitution "prohibiting slavery forever."[78] In January 1850 Wilson along with Apostle Amasa Lyman presented this petition to California officials, indicating Mormon support for "a temporary coalition with California to sue for admission into the Union as a free and sovereign state."[79] The Deseret petition, however, was rejected by the Californians as impractical because of problems inherent in governing two such distant settlements.[80]

Such antislavery sentiments notwithstanding, Mormon thinking after 1846 was dominated by a basic desire to remain aloof from the entire slavery controversy. This attempt at Mormon noninvolvement was somewhat reminiscent of the position taken by W. W. Phelps and the Missouri-based Saints during the early 1830s. The later Mormon quest for detachment was reflected in the Mormon approach to the problem of the run-

away slave. This problem confronted those Saints encamped at Council
Bluffs, Iowa, just across the border from the slave state of Missouri. This
settlement was under the direction of Apostle Orson Hyde.[81] Through
The Frontier Guardian, which he edited, Hyde when confronted with the
problem of the runaway slave, instructed those Saints under his authority
to treat such a runaway as they would any other stranger: to feed him if
he was hungry and then send him on his way. Hyde admonished the Saints
to avoid contact with either the fleeing slave or the owner in pursuit. He
told them not to "harbor or secret the runaway," but at the same time not
be "officious to procure" the black fugitive's "arrest" unless he had committed some specific criminal act.[82] In conclusion, Hyde instructed the
Saints to keep themselves "entirely free and unspotted from [this] dark
. . . subject" and not be "partizans [*sic*] . . . to this vexatious question."[83]

The problem of the runaway slave had greater relevance for the Council
Bluffs Saints than for the Utah-based Mormons. But the latter group was
forced to deal with this question on at least one occasion, when it was
disclosed that a fugitive slave was living among them. In response a church
spokesman explained that the Saints did not cause the runaway "to fly
from servitude." At the same time, these same Saints were "not disposed
to . . . causing him to return to slavery." However, if the owner wanted
the slave back, "he would probably meet with no resistance from [the
Saints] in getting him."[84]

As for the larger question of Utah territorial slavery, Utah Mormon
leaders tried to handle it in the same aloof manner. Mormon "Sentiment
from the Salt Lake Valley" was expressed in *The Frontier Guardian.*

> In regard to the Wilmot Proviso, slavery &c., we wish you to dis-
> tinctly understand that our desire is to leave that subject to the
> operation of time and circumstances, and common law; that we
> wish not to meddle with this subject, but leave these to their
> natural course.[85]

A Mormon desire to avoid the slavery issue was also reflected in the
instructions issued to Mormon representatives sent to Washington, D.C.,
to promote Latter-day Saint interests. Brigham Young told these delegates
to reject a territorial "probationary [antislavery] clause. . . ."[86] Apostle
Wilford Woodruff told these same representatives to avoid siding "with
the Democrats, Whigs, Free Soil or any other party."[87]

Almon W. Babbitt and John M. Bernhisel, the Latter-day Saint representatives to Congress, acted on these instructions in contrasting ways. Bernhisel, a circumspect individual whose profession was medicine rather than politics, followed the advice of church leaders and scrupulously avoided the entire slavery controversy.[88] In a letter to Brigham Young, Bernhisel explained, " I made it a *point* not only during my travels last summer and fall, but since my arrival in Washington, *not* to make *slavery* nor politics a *point*."[89] By contrast, Babbitt, a lawyer-politician and a somewhat impulsive, pugnacious personality, did not follow these instructions.[90] Instead, he presented himself as a "pro-slavery man" in a vain attempt to get himself seated in Congress.[91] In addition, Babbitt advertised the Utah Mormon "position" as "ultra-pro-slavery." He characterized the Great Basin as "Slavery Territory," claiming the presence of "four hundred slaves."[92] Babbitt's actions upset Utah Mormon leaders so much that they recalled the errant representative. By contract, Bernhisel, who had followed church instructions, became Utah's permanent delegate in Congress.

A Latter-day Saint desire for noninvolvement in the slavery controversy was also evident in the constitution for a proposed Mormon state. This document, sent to Washington with Bernhisel and Babbitt, did not mention slavery.[93] This omission caused at least three non-Mormon newspapers to observe rather naively that, since "not a word is said in the [Mormon] Constitution about slavery or the Wilmot Proviso," the Saints did not consider "such things . . . important for their welfare."[94] This was not the case. Latter-day Saint leaders recognized the sensitive nature of the slave issue during this critical time. The Saints wanted to avoid alienating partisans on both sides. Therefore Apostle Wilford Woodruff explained in private that the Saints, in forming their constitution, "deemed it expedient" to remain silent on this "vexed question. . . ."[95] Apostle Orson Hyde, through *The Frontier Guardian,* was more direct. He pointed out that the Mormons did not respond to the issues of "Slavery and the Wilmot Proviso" because, "We view these questions as a prolific source of bitterness and strife, the agitation of which would tend to sour and alienate the feelings of our own people one against another."[96]

The Latter-day Saints divorced themselves from the slavery controversy as it involved their territory by embracing the "natural limits" theory. This concept held that Utah, along with other territory recently acquired from Mexico, was geographically and climatically unsuited for black slave labor. This theory, according to Bernhisel, writing from Washington, was endorsed

by "all [of] the leading men in the non-slaveholding states and of all the
moderate men in the Slaveholding States" both in and out of Congress.[97]
Influential congressional leaders like Henry Clay, Daniel Webster, Lewis
Cass, and Stephen A. Douglas endorsed the natural limits theory for the
Mormon-occupied Great Basin.[98] Even southerners who vigorously opposed the Wilmot Proviso conceded the Great Basin to be unsuited for
slavery.[99]

John M. Bernhisel not only chronicled widespread congressional belief
in the "natural limits" theory, but expounded this view himself. When
approached by a sympathetic senator with the question "Is Deseret [Utah]
likely to become the Theatre of slave labor?" Bernhisel answered, "In
my judgment, there is no part of Deseret, so far as it has been explored,
in which slave labor can ever be profitably employed."[100]

Bernhisel further promoted the "natural limits" idea by trying to cover
up Utah's black slave population. Bernhisel was bothered by the presence
in Utah of 60 to 70 black slaves belonging to twelve Mormon masters.[101]
These blacks were mostly household servants with close personal ties to
particular Mormon families who had brought them from the South. They
were not part of a slave vanguard brought in to test Utah as an arena for
large-scale slaveholding.[102] Bernhisel, however, was not reassured by the
limited nature of Utah's Peculiar Institution. He was upset at the mere fact
of its existence. His concern intensified when informed that federal census
takers were on their way to Utah to count all the inhabitants, both free and
slave, for the 1850 Federal Census. He wrote Brigham Young of this fact
and requested that

> no person of African descent be reported as a slave. I make this sug-
> gestion because a large majority of the members of both branches
> of Congress, and a vast majority of the jurists in the United States
> entertain the conviction that slavery does not, and cannot exist in
> the Territory of Deseret without the sanction of positive law, yet to
> be enacted.[103]

Bernhisel's attempt to conceal Utah's black slave population was motivated by a basic desire to keep the Utah Mormons aloof from the slavery
controversy. He was also afraid that the disclosure of Mormon slaves would
jeopardize his own congressional efforts to secure a territorial government
for the Saints. Formation of such a government, Bernhisel later theorized,

would have been thwarted by northern congressmen if they had known of Utah's black slave population.[104]

Bernhisel's efforts to cover up Utah's black slavery failed. When the figures of the 1850 Federal Census were published two years later, Bernhisel learned to his dismay that church leaders in Utah did not follow his suggestions of reporting no black slaves. Instead, the final census figures for Utah recorded twenty-six black slaves.[105] Although this number was somewhat modest when compared with the 60 to 70 slaves actually held in the territory, it was still too high to suit Bernhisel.[106] The Mormon delegate felt that he had been deceived or at least misled by church leaders in Utah. After learning of the disturbing figures, he tersely wrote Brigham Young, "I understood from brother Bullock last summer that there were not slaves in the Territory and I have been asked how they came there, but was unable to answer. Will brother B. explain?"[107]

Even though Bernhisel failed to cover up the existance of Utah's black slave population, he did succeed in securing a territorial government for Utah as part of the Compromise of 1850. This compromise adopted the principle of popular sovereignty for Utah and New Mexico. Popular sovereignty allowed the residents of Utah to decide for themselves whether or not to allow slaveholding in their midst.[108] This principle conformed with the basic Mormon objective of remaining aloof from the vexing issue of slavery by removing this issue from the national political arena.

Despite the formation of the Territory of Utah on the basis of popular sovereignty, there was still the problem of those 60 to 70 black slaves. This problem, if not handled correctly, could complicate Mormon relations with the nonslaveholding North. Among those concerned about such relations was Thomas L. Kane of Pennsylvania, a close friend and political advisor to Brigham Young, despite being a non-Mormon. Kane advised Brigham Young, who had been appointed Utah's first territorial governor, to "avoid passing" legislation regulating this black slave population. Kane suggested that all "affairs affecting" these black slaves could be solved by "other and quiet arrangements," namely, by the removal of Utah's entire black slave population from the territory.[109] Young apparently tried to follow Kane's advice. In 1851, Young organized and sent to California a colonizing expedition containing twenty-six black slaves. This number was reported in the 1850 Census as "on their way to California." Thus the Saints tried to create the impression that as of 1852 there were no black slaves in Utah.[110]

In this way Young hoped to keep the Saints aloof from the entire slavery controversy.

However, in 1852 Brigham Young chose to reveal the presence of Utah's black slave population through the implementation of "An Act in Relation to Service" by the Utah territorial legislature.[111] This measure gave legal recognition to black slaveholding in the territory. There are several possible motives for the enactment of this measure, which seemed at variance with the basic Mormon desire to avoid the slavery issue. First, this measure was a response to the desire for legal recognition of black slaveholding by those Saints who had migrated to the Great Basin with their black slaves.[112] Included among these Mormon slaveholders were Apostle Charles C. Rich, William H. Hooper, a prominent Mormon merchant who later became Utah's territorial delegate, and Abraham O. Smoot, the first mayor of Salt Lake City.[113] Such individuals, in the words of a contemporary observer, constituted a "respectable minority" who were definitely "in favor of slavery."[114]

A second motive behind "An Act in Relation to Service" involved a Mormon desire to court southern congressional favor. Southern members of Congress were making crucial decisions affecting the Great Basin Saints. Sensitive to these interests, Brigham Young assured all southerners, both Mormon and non-Mormon, that their rights as slave holders in Utah would be upheld by law. There were "many Bren [brethren] in the South," Young noted, with "a great amount" invested "in slaves" who might migrate to the Great Basin if their slave property were protected by law.[115] The 1852 Act, in fact, was addressed to those "persons coming to this Territory and bringing with them servants justly bound to them."[116]

More significantly, "An Act in Relation to Service" was the product of Mormon racism—the tendency to look upon black people as inherently inferior and therefore fit subjects for involuntary servitude. The inferiority of black people, according to basic Mormon scriptural beliefs, stemmed from their alleged descent from certain biblical counterfigures, including Ham and Canaan. As a result of this accursed lineage, blacks were divinely destined to be "Servants" or slaves. Reflecting this view, W. W. Phelps described the Great Basin as a place where "the Jehovah Smitten Canaanite [could] bow in humble submission to his superiors."[117] Brigham Young utilized this same line of reasoning in justifying the 1852 "Act in Relation to Service." He proclaimed "the seed of Canaan will inevitably carry the curse which was placed upon them until the same authority which placed it there, shall see proper to have it removed."[118] In fact, Young went one step further. He justified black servitude because of a relationship between blacks and the biblical counterfigures of Cain and the Devil.[119]

Although Brigham Young and other Latter-day Saints looked upon the handful of blacks in their midst as inherently inferior and natural subjects for servitude, they never considered Utah as an arena for large-scale slaveholding. Geographically Utah was beyond the "natural limits" of slavery. Culturally most Latter-day Saints opposed slavery as a viable institution in their midst. Even Brigham Young confessed that his "own feelings" were "that no property can or should be recognized as existing in slaves." He further explained that "no person can purchase [slaves] without their becoming as free so far as natural rights are concerned."[120]

Brigham Young and other Mormons reflected this same antislavery position in the way they interpreted the 1852 "Act in Relation to Service" and the status of Utah's so-called black servants. These Saints looked upon Utah's institution of servile bondage as something like the practice of black indentured servitude that existed in Mormonism's former gathering place of Illinois.[121] Young rejected the slaveholding South as a model for Latter-day Saint slaveholders to follow. He opposed "the present system of [Southern] slavery" because of "its cruelties and abuses," which he found "obnoxious to humanity." Young, however, felt that the "Negro should serve."[122] Young pictured Mormon slaveholders as "masters" over "servants" in a personal, benevolent way. In this spirit he called upon Mormon slaveholders to use their black servants, "with all the heart and feeling, as they would use their own children . . . and treat them as Kindly, and with that humane feeling necessary to be shown to mortall [sic] beings of the human species."[123] In this benevolence, Young saw the Saints in the tradition of other "chosen" individuals who had held "servants" as described in the Old and New Testaments. This mood of "benevolent servitude" was reflected in the use of the term "servants" rather than slave throughout "An Act in Relation to Service."[124] Brigham Young summed up the rationale for "black servitude" in the Mormon Kingdom.

> Thus, while servitude may and should exist, and that too upon
> those who are naturally designed to occupy the position of "servant

of servants" yet we should not fall into the other extreme and make them as beasts of the field, regarding not the humanity which attaches to the colored race, nor yet elevate them, as some seem disposed, to an equality with those whom Nature and Nature's God has indicated to be their masters, their superiors.[125]

Finally, there was a fourth, albeit more subtle, motive behind the implementation of "An Act in Relation to Service." This act was an instrument to discourage any large-scale slaveholding in Utah, by which the Saints could achieve their basic aim of isolating themselves from the whole slavery controversy. This Act consisted primarily not of regulations on black slaves, as one might expect, but instead of rules to control the slaveowners. Utah slaveowners had to prove that their black servants had come into the territory "of their own free will and choice." Moreover, the slaveowner could not sell his black servants or remove them from the territory without the servants' own consent. In addition, a master was required to provide his servants with "comfortable habitations, clothing, bedding, sufficient food, and recreation." A master was even restricted in his right to "correct and punish his servant." He must be "guided by prudence and humanity" and not be cruel or abusive. Masters were, moreover, required "to send their servant or servants to school" for "not less than eighteen months, between the ages of six and twenty years." Finally, in contrast to prevailing practices in the slaveholding South, Utah masters were forbidden to engage in "sexual intercourse with any of the African race." A master found in violation of this provision was subject to a fine ranging from $500 to $5,000 and/or a term of imprisonment from three to five years. More important, the offending master could be compelled to "forfeit all claims to said servant or servants."[126] All of these regulations were subject to enforcement by the all-important territorial probate courts.[127]

The restrictive provisions of "An Act in Relation to Service" could not help but have a dampening effect on black slaveholding in Utah. Brigham Young seemed to suggest as much in a message delivered before the Utah legislature in late 1852. He noted that this statute, along with a number of antiblack measures, "had nearly freed the territory of the colored population." He could have added that this measure discouraged slaveholding in general.[128] Thus, "An Act in Relation to Service," despite its legal recognition of Utah slavery, was at least partially motivated by a Mormon desire to remain isolated from the slavery controversy.

There are at least three reasons why the Latter-day Saints moved away from their initial antislavery position of the early 1840s and attempted to isolate themselves from all aspects of the slavery controversy by the late 1840s. The first stemmed from the Mormon migration to the Great Basin. This migration threatened to directly involve the Saints in the sectional crisis of 1846-50. This crisis resulted from the North-South conflict over slavery in this Mormon-dominated region and generally in the Mexican Cession, territory acquired in 1848 by the United States through the Treaty of Guadalupe Hidalgo. Extreme northern antislavery partisans wanted through the Wilmot Proviso to completely exclude slavery from the Mexican Cession. By contrast, slaveholding southerners wanted this region left open to slavery. In between these two groups stood a number of northern and southern moderates willing to compromise. One moderate suggestion involved extending the Missouri Compromise line 36° 30′ through the Mexican Cession to the Pacific Ocean. This proposal, however, would have confounded the slave issue in the proposed Mormon State of Deseret, which included territory both north and south of the line 36° 30′. The Saints, as recent arrivals to this contested region, found themselves under close national scrutiny and pressure to state their position on this vexing issue. The Mormons, therefore, welcomed the 1850 establishment of the Utah territory based on the concept of popular sovereignty. As a result, the issue of Utah slavery was removed from the national political arena. This development aided the Utah Mormons in their efforts to remain as isolated as possible from the slave controversy.[129]

In addition to events in the Great Basin, a Mormon quest for noninvolvement was encouraged by the general national crisis over slavery during the late 1840s and early 1850s. The Mormons were alarmed by reports predicting the breakup of the Union. The "grave and great question of slavery" was generating "feelings of deepest hatred" between the North and the South.[130] Some Latter-day Saints interpreted this national crisis in millennialistic-apocalyptic terms. In doing so, the Mormons moved away from the optimistic post-millennialistic belief that earlier had dominated Mormon thinking during the early 1840s, that is, a belief that the millennium was at least several decades away. By the late 1840s the Mormons returned to their earlier pre-millennialistic beliefs that the apocalyptic end of time was imminent. Expressing this view, Apostle Wilford Woodruff prophesied "War, blood and thunder" between the North and South, leading to "the overthrow of this government."[131] John M. Bernhisel expected "the great and grave question of slavery" to "shake this Union to its centre," and possibly to break it "into as many fragments as there are States composing it."[132] The North and the South, according to Apostle Orson Pratt, were rushing "headlong into the opening vortex that has swallowed up nations and generations." Pratt predicted that:

> The people of the United States are to be divided among themselves—the North against the South; the Southern states will call on Great Britain for help: Great Britain will call on other nations ... and thus war shall be poured out upon all nations, and no people under heaven shall be at peace except the Lord's people—the children of Zion.[133]

The predictions of Pratt, as well as those of Bernhisel and Woodruff, were remarkably similar to Joseph Smith's millennialistic—apocalyptic 1832 "Revelation and Prophecy on War." This revelation, in fact, was incorporated into the *Pearl of Great Price,* published for the first time in 1851.[134] Therefore, the Latter-day Saints in response to these "signs of the times" wanted to remain apart from the destructive, apocalyptic events associated with the slave controversy.

Finally, a Mormon quest for isolation from the slavery controversy was stimulated by a third factor, a change in church leadership after 1844. Following the assassination of Joseph Smith, Brigham Young, president of the Council of Twelve Apostles, emerged as the acknowledged leader of those Latter-day Saints who migrated westward. In 1847, following the arrival of the Saints in the Great Salt Lake Valley, Young was sustained as president of the whole church, thereby inheriting the post of "Prophet, Seer, and Revelator" held by his predecessor, Joseph Smith. But Young differed from Smith in that he avoided national political issues in general, including slavery, and presidential politics in particular. There was no Young counterpart of Joseph Smith's 1844 campaign for the presidency.[135] Instead, the new church president and his assistants concerned themselves primarily with the problems of establishing their Zion in the Rocky Mountains. Young did not want slavery or any other issue to distract the Saints from this primary task.

The flow and ebb of Mormonism's antislavery impulse represents an important turning point in the evolution of attitudes and practices toward black people. During the early 1840s, when Mormon antislavery sentiments were in the ascendancy, it was possible that the Latter-day Saints might have looked at black people in a more favorable light. Perhaps the Saints would soften their earlier racist concepts as articulated in the Books of Moses and Abraham. This, however, was not to be. Instead, by the late 1840s, the Saints moved away from this antislavery position and, by 1852, gave legal recognition to black slaveholding in the Great Basin. This Latter-day Saint recognition was an important development in that it represented a Mormon willingness to transpose racist concepts into a specific practice directed against black people. Such a transposition was also reflected in the emergence of black priesthood denial by the late 1840s, a development that would have fateful consequences for all blacks involved with the Mormons.

NOTES

1. For a consideration of the various motives attributed to Joseph Smith in his quest for the presidency of the United States, see Fawn M. Brodie, *No Man Knows My History* (New York, 1944), pp. 362-66; and "Joseph Smith's Presidential Platform," *Dialogue* 3 (Autumn 1968): 17-27.

2. Joseph Smith, Jr., *Views on the Government and Policies of the United States* (Nauvoo, Illinois, 1844), p. 3. This pamphlet was distributed throughout the United States. It was also reprinted in various periodicals edited by church spokesmen. See *Times and Seasons* (Nauvoo, Illinois), 15 May 1844; *Nauvoo Neighbor,* 8 May 1844; and *Prophet* (New York City), 8 June 1844.

3. Smith, *Views on the Government,* pp. 3, 7-8. The feasibility of Smith's proposal to liberate the black slaves through the payment of a "reasonable price" to southern slaveholders with funds obtained from the sale of public lands has been questioned by at least one writer, who explained, "There were almost 3,000,000 slaves in 1844, with an average value in excess of $500. Total public land sales in the 1840s averaged approximately $2,000,000 yearly, and the proposed cutbacks in congressional membership and pay (which Smith suggested as an additional source of revenue) would have produced perhaps $500,000." According to these figures, at 1840s rates it would have taken about 700 years, rather than the 5 to 6 estimated by Smith, to carry out his program. See Martin B. Hickman, "Editorial Footnotes to General Smith's Views . . . ," *Dialogue* 3 (Autumn 1968): 28.

4. Fredrick Merk, *Manifest Destiny and Mission in American History* (New York, 1963), pp. 24-88; Louis Filler, *The Crusade Against Slavery 1830-1860* (New York, 1960), pp. 176-77.

5. Joseph Smith, Jr., *History of the Church*, 2d ed. (Salt Lake City, 1978) 6: 244. Another Mormon official, Apostle Wilford Woodruff, made a similar suggestion that he "would liberate two or three states to pay them for their slaves and let them go to Mexico where they are mixed blacks." Wilford Woodruff, "Journal," March 7, 1844. It is not clear what Woodruff meant by the phrase "Mexico where they are mixed blacks."

6. *Nauvoo Neighbor*, 22 May 1844.

7. *Times and Seasons*, 1 June 1844.

8. Ibid.

9. Willard Richards, "Journal," 30 December 1842, Willard Richards Papers, LDS Archives, Salt Lake City.

10. Joseph Smith, *History of the Church*, 5:217-18.

11. For one view of John C. Bennett and his activities see Brodie, *No Man Knows My History*, pp. 266-68, 271, 273, 314.

12. For a brief biographical sketch of Dyer see George P. Upton and Elias Colbert, *Biographical Sketches of the Leading Men of Chicago* (Chicago, 1868), pp. 73-80. It appears that Bennett and Dyer knew each other through their common practice of medicine in the Chicago area prior to Bennett's conversion to Mormonism and migration to Nauvoo.

13. *Times and Seasons*, 15 March 1842.

14. Ibid., 1 February 1844.

15. *Prophet*, 20 July 1844; "An Epistle of Demetrius Jr., the Silversmith," as reprinted in *Prophet*, 28 September 1844.

16. *Prophet*, 29 June 1844.

17. For the most recent treatment of John Taylor see Samuel W. Taylor, *The Kingdom or Nothing: The Life of John Taylor, Militant Mormon* (New York, 1976).

18. *Times and Seasons*, 1 July 1843; *Nauvoo Neighbor*, 17 April 1844.

19. *Nauvoo Neighbor*, 21 August 1844.

20. Ibid., 10 September 1845. On another occasion he compared the "freedom" in the United States with a "stool pigeon, it flutters by force to decoy others." *Times and Seasons*, 15 February 1846.

21. *Nauvoo Neighbor*, 29 October 1845; 7 April 1845.

22. *Prophet*, 22 February 1845.

23. *Latter Day Saints Millennial Star* (Liverpool, England), September 1843.

24. As noted by Leonard L. Richards, *Gentlemen of Property and Standing: Anti-Abolition Mobs in Jacksonian America* (New York, 1970), pp. 156-70.

25. Theodore Calvin Pease and Marguerite Jenison Pease, *The Story of Illinois*, 3d ed. (Chicago, 1965), pp. 149-50. Merton L. Dillon, "Abolitionism Comes to Illinois," *Journal of the Illinois State Historical Society* 53 (Winter 1960): 403.

26. Pease and Pease, *The Story of Illinois,* p. 150.

27. *Times and Seasons,* April, August, 1840.

28. Smith, *History of the Church,* 3: 222.

29. *Times and Seasons,* 15 March 1842.

30. *Wasp* (Nauvoo, Illinois), 17 September 1842; *Nauvoo Neighbor,* 20 August and 13 September 1843. It is interesting to note that "negro burnt alive" to which the *Neighbor* made repeated references, was one McIntosh, who was seized by a Missouri mob and killed in this grotesque manner over a slow-burning wood fire for his part in killing a law officer some years before. Elijah Lovejoy, the noted abolitionist, expressed his abhorrence at McIntosh's execution in his St. Louis newspaper. This concern generated additional Missouri hostility against Lovejoy, who was driven from the state and forced to take up residence in Alton, Illinois. For a discussion of the events surrounding this incident and the activities of Elijah Lovejoy in general, see Merton L. Dillon, *Elijah P. Lovejoy, Abolitionist Editor* (Urbana, Illinois, 1961).

31. *Wasp,* 27 August 1842.

32. Smith, *History of the Church,* 5: 472; *Nauvoo Neighbor,* 13 December 1843.

33. *Nauvoo Neighbor,* 7 April 1845.

34. Ibid., 20 December 1843.

35. W. Sherman Savage, "The Contest over Slavery between Illinois and Missouri," *Journal of Negro History* 28 (July 1943): 318. Larry Gara, "The Underground Railroad in Illinois," *Journal of the Illinois State Historical Society,* 66 (Autumn, 1963): 515-16. For an excellent discussion of antislavery sentiment in Illinois as it existed among various religious denominations, including the Mormons, see Linda Jeanne Evans "Abolitionism in the Illinois Churches, 1830-1865 (Ph.D. diss., Northwestern University, 1981).

36. Savage, "Contest over Slavery," p. 318. It is interesting to note that Missouri's demands for Eells were remarkably similar to demands made by Missouri authorities for the custody of Joseph Smith to stand trial on charges of insurrection in connection with the Mormon-non-Mormon hostilities of 1838-39. See George R. Gayler, "Attempts by the State of Missouri to Extradite Joseph Smith, 1841-1843," *Missouri Historical Review* 53 (1963): 21-36.

37. *Doctrine and Covenants,* 130:15-17. Also see Joseph Smith, Jr., "Discourse," 19 July 1840, Joseph Smith Papers, LDS Church Historical Department. Smith felt that the Second Coming of Christ was at least fifty years away. However, such feelings were not held among all Saints. At least one Mormon saw the divisions over slavery among various religious denominations as indicators of the approaching millennium (*Times and Seasons,* August 1845). The continuation of apocalyptic anxieties as it involved the

millennium and the slave question was reflected in a revelation purportedly received by Joseph Smith in April 1843.

> I prophesy, in the name of the Lord God, that the commencement of the difficulties which will cause much bloodshed previous to the coming of the Son of Man will be in South Carolina.
>
> It may probably arise through the slave question. This a voice declared to me, while I was praying earnestly on the subject, December 25, 1832.

This is found in *Doctrine and Covenants,* 130:12-13. The last part of this revelation referred to Smith's famous "revelation and Prophecy on War" (*Doctrine and Covenants,* 87:1, 3-4), allegedly received in 1832. The origins and contents of this earlier revelation were discussed in Chapter 2.

38. Ernest L. Tuveson, *Redeemer Nation* (Chicago, 1968), pp. 51, 64, 67, 79. Also see Klaus J. Hansen, "The Millennium, the West, and Race in the Antebellum American Mind," *Western Historical Quarterly* 3 (October 1972): pp. 376-78. However, the millennialistic interpretation of Tuveson has been challenged by Ernest R. Santeen in *The Roots of Fundamentalism: British and American Millennialism, 1800-1930.* (Chicago, 1971). According to Santeen millenarian or pre-millennialist rather than post-millennialistic expectations predominated throughout this period. Moreover, Santeen argues that the Mormons moved from a pre- to a post-millennialistic position in order to differentiate themselves from William Miller, their principal millennialistic rival.

39. *Times and Seasons,* February 1840.

40. Ibid., 15 March 1842 (italics in original).

41. *Latter Day Saints Millennial Star,* September 1842.

42. *Times and Seasons,* 1 March 1844; *Nauvoo Neighbor,* 6 March 1844, 6 November 1844.

43. S. George Ellsworth, "A History of Mormon Missions in the United States and Canada, 1830-1860" (Ithaca, N.Y., 1966); (Ph.D. diss., University of California, 1951), pp. 226-95.

44. P.A.M. Taylor, *Expectations Westward* (Ithaca, N.Y., 1966); Richard L. Evans, *A Century of Mormonism in Great Britain* (Salt Lake City, 1937).

45. La Mar C. Berrett, "History of the Southern States Mission, 1831-61," (M.A. thesis, Brigham Young University, 1960), pp. 45-46; Ellsworth, "A History of Mormon Missions in the United States and Canada, 1830-1860," pp. 257, 335.

46. Berrett, "History of the Southern States Mission," p. 46.

47. Baltimore, *Niles Register,* 28 June 1841 (italics in original). It is interesting to note that one Mormon editor expressed somewhat the reverse argument with regard to Mormon attitudes toward the South. "It is to the credit certainly of the Mormons that their sect was originated and has flourished in the North where the greatest degree of intelligence is supposed to prevail" (*Wasp,* 9 July 1842).

48. Wilford Woodruff, "Journal," 4 August 1842. However, at least one Mormon leader, Apostle Lyman Wight, looked toward the slaveholding South as playing a significant future role. Wight believed that Texas could serve as a Mormon "gathering point for all the South." According to Wight there were "thousands of . . . rich planters who would embrace the Gospel . . . if they had . . . some slave holding point" where they could "plant their slaves." Joseph Smith's response to Wight's plan is not known because Wight's proposal came just prior to Smith's untimely death in 1844. Wight himself felt that the Mormon Prophet had given his approval to a southern gathering just prior to his death. See Letter from Lyman Wight, George Miller et al., to the First Presidency and the Quorum of the Twelve, 15 February 1844; Letter from Wight to Smith, 15 February 1844; Letter from George Miller to President and Quorum of the Twelve Apostles, 17 March 1847; and Letter from Orson Hyde to Joseph Smith, 26 April 1844, all reprinted in "Journal History," LDS Church Archives. For two accounts of Lyman Wight and his subsequent activities in Texas as a leader of a schismatic Mormon group see Davis Bitton, "Mormons in Texas: The Ill-Fated Lyman Wight Colony 1844-1858," *Arizona and the West* 11 (Spring 1969): 6-26; and C. Stanley Banks, "The Mormon Migration into Texas," *Southwest Historical Quarterly* 49 (October 1945): 233-44.

49. *Latter Day Saint Millennial Star,* August 1841.

50. Irving Stoddard Kull, "Presbyterian Attitudes Toward Slavery," *Church History* 7 (1938): 107-8; C. Bruce Staiger, "Abolitionism and the Presbyterian Schism of 1837-38," *Mississippi Valley Historical Review* 36 (1949-50): 391-414.

51. Donald G. Matthews, *Slavery and Methodism: A Chapter in American Morality 1780-1845* (Princeton, N.J., 1965), pp. 231, 240, 281.

52. Mary B. Putnam, *The Baptists and Slavery 1840-1845* (Ann Arbor, Mich., 1950), p. 30.

53. Madeleine H. Rice, *American Catholic Opinion in the Slavery Controversy* (New York, 1944), p. 87; Thomas E. Drake, *Quakers and Slavery in America* (New Haven, Conn., 1950), pp. 162-74.

54. Clifford S. Griffin, *Their Brother's Keeper,* (New Brunswick, N.J., 1960), p. 185.

55. *Times and Seasons,* 1 June 1842, 1 October 1842; *Nauvoo Neighbor,* 8 January 1844.

56. *Wasp,* 27 August 1842. Also see letter from George Backman to General Moses Wilson, 20 January 1843, George Backman Papers, LDS Church Archives.

57. *Nauvoo Neighbor,* 25 October 1842. However, such antiabolitionist feelings did not prevent certain Saints from identifying with the problems of the abolitionists. For example, the Saints compared the failure of the United States Congress to respond to their petition for redress from the Missouri difficulties with the nonresponse of this same body to the petitions of the abolitionists. On another occasion, the Saints saw parallels between Missouri's efforts to extradite Joseph Smith and a similar case involving a New York abolitionist fighting extradition to the South. See the *Nauvoo Neighbor,* 12 June 1844, and *Times and Seasons,* 5 December 1842.

58. *Times and Seasons,* 1 April 1845.

59. *Prophet,* 22 February 1845. Also see the *Wasp,* 15 October 1842.

60. *Doctrine and Covenants.*

61. *Times and Seasons,* 1 October 1844.

62. Ibid., 1 April 1845.

63. *Nauvoo Neighbor,* 21 May 1845.

64. Ibid., 4 June 1845.

65. Brigham Young to John M. Bernhisel, 19 July 1849, Brigham Young Papers, LDS Church Archives. It is possible that Young's basic dislike for slavery, which manifested itself throughout the twenty-year period from 1846 to 1865, might have been influenced by his family background. Brigham Young's father as a youth had been " 'bound out' to a man . . . who had both white and black servants." This man, according to the stories handed down, treated the elder Young and his other servants "cruelly." See S. Dilworth Young, *Here Is Brigham* (Salt Lake City, 1964), pp. 14- 37.

66. Orson Hyde to Brigham Young, 12 June 1849, Orson Hyde Papers, LDS Church Archives; Wilford Woodruff to Thomas L. Kane, 27 November 1849, Wilford Woodruff Papers, LDS Church Archives.

67. *Latter Day Saints Millennial Star,* 1 January 1849.

68. Ibid., 1 December 1849.

69. *Deseret News* (Salt Lake City), 10 August 1850.

70. Ibid., 16 November 1850.

71. George A. Smith to Brigham Young, 2 October 1848, George A. Smith Papers, LDS Church Historical Department. Willard Richards to Thomas Kane, 25 July 1849, Willard Richards Papers, LDS Church Historical Department. Potential Mormon support for the Free-Soil party, however, was far from complete because of the Latter-day Saint hostility toward its standard bearer, Martin Van Buren. The *Latter Day Saints Millennial Star* referred sarcastically to the members of this party as "half-blood Abolitionists," 1 February 1848.

72. For a discussion of the political activities of the Iowa-based Saints see J. Keith Melville, *Conflict and Compromise: The Mormons in Mid-Nineteenth-Century American Politics* (Provo, Utah, 1974).

73. Willard Richards to Thomas Kane, 2 May 1849. Richards Papers (italics in original).

74. Daniel H. Wells to Orson Hyde, 5 March 1849, Daniel H. Wells Papers, LDS Church Archives. Also, church leaders hoped that the growing debates over Free-Soil and slavery in the territories would divert political attention away from the Saints and their activities.

75. This goal of immediate statehood was based on Taylor's desire to bring an end to all Congressional debate over the question of slavery in the Mexican Cession, thus restoring domestic tranquility. See Holman Hamilton, *Zachary Taylor: Soldier in the White House* (New York, 1951), pp. 263-79. Also see Hamilton's *Prologue to Conflict: The Crisis and Compromise of 1850* (New York, 1966), pp. 20, 47-48. The Saints, however, in pursuing this same goal of immediate statehood looked at the current North-South crisis in a different light. Brigham Young summed up the view of some Saints. "Should the Wilmot Proviso or slave question, by any means, become settled before our admission into the Union, politicians might feel themselves more independent, and our interests might not lay so near their hearts." Brigham Young to Amasa Lyman, 6 September 1849, Young Papers.

76. Hamilton, *Prologue to Conflict,* p. 20; J. Keith Melville, *Highlights in Mormon Political History* (Provo, Utah, 1967), pp. 61-62; Leland H. Creer, *Utah and the Nation* (Seattle, Washington, 1929), pp. 80-81. The main motives behind the idea of combining these two regions was the feeling that each of these two regions, alone, lacked sufficient population for statehood.

77. Brigham Young to Amasa Lyman, 6 September 1849, Young Papers.

78. As quoted in Frederic A. Culmer, " 'General' John Wilson, Signer of the Deseret Petition," *California Historical Society Quarterly* 26: 330.

79. "Journal History," LDS Church Archives, 31 January 1850.

80. Melville, *Highlights in Mormon Political History,* p. 64; Creer, *Utah and the Nation,* p. 81.

81. For the best account of Orson Hyde, see Marvin S. Hill, "A Historical Study of the life of Orson Hyde, Early Mormon Missionary and Apostle from 1805-1852" (M.A. thesis, Brigham Young University, 1955)

82. Kanesville (Iowa) *Frontier Guardian,* 17, 21 October 1849.

83. Ibid., 17 October 1849.

84. Ibid., 8 August 1849.

85. Ibid., 18 September 1849. It is interesting to note that the original correspondence from Daniel H. Wells to Orson Hyde, 19 July 1849, Wells

Papers, is somewhat different in its contents and implication from that reprinted in the *Guardian*. The unpublished portion of the correspondence noted that "You might safely say (if it was of any *particular* case) that as a people We are adverse to Slavery, but we wish not to meddle with this subject at present but leave things to take their natural course" (italics and crossing out in original).

86. Brigham Young to John M. Bernhisel, 19 July 1849, Young Papers.

87. Wilford Woodruff to Almon W. Babbitt, 27 November 1849, Woodruff Papers; Conversation between Thomas L. Kane, John M. Bernhisel, and Wilford Woodruff, 26 November 1849, as recalled and noted by Woodruff, Thomas L. Kane Papers, LDS Church Archives.

88. Gwynn William Berrett, "John M. Bernhisel: Mormon Elder in Congress" (Ph.D. diss., Brigham Young University, 1968).

89. John M. Bernhisel to Brigham Young, 21 March 1850, John M. Bernhisel Papers, LDS Church Historical Department (italics in original).

90. Jay Donald Ridd, "Almon Whiting Babbitt: Mormon Emissary" (M.A. thesis, University of Utah, 1953).

91. *Congressional Globe* (Washington, D.C.), 19:2, 21 July 1850. Babbitt in his proslavery approach may have been influenced by the unsuccessful efforts of a delegate from New Mexico to get himself seated by virtue of his opposition to slavery for his territory.

92. Ibid., 19:2, 29 August 1850. Thomas L. Kane to Brigham Young, 19 February 1851, Kane Papers. Another source gave the figure of "some two hundred slaves." (see Robert W. Johannsen's *Stephen A. Douglas* [New York, 1973], p. 267). These two sets of figures were a gross exaggeration. See Appendix C. Babbitt, in his quest for southern support for the Saints, may have also been encouraged by what he perceived as underlying southern sympathy for the Mormon cause as suggested in the speeches given by at least two southerners in Congress. See *Congressional Globe*, 19 Appendix, 5 June 1850 and 9 July 1850.

93. First printed in *Latter Day Saints Millennial Star*, 1 January 1850.

94. *Daily Missouri Republican*, 1 October 1849. *New York Herald*, 10 October 1849, and the *Alta Californian*, 15 December 1849, as quoted in Culmer, " 'General' John Wilson, Signer of the Deseret Petition," p. 331.

95. Wilford Woodruff to Thomas L. Kane, 27 November 1849, Woodruff Papers.

96. *Frontier Guardian*, 23 January 1850. He went on to explain that divine providence had not foreordained "the Mormons to work up the knotty and crossgrained lumber of Slavery and the Wilmot Proviso" but had left this task for those outside the true faith.

97. John M. Bernhisel to Brigham Young, 21 March 1850, Bernhisel Papers. He felt that only the "ultra-fanatics of the South" held an opposite opinion.

98. *Congressional Globe,* 19 Appendix, 23 January 1850, 7 March 1850, 13 May 1850, 14 March 1850.

99. Ibid., 17 Appendix, 28 June 1848, 12, 20 July 1848; 18 Appendix, 10 February 1849; 19 Appendix, 21 May 1850, 24, 27 June 1850. This southern belief that the Great Basin was *not* a fertile ground for the expansion of the Peculiar Institution was perhaps best illustrated by the lack of concern at the Nashville Convention of 1850. Even in the emotion-charged proceedings of this gathering, partisan southerners did not consider it worth their effort to promote even the symbolic right to hold slaves in the Mormon-dominated Great Basin.

100. Ibid., 19 Appendix, 8 July 1850. Bernhisel's answer as printed in the *Globe* was somewhat different from the description that Bernhisel gave President Young. To Young, he said, "Slave labor can never in *our* opinion be profitably employed in Deseret so far as it has been explored." (italics mine, John M. Bernhisel to Brigham Young, 21 March 1850, Bernhisel Papers).

101. For a list of Mormon slaveholders during this period see Appendix C, particularly tables 1 and 4.

102. As pointed out by Dennis L. Lythgoe in "Negro Slavery in Utah," *Utah Historical Quarterly* (Winter 1971). Also see his "Negro Slavery in Utah" (M.A. thesis, University of Utah, 1966).

103. Bernhisel to Young, 3 July 1850, Bernhisel Papers.

104. Bernhisel to Young, 12 September 1850, 9 November 1850, Bernhisel Papers.

105. U.S. Bureau of the Census, *The Seventh Census of the United States: 1850* (Washington, D.C., 1853), p. 993.

106. See Appendix C.

107. Bernhisel to Young, 13 February 1852, Bernhisel Papers.

108. Hamilton, *Prologue to Conflict.*

109. Kane to Young, 13 February 1852, Kane Papers.

110. *Statistical Views of the U.S. and Compendium of the Seventh Census,* 1850, p. 83. *Deseret News,* 12 June 1852, following the publication of the census, further explained that the twenty-six slaves in the report "were in the Territory at the date of the census, in 1850, en route for California and were so marked on the census papers; they left the Territory in the spring of 1851." For names of those slaves contained in the census figures of 1850 see Appendix C.

111. "AN ACT in relation to Service," *Acts, Resolutions and Memorials of the Legislative Assembly of the Territory of Utah* (Salt Lake City, 1855), pp. 160-62.

112. See Dennis L. Lythgoe, "Negro Slavery in Utah."

113. See list of Mormon slaveholders as contained in Appendix C.

114. As quoted in Culmer, " 'General' John Wilson, Signer of the Deseret Petition," p. 330.

115. "Speach [sic] by Gov. Young in Counsel on a Bill relating to the Affrican [sic] Slavery," 23 January 1852, Brigham Young Papers.

116. "AN ACT in Relation to Service," pp. 160-62.

117. *Deseret News*, 26 July 1851.

118. Brigham Young, "Speech to the Joint Session of the Legislative Assembly, January 5, 1852," *Journals of the Legislative Assembly of the Territory of Utah* (Salt Lake City, Utah, 1852).

119. As recorded by Wilford Woodruff in his "Journal," 16 January 1852.

120. Brigham Young, "Speech of the Joint Session of the Legislative Assembly, January 5, 1852." Also reprinted in *Deseret News,* 10 January 1852.

121. In fact, there were a number of provisions in the 1852 Statute that were remarkably similar to legislation adopted by Illinois in 1819 regulating indentured servants in that state. See Paul M. Angle, "The Illinois Black Laws," *Chicago History* 8 (Spring 1967): 66-67.

122. As recorded by Wilford Woodruff in his "Journal," 16 January 1852, and as recorded in the "Manuscript History of the Church" for that same date.

123. "Speach by Gov. Young in Joint Session of the Legislature . . . giving his views on slavery," 5 February 1852.

124. In this regard it is interesting to note that when the first draft of this act was initially presented as "a Bill relating to Affrican slavery," Brigham Young remarked: "The Caption of this Bill I don't like, I have therefore taken the liberty to alter it. I have said 'an act in relation to manual service' instead of Affrican Slavery" (23 January 1852, Brigham Young Papers).

125. Brigham Young, "Speech to the Joint Session of the Legislative Assembly, January 5, 1852." Also reprinted in *Deseret News,* 10 January 1852.

126. "AN ACT in relation to Service," pp. 160-62.

127. Contrary to their title, the county probate courts in Utah had judicial authority not simply relating to property but granted power over original jurisdiction in all types of civil and criminal actions. For a discussion of the role and power of this unique judicial authority see James B. Allen, "The Unusual Jurisdiction of County Probate Courts in the Territory of Utah," *Utah Historical Quarterly* 36 (1968): 133-42.

128. Brigham Young, "Message to the Joint Session of Legislature," 13 December 1852, Brigham Young Papers. Also reprinted in the *Deseret News,* 25 December 1852.

129. For a good discussion of the national crisis over slavery in the ter-

ritories from 1846 to 1850, see Hamilton, *Prologue to Conflict.* A less satisfactory treatment of the Mormon position during this period is Melville, *Conflict and Compromise.*

130. *Latter Day Saints Millennial Star,* 25 April 1847, 1 October 1847, 15 October 1848, 1 February 1849; Bernhisel to Young, 5, 15 March 1850, Bernhisel Papers.

131. Ibid., 1 March 1850. See letters from Wilford Woodruff to Orson Pratt reprinted in *Latter Day Saints Millennial Star,* 15 April 1849; Wilford Woodruff to George A. Smith, 22 February 1849; Woodruff to Young, 15 February 1849, Woodruff Papers.

132. Bernhisel to Young, 21 March 1850, Bernhisel Papers.

133. *Latter Day Saints Millennial Star,* 15 November 1848, 15 December 1850.

134. *Pearl of Great Price.* The background and contents of this prophecy were discussed in Chapter 2.

135. John Henry Evans in *Ezra T. Benson* (Salt Lake City, 1941), pp. 127-38, alludes to the contrasting personalities and interests of Smith and Young as well as the shifting focus of church leadership following Joseph Smith's death in 1844.

5 | The Beginnings of Black Priesthood Denial, 1839-1852

> this black man has got the blood of Ham in him which lineage [*sic*] was cursed as regards [to] the Priesthood. . . .
>
> Parley P. Pratt, April 1847

> because Cain cut off the lives [*sic*] of Abel . . . the Lord cursed Cain's seed and prohibited them the priesthood. . . .
>
> Brigham Young, February 1849

The spring of 1847 was a critical time for Brigham Young and his Mormon followers, encamped at Winter Quarters in present-day Nebraska. These Latter-day Saints had migrated to this temporary settlement after their forced exodus from Nauvoo early in 1846. Many of these migrants had arrived in Winter Quarters with little more than the clothes on their backs. As the result of an inadequate diet an alarming number of individuals had perished of scurvy, consumption, and chills and fever during the summer of 1846. The severe winter of 1846-47 brought further discomfort to those Saints who lacked adequate housing. On top of these difficulties, the Winter Quarters Saints had to somehow prepare for their long, arduous trek across the Rockies and the Great Plains to their new home in the remote reaches of the Great Salt Lake Basin.[1]

As if these difficulties were not enough, Young and his Winter Quarters followers were forced to deal with the disruptive activities of one William McCary, a self-proclaimed black Indian prophet. McCary had arrived in the Mormon Camp sometime during that bleak winter of 1846-47. At first,

Brigham Young and other Church leaders welcomed or at least accepted McCary into their midst. McCary, an accomplished musician, entertained the encamped Saints during the months of February and March 1847.[2]

However, by late March 1847, McCary fell from Mormon favor. Young and others were apparently upset with McCary for using his powers as a musician and ventriloquist to claim supernatural powers of transmigration, that is, the ability to assume the "identity" of certain Old and New Testament peoples. At a "meeting of the twelve and others" McCary exhibited "himself in Indian costume" and purported "to be Adam, the ancient of days." He "claimed to have an odd rib which he had discovered in his wife."[3] Then McCary "showed his body to the company to see if he had a rib gone." At this same meeting, McCary also tried to pass himself off as the ancient Apostle Thomas. He did this by throwing his voice and announcing that "God spoke unto him and called him Thomas."[4] Young and other church leaders were not impressed. They expelled McCary from Winter Quarters, and Apostle Orson Hyde preached a sermon "against his doctrine."[5]

Undaunted, McCary remained in or returned to the area around Winter Quarters and proceeded to set up his own rival Mormon group, drawing followers away from Brigham Young.[6] According to a July 1847 account, the "negro prophet" exerted his influence by working "with a rod, like those of old."[7] By the fall of 1847, McCary's religious practices took a new turn when the black Indian taught his own form of plural marriage or polygamy.[8] McCary's ritual involved a number of women,

> seald to him in his way which was as follows, he had a house in which this ordinance was preformed his wife . . . was in the room at the time of the proformance no others was admited the form of sealing was for the women to go to bed with him in the daytime as I am informed 3 diforant times by which they was seald to the fullist extent.

These activities angered Brigham Young and his followers, particularly the relatives of McCary's female disciples. One irate Mormon threatened "to shoot" McCary for trying "to kiss his girls." But McCary, aware of the ruckus caused by the disclosure of his unorthodox practices, "made his way to Missouri on a fast trot."[9]

The storm caused by William McCary, however had consequences far beyond the black Indian and his small following. In the wake of McCary's activities at least two Mormon leaders were willing to affirm that blacks could not hold the Mormon priesthood. The earliest-known statement came from Apostle Parley P. Pratt in the spring of 1847. Before a gathering of Latter-day Saints, Pratt maintained that "McCary had 'got the blood of Ham in him which linege [*sic*] was cursed as regards [to] the priesthood.' "[10] Brigham Young alluded to this same position during the fall of 1847 when he suggested that blacks in general were ineligible to participate in certain sacred temple ordinances.[11]

The affirmation of black priesthood denial by the late 1840s represents a crucial turning point in the Mormon treatment of black people. It marked the transformation of Mormon racist concepts into a specific racist practice that, in turn, assured a subordinate place for all black people within Mormonism. However, black priesthood denial did not emerge simply as the result of William McCary's bizarre activities. A number of factors, complex and interrelated, caused Mormon leaders to deny blacks the priesthood. To a large extent black priesthood denial was the end product of a Mormon religion whose racist concepts looked at blacks in an increasingly unfavorable light. Joseph Smith had lain the ground work for such concepts. He asserted in 1841 that the "curse" on Ham, the alleged ancestor of black people, was promoted by Noah, not simply in a fit of drunken anger, but rather in a calm and deliberate fashion, utilizing his divinely vested priesthood authority. Although Smith was vague in describing the exact nature of Ham's "curse," he maintained that it "remains upon the posterity of Canaan until the present day."[12] The following year the Mormon prophet parenthetically labeled contemporary "negroes . . . the sons of Cain."[13] Smith's identification of blacks with the alleged first murderer stood in contrast to prevailing Mormon views, which previously had emphasized the black man's relationship with the less unfavorable biblical figures of Ham and Canaan.[14] In December 1842, Smith expressed doubts about the capacity of blacks for self-government. He feared that if blacks were "organized into an independent government they would become quarrelsome."[15] A few days later, Smith again discussed "the situation of the negro." He indicated that though blacks had the potential for achievement, they were in practice inferior because they "came into the world slaves mentally and physically."[16] In May 1844, just prior to his death, the Mormon prophet metaphorically declared that "Africa, from the curse of God had lost the use of her limbs. . . ."[17]

Following Smith's assassination, Mormon leaders through their racist concepts viewed black people in an even more negative light. In 1845, the *Times and Seasons* editorialized that blacks as "the descendants of Ham" were burdened not only with "a black skin, which has ever been the curse that has followed an apostate of the holy priesthood," but also "a black heart." Blacks, moreover, were characterized as "servants to both Shem and Japheth."[18] In that same year Apostle Orson Hyde carried the Mormon notion of black inferiority one step further. Hyde claimed that the subordinate status of black people in this life had been "predetermined" or foreordained by events during the premortal existence. Hyde expanded on a basic belief developed by Joseph Smith through the Book of Abraham.[19] According to Hyde certain premortal spirits were doomed to receive black bodies because of their less than valiant activities during a premortal war that had taken place between God and Lucifer. These premortal spirits, Hyde said, "did not take a very active part on either side. . . ." Despite this behavior, they "were not considered bad enough to be cast down to hell and never have bodies," as were those spirits who had sided actively with Lucifer. But, at the same time, they were not "considered worthy of an honorable [white] body on this earth as were those who had fought for God."[20] As a result these spirits "were required . . . to take bodies in the accursed lineage of Canaan; hence the negro or African race."[21] Therefore, by the time William McCary caused turmoil among the Winter Quarters Saints in 1847, the Mormons tended to view blacks generally in a more unfavorable light than had been the case just a few years before.

The Mormon transformation of such racist concepts into black priesthood denial was motivated by several factors. First, black priesthood denial was a response to the problems created by black people among the Saints. William McCary was, of course, a case in point. However, long before the black Indian burst upon the Mormon scene, the Saints had to deal with the problems created by other black Mormons. One of these was Elijah Abel, Mormonism's first known black priesthood holder, whose disruptive behavior during his mission in upstate New York and Canada had attracted the attention of church leaders in Nauvoo in 1839.[22]

Despite these earlier difficulties, Abel managed to avoid controversy during the three-year period following his arrival in Nauvoo in 1839. In fact, Abel developed a close, congenial relationship with Joseph Smith and his immediate family. Abel, according to one account, was "intimately

acquainted" with Smith, living in the home of the Mormon Prophet.[23]
Abel was also present at the bedside of Patriarch Joseph Smith, Sr., father
of the Mormon prophet, "during his last sickness" in 1840. The following
year Abel, along with six other Nauvoo Mormons, attempted to rescue
Joseph Smith in the wake of his arrest for earlier Missouri difficulties.[24]

Abel's close relationship with the Joseph Smith family made it easier
for him to be accepted by Nauvoo Saints in full fellowship despite his
blackness. Abel pursued the occupation of a carpenter and in February
1840 got together with six other individuals who described themselves
as "the House Carpenters of the Town of Nauvoo" and had printed a small
"book of prices." This pamphlet outlined the uniform rates to be charged
by these Nauvoo carpenters.[25] Abel was also "appointed" by Joseph Smith
"to the calling of an undertaker in Nauvoo."[26] He was kept busy in this
calling by the appallingly high number of deaths from malaria during the
early years of Nauvoo's settlement.[27]

However, in 1842 Abel, for some unknown reason, left Nauvoo and
settled in Cincinnati.[28] Here he encountered new difficulties because of
his blackness. Abel's activities as a black priesthood holder were called
into question during a church conference on July 25, 1843. Present at this
meeting were three Mormon apostles, Heber C. Kimball, Orson Pratt, and
John E. Page. Apostle John E. Page wanted to restrict Abel's activities as
a black Mormon. Page maintained that while "he respects a coloured Bro,"
i.e., Abel, "wisdom forbids that we should introduce [him] before the
public." Apostle Orson Pratt then "sustained the position of Bro Page."
Apostle Kimball also worried about Abel's visibility as a black Mormon.
Abel tried to reassure these leaders that "he had no disposition to force
himself upon an equality with white people." Nevertheless, the conference
adopted a resolution limiting Abel in his church activities. Thus, in con-
forming with the established "duty of the 12 . . . to ordain and send men
to their native country Bro Abels [*sic*] was advised" to limit his activities
to "the coloured population. . . . Instructions were then given him concerning his mission."[29] It is not clear whether Abel made a deliberate effort to limit his activities to the blacks of Cincinnati or anywhere else.
Despite these difficulties Abel remained active in the Mormon branch
in Cincinnati. In June 1845 "Elder Elijah Abel preferred a charge"
against three women for their failure to attend church meetings and for
"speaking disrespectfully of the heads of the Church."[30]

Back in Nauvoo, Mormon-black relations were complicated by other problems. This was the case despite a Mormon "desire" to gather all races and ethnic groups, including the "degraded Hottentot," to the Saints' Illinois Zion.[31] This was an impossible goal because Illinois state laws precluded the possibility of any large-scale black gathering. One statute required any free black entering the state to furnish notarized proof of his or her freedom and to post a $1,000 bond. This Illinois statute and other problems confronted a group of nine Mormon blacks who migrated from Connecticut to Nauvoo in the fall of 1843. These blacks, part of a larger Mormon group under the leadership of Charles Wesley Wandell, became separated from the main Mormon group in Buffalo, New York, because they did not have the fares necessary to travel by canal to Columbus, Ohio. Instead, these black Mormons, without adequate preparation, were forced to make the entire journey to Nauvoo on foot. According to one account they walked until their "shoes were worn out, and [their] feet became sore and cracked open and bled until you could see the whole print of [their] feet with blood on the ground." Upon their arrival in Illinois they encountered further difficulties. They were stopped by authorities in Peoria who "threatened to put [them] in jail" when they failed to produce their "free papers." In the end, however, Peoria officials had a change of heart and allowed the besieged black Mormons to continue their journey to Nauvoo.[32] This incident dramatizes the fact that existing Illinois antiblack statues would have discouraged any large-scale black Mormon migration to Illinois, had there been one. Actually, there were probably no more than a handful of blacks in the entire Mormon movement during the 1840s. In all, only about twenty blacks settled in Nauvoo, which by the mid-1840s was a bustling community of 15,000 to 20,000.[33]

Nauvoo, moreover, was not the most congenial environment for prospective black migrants. The Saints through their Nauvoo city charter prohibited blacks from voting, holding municipal office, or belonging to the militia, the famed Nauvoo Legion. These privileges were limited to "free white males."[34] Another Nauvoo statute prohibited black-white intermarriage. This statute was enforced on at least one occasion by Joseph Smith, acting in his capacity as mayor of Nauvoo. Smith presided over the trial of two blacks for attempting "to marry white women." In the final judgement Smith "fined one $25 and the other $5."[35]

A willingness to recognize legally the inferior status of blacks within the secular realm was no new thing for the Saints. Throughout the first decade of Mormonism's existence the Saints were forced to recognize and to obey various non-Mormon, antiblack statutes during their sojourn in Ohio and Missouri. What was different about Latter-day Saint actions in Illinois was that the Saints, themselves, for the first time and on their own initiative enacted antiblack statutes. This Mormon implementation of statutes affirming a subordinate status for Nauvoo blacks made it easier for Mormon leaders to relegate blacks to a subordinate church position through black priesthood denial. Mormon leaders tended to "blur over" and interrelate secular and ecclesiastical matters during this period.[36]

The Nauvoo Saints were not unique in their desire to limit the civil and political rights of blacks living in their midst. Americans living in the Midwest enacted all types of antiblack laws and statutes during the 1840s. Like the Saints, non-Mormon residents in this region passed legislation limiting the civil and political rights of black people—prohibiting them from voting, holding public office, belonging to the militia, or intermarrying with whites. In fact, antiblack discrimination "intensified" during the late 1840s and early 1850s. Illinois, just after the Mormon exodus from Nauvoo, approved a statute that absolutely prohibited black migration into the state.[37] Therefore, Nauvoo antiblack statutes conformed with those of a larger American society that routinely discriminated against blacks in the political realm.

Outside of Nauvoo itself, church officials dealt with the priesthood status of another black man who, like Abel, was ordained during Joseph Smith's lifetime. Walker Lewis, a black barber in Lowell, Massachusetts, had been ordained an elder by William Smith, a younger brother of the Mormon prophet.[38] At first, various church officials did not question the priesthood status of this black elder.[39] Apostle Wilford Woodruff, during a November 1844 visit to Lowell, merely observed that "a Coloured Brother who was an Elder," presumably Lewis, manifested his support for the established church leadership during this time of great internal division within Mormonism.[40]

By 1847 this had all changed. Lewis' priesthood status was questioned by William L. Appleby, a Mormon official in charge of church activity in the eastern states. Appleby did not think that Lewis, or any other black man, had the right to the priesthood. In a terse letter to Brigham Young,

Appleby asked if it was "the order of God or tolerated, to ordain negroes to the Priesthood. . . . If it is, I desire to know it as I have yet got to learn it." Unfortunately, Young was unable to reply in writing to Appleby's question because by the time Appleby's letter arrived at Winter Quarters, the Mormon leader was on his way to the Great Basin with the first group of Mormon settlers.[41] After Young returned to Winter Quarters from the Great Basin during the fall of 1847, he did affirm a subordinate status for blacks within Mormonism. This affirmation might have been a response to Appleby's inquiry or a reaction to William McCary's concurrent controversial behavior in and around Winter Quarters or a combination of the two.[42]

Besides the problems generated by Walker Lewis, Elijah Abel, and other black Mormons, other factors influenced the Latter-day Saints in their decision to deny blacks the priesthood. One of these, evident before Joseph Smith's assassination and the Mormon abandonment of Nauvoo, involved a continuing Mormon interest in black biblical counterfigures. This scriptural preoccupation had been first evident in the *Book of Mormon* and later in the books of Moses and Abraham. This scriptural awareness continued into the 1840s, as reflected in two events. The first involved the publication of the Book of Abraham in 1842. This work, initially published in the *Times and Seasons*, allowed the general church membership for the first time to follow scripturally the deeds (or rather misdeeds) of some of the black man's alleged biblical ancestors, Cain and the people of Canaan, as well as the idolatrous Egyptians.[43] Most important, the Saints were exposed to the idea that these Egyptians—as the literal descendants of Ham, the accursed son of Noah—were "cursed as pertaining to the priesthood."

A Mormon interest in black biblical counterfigures was also evident in the events surrounding the so-called Kinderhook plates. These plates were "discovered" along with a human skeleton by some non-Mormons near Kinderhook, Illinois. These artifacts were then taken to Joseph Smith in the hopes that he could use his reputed powers as a translator to decipher their meaning.[44] Smith obliged and declared that they contained, "the history of the person [skeleton] with whom they were found. He was a descendant of Ham, through the loins of Pharaoh, King of Egypt, and that he received his Kingdom from the Ruler of heaven

and earth."[45] Apostle Parley P. Pratt also took an interest in the plates.
He suggested that they had been written by the Jaredites, a *Book of
Mormon* people.[46] According to Pratt the "genealogy" of these "ancient
Jaredites" could be traced "back to Ham the son of Noah."[47] Pratt's
observations represented a unique Mormon suggestion that the Jaredites,
who ultimately perished because of their unrighteousness, had the same
Hamitic racial lineage as contemporary black people.

A third, somewhat more subtle factor, however, was probably even
more important in causing the Saints to deny blacks offices within the
Mormon priesthood. Black priesthood denial was the by-product of a
Mormon tendency to impose "unfavorable"—often black—racial characteristics on their enemies and opponents. The Mormons had projected such
negative racial characteristics on their enemies during the 1830s,[48] but this
practice intensified after 1839 as the Mormons rhetorically lashed out at
a widening circle of enemies and opponents in both Missouri and Illinois.
This practice compensated for the Mormon inability to physically punish
or get economic redress from these enemies. At the same time it had the
unfortunate side-effect of creating an intellectual environment conducive
to the implementation of black priesthood denial.

The first group to which the Latter-day Saints imputed "unfavorable"
racial characteristics were those Missourians responsible for expelling the
Mormons from the state in 1838-39.[49] The Saints, as they had done during
the 1830s, compared these Missouri opponents with certain scriptural
countergroups who had opposed God's chosen people in the past. Thus
Missouri became "Western Egypt" and its citizens "Egyptians" or "un-
circumcised Philistines," while their hostile acts were compared with those
of "Pharaoh, Nebuchadnezzer, and Herod."[50] The Saints characterized
Governor Boggs as an "Edomite . . . led captive by the devil."[51] Moving
beyond biblical analogies the Saints described the offending Missourians
as a "blood-thirsty and savage race of beings in the shape of men" who
were "profaning the refinements of civilization."[52] The anti-Mormon actions
of Missouri's governor Libern Boggs, explained the *Times and Seasons,* had
"shed a darker polish on the blackened aspect of that disgraced state."[53]

The Mormon practice of identifying their enemies with negative racial
figures intensified as Mormon-non-Mormon conflicts increased within
Illinois during the mid-1840s. The *Nauvoo Neighbor* criticized Mormon

opponents in the nearby town of Carthage, Illinois for their "barbarous notions."[54] These Carthaginians, explained the *Neighbor,* lacked the capacity to learn "good neighborship" as " 'an Ethiopian' cannot change his skin, nor a leopard his spots." The *Neighbor* suggested that these Carthaginians migrate to a "more congenial clime"—Missouri—where they could be with their own kind.[55] As the Saints continued to clash with the citizens of Carthage, the *Neighbor* seized upon what it perceived as the metaphoric significance of the name "Carthage," comparing the contemporary Illinois community with its ancient African namesake. This rival community, led by a modern "Hannibal," was plotting "to swallow up Nauvoo."[56] Through the use of biblical counterfigures, the Saints drew racial analogies between Carthaginian anti-Mormons and the inhabitants of ancient Carthage. Alluding to the alleged biblical-Hamitic racial origins of ancient Carthage, the *Neighbor* constructed metaphoric parallels with the anti-Mormons of Carthage, Illinois, and assigned them figurative "black" racial characteristics.[57] Thus, an anti-Mormon gathering in Carthage was labeled a "Nigger meeting" and its proceedings given in terms of a "Sambo" story.[58]

Following Joseph Smith's assassination in 1844, the Saints drew even sharper analogies between their enemies and black people. Certain church spokesmen expressed their hope and expectation that their enemies would be divinely cursed with a dark skin. Smith's assassins, who had blackened their faces prior to their violent act, were characterized as "Artificial black men."[59] Another spokesman explained that "the murderers no doubt are sorry they have white skins." They "wanted to make their faces correspond with their hearts." He warned that "God will paint them by and by with a color that soap will not wash off."[60]

Other Mormon adversaries were also slated to receive the curse of a dark skin. According to the *Nauvoo Neighbor,* "Artificial black men" included not just individuals who "paint" themselves and "murder," but also those individuals who "justify and approve those who do." "Such 'an apologist,' " according to the *Neighbor,* "has . . . a little of the 'blackening' unwashed from his body—and a few drops of innocent 'blood' in his skirts, to witness what has been and *what will be.*"[61] The divine curse of a dark skin would also befall other anti-Mormon adversaries. Apostle Orson Hyde, admitting that current anti-Mormon persecutions were "bringing grey hairs upon the Saints," warned that in due course "the Heads of the persecutors will be covered with blackness."[62] Such racial ideas, of course, conformed with scriptural beliefs in the *Book of Mormon* and Book of Moses, which described the curse of a dark skin that befell the wicked opponents of God's chosen people.

In addition to their enemies, the growing divisions within Mormonism itself after Joseph Smith's assassination caused those Saints who followed Brigham Young to project "unfavorable" racial characteristics on their various Mormon rivals. Among the most prominent rivals was Sydney Rigdon, former counselor and assistant to Joseph Smith, who established a Mormon following in western Pennsylvania.[63] A second rival, Lyman Wight, a former Mormon apostle, led a small group of dissident Saints to Texas.[64] Brigham Young's most serious challenger for Mormon authority was James J. Strang, a charismatic leader who drew a significant number of followers away from Young and established a flourishing Mormon settlement in Wisconsin during the late 1840s.[65] Brigham Young, in response to these various divisions, labeled his rivals as "faltered and . . . darkened" individuals.[66] A pro-Brigham Young letter to the editor of the *Times and Seasons* compared Sydney Rigdon with Cain, denouncing him as a false prophet or "Kind of god that [would] trouble none but the Ethiopians, Egyptians, Lybians, etc. . . ."[67] Another Young loyalist, Elder Orson Spencer, condemned all Mormon rivals as "false Preachers" or "the daring Sons of Pharaoh, Cain and Judas." Those who had departed from the true faith in the past, continued Spencer, had "deteriorated" and become "an inferior race of beings."[68] In probably the most famous church tract condemning dissident Mormons, Apostle Orson Hyde held up the specter of a dark skin for such individuals. Hyde rejected the rival claims of Sydney Rigdon, whom he compared with the devil, and, more important, issued a warning to those Saints who were "halting" or unsure as to who had "the right to govern" the church. Such doubting individuals, cautioned Hyde, should take a lesson from "the accursed lineage of Canaan . . . the negro or African race." According to Hyde the blacks were suffering their earthly curses, specifically their servile status—but by implication skin color and debased condition—as a consequence of their reluctance to choose the right side during the premortal war in Heaven.[69] Thus, a Mormon tendency to associate the "curse" of a dark skin with Mormon enemies and rivals made it easier for the Saints to deny the priesthood to the actual black men in their midst.

At the same time, Mormon black priesthood denial was encouraged by an important fourth factor, a Latter-day Saint practice of emphasizing their status as white people who were racially "chosen." This practice was the byproduct of Mormon-non-Mormon conflicts in which various enemies tried to besmirch the Saints by drawing parallels between the Mormons and black people. In response Church spokesmen lashed out at these enemies for their failure to treat the Saints as "white people."[70] Apostle William Smith, in defending the "whiteness" of the Saints, discounted the

> many faint and incorrect descriptions . . . given Nauvoo and the temple by travellers, passers by, and others until some have thought the temple build upon moonshine, and the city a barbarian—ugly, formal, with heads and horns and stuck into the nethermost corner of the universe where none but Indians, Hottentots, Arabs, Turks, wolverines, and Mormons dwell.[71]

By 1845, just before the Saints were forced to leave Illinois, Apostle Heber C. Kimball sarcastically noted that the Saints were "not considered suitable to live among 'white folks.'" and "not accounted as white people."[72]

The Saints in addition to affirming their own "whiteness," identified themselves with various "chosen" peoples of the Old Testament—the Hebrews, the Children of Israel, and the Seed of Abraham.[73] Church spokesmen suggested that a spiritual link existed between the Saints and the "Seed of Abraham." "There is neither Jew nor Greek, there is neither bond nor free, there is neither male nor female; for ye are all one in Christ Jesus. And if ye be Christ's then ye are Abraham's seed and heir according to the promise."[74] Apostle Orson Pratt believed that an individual could become "a citizen of the Church" or kingdom of God, and by implication the "Seed of Abraham," through the "law of adoption."[75]

Physical suffering at the hands of non-Mormon enemies strengthened the Mormon desire to identify with Old Testament "chosen peoples." In the wake of their forced expulsion from Missouri and their arrival in Illinois in 1839, the Saints saw themselves like the Children of Israel who had come out of Egypt. After the Saints came into conflict with their Illinois neighbors, Apostle Parley P. Pratt expected the Lord to lead the Saints "out of Egypt into some [new] Canaan."[76] Following their exodus

from Illinois and the establishment of a temporary Mormon camp at Winter
Quarters, Nebraska, the Saints designated themselves the "Camp of Israel."[77]
The persecutions and difficulties faced first by Joseph Smith and then by
Brigham Young were compared to those endured by Abel, Moses, and other
Old Testament leaders.[78]

Following the death of Joseph Smith, the Mormons moved beyond their
earlier claims of a spiritual link between themselves and the "Seed of Abraham." They claimed a literal relationship between themselves and this
chosen seed. In asserting this claim, Brigham Young followed the practices
of Joseph Smith. The Mormon Prophet had established a literal Abrahamic
relationship for himself and the Lamanites—contemporary American Indians—
through the *Book of Mormon*.[79] However, Smith did not promote such an
ethnic relationship for other church leaders and the general church membership during the 1830s. This all changed by the mid-1840s in response to the
leadership crisis within the church following Smith's death. Brigham Young
and his followers wanted to refute the leadership claims of various rivals.
These rivals, including Sydney Rigdon, Lyman Wight, and others, based
their claims on the concept of proper Abrahamic descent. That is, they
believed that church leadership should be vested in the lineage of Joseph
Smith, an acknowledged descendant of the seed of Abraham. Therefore,
these rivals looked toward Joseph Smith III, the son of the slain Mormon
prophet, as the logical successor to his father. However, as the younger
Smith was an adolescent at the time of his father's death, an interim church
guardian would be necessary until he came of age.

Brigham Young and his followers agreed with Rigdon, Wight, and others
that literal Abrahamic descent was an essential prerequisite for church
leadership. But they disagreed with these rivals' assertion that such literal
descent was limited to the family of Joseph Smith. Instead, Young and
his followers claimed to be literal descendants from this chosen seed. In
addition, Young and his backers bolstered their leadership claims by making literal Abrahamic descent an essential prerequisite for priesthood
authority. Therefore, "the honors and power of the priesthood are not
obtained, by money or craft. They are handed down by lineage from
father to son, according to the order of the Son of God."[80] Throughout
the late 1840s Mormon leaders described the Saints as the pure and un-
mixed "Seed of Abraham" or "Ephraim," asserting their right to the
priesthood by virtue of this "royal lineage."[81] Brigham Young, in ad-
vancing his own rights to the mantle of Joseph Smith, declared that he,

like the slain Mormon Prophet, was "entitled to the Priesthood according to lineage and blood." Likewise, Young believed that members of the Council of Twelve Apostles and "many others" in the church were also entitled to the "keys and powers" of priesthood authority by virtue of their "lineage & blood."[82]

The efforts of Brigham Young and his followers to assert their literal descent from the "Seed of Abraham" and link it to church membership and priesthood authority could not help but have a negative effect on the status of black people within Mormonism. Blacks, unlike the white Saints, could not trace their lineage back to the "chosen seed" of Abraham because, according to the popular beliefs of the Saints and other nineteenth-century biblical literalists, they were direct descendants of Ham, the accursed son of Noah. By making Abrahamic lineage a prerequisite for the Mormon priesthood, the Saints weakened all actual and potential black claims to such power and authority.

Therefore, by the spring of 1847, the first concrete indications of Mormon black priesthood denial were evident. The exact date this practice began is not known, but it appears that it was sometime after the 1844 assassination of Joseph Smith. Although some questions remain about the initial extent of its application, the universal application of black priesthood denial was clearly enunciated by Brigham Young in 1849 through his unequivocal statement that "the Lord Cursed Cain's seed with blackness and prohibited them the priesthood. . . ." Despite uncertainty concerning its exact timetable, it is clear that this practice was brought about by a number of developments that occurred both before and after Smith's death. These included the problems generated by the few blacks associated with the Mormon movement—including William McCary, Elijah Abel, and others; the Mormon enactment of secular statutes asserting the inferior political status of blacks within Nauvoo; and by a continuing Mormon interest in black biblical counterfigures as reflected in the Kinderhook plates and publication of the Book of Abraham. Finally, and of crucial importance, black priesthood denial was encouraged by the Mormon practice of projecting unfavorable racial characteristics on their opponents and a concurrent Mormon willingness to picture themselves as the literal "Seed of Abraham."

The Mormon decision to deny blacks the priesthood was reinforced after 1847 by the traumatic Mormon experience of migrating to and settling the wild and uncivilized areas of the Great Basin. The Saints, like other westward-migrating Americans, had anxieties about the untamed, barbarian influences of the frontier. They could not let the frontier pull them down into a barbarian state.[83] Such Mormon anxieties were reflected in a speech given by Brigham Young in 1847 during the first Mormon migration to the Great Basin. Young, chastising some misbehaving Saints, declared

> Here are the Elders of Israel who have got the Priesthood who have got to preach the gospel, who have to gather the nations of the earth, who have to build up the Kingdom, so that the nations can come to it; they will stoop to dance as niggers: (I don't mean this as speaking disrespectfully [*sic*] of our colored friends amongst us by any means) they will hoe down all, turn summersets, dance on their knees, and haw, haw, out loud; they will play cards, they will play checkers and dominoes; they will use profane language; they will swear.[84]

Another Mormon apostle remarked that it "had made him shudder when he had seen the Elders of Israel descend to the lowest and dirtiest things imaginable—the last end of everything." One of the offending elders confessed his shortcomings, admitting that "He knew his mind had become darkened."[85] It is interesting to note that Young compared the misbehaving "Elders of Israel" with black people rather than Indians.

Mormon worries about the barbaric influences of a frontier environment intensified as a result of the Saints' own deep-seated sexual anxieties. Such anxieties were rooted in Mormon worries about black-white racial intermixture. Even before the Mormon migration west, Joseph Smith articulated his fears about racial miscegenation.[86] Such fears intensified in the wake of the Mormon migration. William McCary's sexual behavior at Winter Quarters in 1847 struck at the core of this Mormon fear. In that same year, moreover, the case of Walker Lewis—the black Mormon elder in Lowell, Massachusetts— drew added attention because his son was married to a white woman. The Saints were not unique in such fears. Victorian Americans, generally, manifested an "almost obsessive preoccupation with the temptations and evils of miscegenation between whites and blacks."[87] The Saints were particularly prone to such sexual anxieties because of their acceptance of plural marriage as an essential feature of their religion by the mid-1840s.

Mormon fears about racial intermixture in an uncivilized barbarian frontier environment reached a peak as a relatively large number of blacks migrated into the Great Basin during the years 1847-50. Between 88 and 106 blacks migrated to or were brought into this region during these years. Thus the Great Basin Saints came into contact with a significantly larger number of blacks than had been the case in Nauvoo just a few years before.[88] Brigham Young was particularly emphatic in opposing racial intermixture. According to Young, any white man guilty of mingling "his seed with the seed of Cane [*sic*] . . . could redeem himself" or "have salvation" only by having "his head cut off" and "his Blood [spilt] on the ground."[89]

The enforcement of Mormon black priesthood denial helped to allay Mormon fears over possible racial intermixture with this black population, at least through marriage. No man without the priesthood could have a fully sanctioned Mormon marriage ceremony. As these marriages were performed in Mormon temples, the doors of these sacred Mormon sanctuaries were closed to blacks. Thus Mormon blacks, in contrast to other Saints, were denied the full blessings and privileges that a temple marriage brought, namely, the "sealing" of the Mormon couple to each other and to their family not just for this life but for all "time and eternity." This restriction, while helping to allay Mormon anxieties over racial intermixture, had the effect of placing Mormon blacks "beyond the pale" of true believers, in both this life and the next.

To further safeguard racial purity, the Utah territorial legislature in 1852 enacted a statute outlawing all black-white racial intermixture. The Saints also moved to control the behavior of blacks in other ways. Utah blacks were prohibited from voting, holding public office, and belonging to the territorial militia.[90]

Even more important, the Mormon implementation of "An Act in Relation to Service" in 1852 legalized black slavery in Utah and thus gave the Utah Saints one more reason to look at blacks in an inferior light.[91] This measure, enacted in 1852 as the Saints were publicizing, for the first time, their practice of black priesthood denial, provided an important support for this practice and helped to make it irreversible.

These various Mormon antiblack actions—secular as well as ecclesiastical—made the subordinate status of Mormon blacks complete by 1852. At the same time as the Saints gave legal recognition to the black slavery in their midst, they made every effort to remain detached from the larger slavery controversy that was racking the country during the late 1840s and early 1850s. This, however, changed after 1852 as the Saints moved away from their detached position and publicly lashed out at northern abolitionists,

while at the same time expressing dislike for the south's Peculiar Institution. Concurrent Mormon antiabolitionist and antislavery feelings would
predominate during the troubled period from 1852 to 1865 as the slavery
controversy intensified on the national level, culminating in southern secession and civil war.

NOTES

1. For a brief description of the difficulties faced by these Winter
Quarters Saints, see Wallace Stegner, *The Gathering to Zion: The Story
of the Mormon Trail* (New York, 1964), pp. 99-108.

2. Juanita Brooks, ed., *On the Mormon Frontier: The Diary of Hosea
Stout, 1844-1861* (Salt Lake City, 1966), 2:244; Journal of John D. Lee, 27
February 1847, John D. Lee Papers, LDS Church Archives.

3. "Manuscript History of the Church," 26 March 1847, LDS Church
Archives. A brief mention of the confrontation between McCary and church
leaders was also contained in the journal of Willard Richards, 26 March
1847, Willard Richards Papers, LDS Church Archives.

4. Journal of Wilford Woodruff, 26 March 1847, Woodruff Papers,
LDS Church Archives; *The True Latter Day Saints Herald* (Cincinnati,
Ohio), March 1861.

5. Journal of Lorenzo Brown, 27 April 1847, Lorenzo Brown Papers,

6. Ibid.; Journal of Nelson W. Whipple, 14 October 1847, Nelson W.
Whipple Papers, LDS Church Archives; Brooks, *On the Mormon Frontier*,
entry for 25 April 1847. However, there is some confusion as to McCary's
comings and goings prior to this time. According to one account, McCary
joined Lyman Wight, then on his way to Texas. Other sources claimed that
McCary joined Charles B. Thompson, the leader of a minor Mormon schismatic sect based in Iowa. Another witness reported that McCary traveled
"South to his own tribe." See Journal of John D. Lee, 7 May 1847. Along
this line the *Latter-day Saints Millennial Star*, 1 January 1849, notes the
interaction between Wight and the "Pagan Prophet." Also see *Gospel Herald*,
5 October 1848, and *The True Latter Day Saints Herald*, March 1861.
Thompson throughout his career manifested a lively interest in the issues
of slavery, race, and blacks. See C. R. Marks, "Monona County, Iowa, Mormons," *Sioux City Academy of Science and Letters* 1 (1903-04): 85-116
(later reprinted in the *Annals of Iowa*, April 1906). George Bartholomew
Arbaugh, *Revelations in Mormonism* (Chicago, 1932), pp. 159-71; and
Newell G. Bringhurst, "Forgotten Mormon Perspectives: Slavery, Race,
and the Black Man as Issues Among Non-Utah Latter-day Saints, 1844-75,"

Michigan History 61 (Winter 1977): 352-70; Journal of Lorenzo Brown, 27 April 1847, Brown Papers.

7. *Zion's Revelle*, 29 July 1847.

8. However, there are suggestions that McCary promoted polygamy as part of his religious ritual during his sojourn in Cincinnati in late 1846 and early 1847 prior to his migration to Winter Quarters. See *Cincinnati Commercial*, 27 October 1846.

9. Journal of Nelson W. Whipple, 14 October 1847, Whipple Papers.

10. General Minutes, 15 April 1847, LDS Church Archives.

11. According to a copy of the document in possession of Ronald K. Esplin. The original is contained in LDS Church Archives.

12. Joseph Smith, Jr., *History of the Church*, 2d ed. (Salt Lake City, 1978) 4: 445-46, 7 November 1841.

13. Ibid., 4: 501, 25 January 1842.

14. Although, as noted in Chapter 3, such a possibility was hinted at. However, a basic Mormon belief that blacks were of the lineage of "Cainan" rather than Cain probably predominated during the period 1839-52, as reflected in the fact that three Mormon blacks were assigned the lineage of "Cainan" through patriarchical blessings given during these years. See Patriarchical Blessing Indices, CR5001 #64; citations for Jane Manning, 6 March 1844, and Anthony Stebbins for 6 March 1844, both given by Hyrum Smith and for Walker Lewis given 4 October 1851 by John Smith. Index in LDS Church Archives.

15. Journal of Joseph Smith, 30 December 1842. Original in LDS Church Archives.

16. Smith, *History of the Church*, 5: 217-18, 2 January 1843. At the same time, however, Smith declared "Change their situation with the whites and they would be like them."

17. *Times and Seasons*, 13 May 1844.

18. Ibid., 1 April 1845.

19. The Book of Abraham, while not directly concerned with the transgressions of blacks during this "pre-existence," hinted at future mortal gradations, including the establishment of the Seed of Abraham as the "chosen" seed. "Now the Lord had shown unto me, Abraham, the intelligences that were organized before the world was; and among all these there were many of the noble and great ones." In this account, "God saw these souls that were good and . . . he said: these I will make my rulers . . . Abraham, thou art one of them; thou was chosen before thou was born." See *Pearl of Great Price*, Abraham, 3:22-23.

20. Orson Hyde, *Speech Given Before the High Priests Quorum in Nauvoo, April 25, 1845* (Liverpool, England, 1845), p. 30.

21. Brigham Young in 1869 rejected Hyde's argument that preexistent behavior contributed to the unfavorable status of blacks. When asked "if the spirits of negroes were neutral in Heaven," Young answered "No . . . there were no neutral [spirits] in Heaven at the time of the rebellion, all [spirits] took sides. . . . The posterity of Cain are black because he committed murder." "Journal History," 25 December 1869.

22. See Chapter 3 for a discussion of this incident and Abel's other activities up to June 1839.

23. Kate B. Carter, *The Negro Pioneer* (Salt Lake City, 1965), p. 15; Andrew Jenson, *Latter-day Saint Biographical Encyclopedia,* (Salt Lake City, 1920), 3:577. It is somewhat unclear what Carter meant by "lived in the home" of Joseph Smith. It seems unlikely that Abel resided with the Smith family itself. Probably Abel lived in the Nauvoo House, a hotel guest-house run by the Smith family. In addition, Isaac Lewis Manning and his sister Jane Manning James were described as "servants" of Joseph Smith who both "lived for many years in the household of Joseph Smith." See Carter, pp. 9-13.

24. Smith, *History of the Church,* vol. 4, 6 June 1841.

25. See Elijah Abel Papers, LDS Church Archives for a description of this pamphlet, which was printed according to an "Agreement," 20 February 1840, between E. Robinson and D. C. Smith—the Nauvoo town printers—and "Elijah Abel, Levi Jackson, Samuel Rolf, Alexander Badlam, Wm. Cahoon, Wm. Smith and Elijah Newman." Robinson and Smith agreed "to Print for Abel, Jackson & Co., small pamphlet of 200 copies 'Book of Prices of Work adopted by the House Carpenters of the Town of Nauvoo' to be paid upon in labor or putting up a building when called upon." The sum agreed upon was $58. I have not had the opportunity to look at the original, but according to this reference the "original is in the possession of Mrs. Alfred M. Henson, St. George."

26. As recorded in "Minutes of First Council of Seventy, 1859-1863," p. 494, 5 March 1879, LDS Church Archives.

27. As noted by W. Wyl, *Mormon Portraits* (Salt Lake City, 1886), pp. 51-52.

28. As noted in the Cincinnati City Directories for 1842, compiled by Charles Cist (GS 194001) and for 1849-50 (GS 194002).

29. Minutes of a conference of the Church of Jesus Christ of Latter-day Saints held in Cincinnati, 25 June 1843, original in LDS Church Archives.

30. "Minutes of a special conference of the Cincinnatti [*sic*] branch of the Church . . . held at Elder Pugh's on the 1st day of June, 1845" as noted by *Times and Seasons* (Nauvoo, Illinois), 1 June 1845. The spellings "Abel" and Able" were used interchangeably throughout this period.

Such differences in spelling caused certain defenders of the practice of priesthood denial to claim that there were *two* Elijah Abels (or Ables) in the church at Nauvoo during the 1840s—one white and the other black—spelling their names differently. See Joseph Fielding Smith to Mrs. Floren S. Preece, 18 January 1955, S. George Ellsworth Papers, Utah State University, Logan, Utah.

31. For Mormon universalistic rhetoric which looked forward to the gathering of blacks, along with other peoples of Nauvoo, see *Times and Seasons,* October, 1840, 15 May 1843, 1 November 1843, 1, 15 January 1844.

32. For an excellent discussion of Jane Manning James and these Connecticut blacks and their later involvement in the origins of Utah's black community, see Henry J. Wolfinger, "A Test of Faith, Jane Elizabeth James and the Origins of the Utah Black Community," in *Social Accommodation in Utah* (American West Center Occasional Papers, University of Utah, Salt Lake City, 1975), pp. 126-72.

33. As derived from information as compiled in Appendix C, especially tables 7 and 8.

34. As indicated in "An Act to Incorporate the City of Nauvoo," as reprinted in Smith, *History of the Church,* 4: 239-44.

35. Ibid., 6: 210.

36. Leonard J. Arrington, *Great Basin Kingdom* (Cambridge, Mass, 1958), p. 5.

37. Eugene Berwanger, *The Frontier Against Slavery,* (Urbana, Illinois, 1967), pp. 33, 44-46.

38. William L. Appleby to Brigham Young, 2 June 1847; also noted in the journal of William L. Appleby, 19 May 1847, "Journal History," LDS Church Archives. There is, however, some confusion over *who* actually ordained Lewis. According to the recollections of Jane Elizabeth James "Parley P. Pratt ordained Him an Elder." See Jane E. James to Joseph F. Smith, 7 February 1890, as reprinted in Wolfinger, "A Test of Faith," p. 149. Also through an error committed by the compilers of the "Journal History," the impression that Walker Lewis was a member of the Mormon branch at Batavia, New York, was created. See "Journal History," 2 June 1847. Such a false impression was obtained because Appleby's letter describing Walker Lewis was mailed to Brigham Young from Batavia, New York. However, the contents of both this letter and Appleby's journal show Lewis to be a resident of and member of the church at Lowell, Massachusetts.

39. See Wilford Woodruff to Brigham Young, 16 November 1844, Woodruff papers. Woodruff in his journal during late 1844 and early 1845 made note of his numerous visits to Lowell and the areas around Lowell. Both Apostles Brigham Young and Ezra Taft Benson visited these same areas

during 1844-45 and reported nothing unusual in the ethnic or racial qualities of Mormon priesthood holders.

40. Woodruff to Young, 16 November 1844, Woodruff Papers. According to Ezra Taft Benson to Brigham Young, 22 January 1845, Benson Papers, LDS Church Archives, the particular difficulties in the Lowell Branch came about as a result of church finances and the collection of funds.

41. William L. Appleby to Brigham Young, 2 June 1847, William L. Appleby Papers, LDS Church Archives. Also see Appleby's journal, 19 May 1847. In his journal, Appleby acknowledged that the ordination of Lewis was "contrary though to the order of the Church on the Law of the Priesthood as the descendants of Ham are not entitled to that privilege." There are indications, however, that this entry, along with most of his so-called journal, was not written until the mid-1850s, by which time black priesthood denial was well known by people both within and outside of Mormonism.

42. The absence of a written reply by Young to Appleby's inquiry might be due to the fact that when Young returned from the Great Basin to Winter Quarters in the fall of 1847, Appleby was at Winter Quarters. Therefore, Young and/or other church leaders were able to respond personally to any questions that Appleby had on this matter.

43. *Times and Seasons,* March and April, 1842; *Latter-day Saints Millennial Star* (Liverpool, England), July and August, 1842. Although, as discussed in chapter 3, this work was compiled during the 1830s and had an impact on and reflected developing Mormon racial attitudes at that time.

44. Smith, *History of the Church,* 5: 372-79, 1 May 1843.

45. Ibid., p. 372.

46. The Jaredites and their alleged racial origins were briefly described in Chapter 1.

47. Parley P. Pratt to John Van Cott, 7 May 1843, Parley P. Pratt Papers, LDS Church Archives. It is easy to confuse the authorship of this letter by ascribing that portion of the letter describing the Kinderhook Plates to Orson rather than Parley Pratt because Orson wrote his greetings to John Van Cott on the bottom of the front side of the second page and the back side of this same page and signed it with his name. However, both sides of the first page and the top half of the second page (including the discussion of the Kinderhook Plates) were written by Parley.

48. For a discussion of this development, see Chapter 3.

49. A group of Mormons in Missouri, reacting to the persecutions that they had suffered, organized a secret, extra legal group—the Danites. For a discussion of the Danites see Leland H. Gentry, "The Danite Band of 1838," *B.Y.U. Studies* 14 (Summer 1974): 421-50.

50. *Times and Seasons,* September, October, November 1840. *Latter-day Saints Millennial Star,* August 1843. *Wasp* (Nauvoo, Illinois), 17 September 1842.

51. *Times and Seasons,* 1 July 1841.

52. Ibid., September 1840; *Wasp,* 14 May 1842.

53. *Times and Seasons,* October 1840. It is interesting to note that the Saints made these offending Missourians the objects of Mormonism's first effort at collective priesthood denial. Through revelation, Joseph Smith denounced these Missourians for their "dark and blackening deeds" and denied the priesthood not just to those Missourians who had lifted "up the heel against mine annointed," but also to "their posterity after them from generation to generation." See *Doctrine and Covenants,* 121:16 and 21, 124:10. First published in the *Times and Seasons,* May 1840. Also noted in Smith, *History of the Church,* 3: 289-94.

54. *Nauvoo Neighbor,* 30 August 1843.

55. Ibid.

56. Ibid., 13, 20 September 1843.

57. According to the biblical genealogy and origins of nations accepted by nineteenth-century biblical literalists (including the Latter-day Saints), the inhabitants of ancient Carthage had come from Tyre and Sidon. The inhabitants of Tyre and Sidon, in turn, were believed to be the literal descendants of Ham, who was looked upon as the father of all black and dark-skinned peoples. Hence it was all too easy for the Mormon mind to draw parallels between the "black" ancient Carthaginians and the residents of Carthage, Illinois, who were engaged in "black" or dark deeds. In a more general sense, all areas occupied by real or supposed enemies of the Saints were collectively designated "the land of Ham." See "Journal History," 26 May 1844; *Latter-day Saint Millennial Star,* July 1841.

58. According to the *Nauvoo Neighbor,* 13 September 1843, the proceedings of the "Nigger meeting" were as follows:

I say Sambo;—says Jim, a very interesting Nigger; I says Sambo, and all ob you jemmen ob color;—dis Nigger mobs dat Massa Leopold Agustuni Washington, my uncles nephew, be de presiden ob dese Nited States; what says all ob ye niggers and massa president ha! ha! ha!"

Second de motion of de former jemmen—says De Massa President says Sambo, put it to de meetan.

All ob you jemmen ob color who faber Leopoldi Augustuni Washington, signify it by saying aye. Carried all but one.—jemmen put dat

one dam nigger out for not voting foe de president of de Nited States,
when all ob dese jemmen voted in de firmative.

59. *Prophet,* 10 May 1845.

60. *Nauvoo Neighbor,* 26 March 1845. Although these remarks were
not written by a Mormon but a sympathetic nonmember, the editor of
the *Neighbor* felt that they were important enough to receive prominent
notice in his publication and to be reprinted in the New York-based
Prophet, 15 July 1844.

61. *Nauvoo Neighbor,* 7 August 1844. Speaking in more general terms,
another church writer warned that "the vengeance of God will haunt the
whole gang of assassins and their offspring and abettors." *Times and Seasons,* 15 July 1844 (italics mine.)

62. "Speech of Orson Hyde before Congregation in Nauvoo" as recorded in the journal of Wilford Woodruff, 2 May 1846.

63. For the most recent account of Rigdon, see F. Mark McKiernan,
*The Voice of One Crying in the Wilderness: Sidney Rigdon, Religious
Reformer, 1793-1876* (Lawrence, Kansas, 1972).

64. The actions and activities of Wight as a schismatic Mormon leader
were discussed in Chapter 4.

65. Milo M. Quaife, *The Kingdom of Saint James: A Narrative of the
Mormons* (New Haven, 1930), and O. W. Riegel, *Crown of Glory: The Life
of James J. Strang: Moses of the Mormons* (New Haven, 1935). For an
overview of the various schismatic Mormon groups who opposed the claims
of Brigham Young and the Twelve see Dale L. Morgan, "A Bibliography
of the Churches of the Dispersion," *Western Humanities Review* 1 (Summer 1952): 255-66; and Robert B. Flanders, "The Mormons Who Did Not
Go West: A Study of the Emergence of the Reorganized Church of Jesus
Christ of Latter Day Saints" (M.A. thesis, University of Wisconsin, 1954),
pp. 1-49; and D. Michael Quinn, "The Mormon Succession Crisis of 1844,"
B.Y.U. Studies 16 (Winter 1976): 187-233.

66. "Journal History," 6 October 1844.

67. *Times and Seasons,* 15 November 1844. James J. Strang was identified with Judas Iscariot and Lucifer; see *Latter-day Saints Millennial Star,*
15 November 1846.

68. *Latter-day Saints Millennial Star,* 1, 15 November 1847.

69. Hyde, *Speech Delivered Before the High Priests Quorum in Nauvoo,*
April 27, 1845. According to at least one account, Orson Hyde, in the
wake of his own brief "apostasy" from the church in 1838-39, experienced
a "vision" in which it was revealed that the "curse of Cain" would come
upon him and his posterity if Hyde did not repent and "make immediate
restitution to the quorum of the Twelve." See journal of Allen Joseph

Stout, p. 9 (typescript copy in the library of the Utah State Historical Society). Also see J. W. Gunnison, *The Mormons* (Philadelphia, 1852), p. 51.

70. *Times and Seasons,* February 1840. Smith went on to note that the Saints wouldn't have deserved such treatment even if they "had been Mohamedans [*sic*], Hottentots, or Pagans."

71. *Prophet,* 23 November 1844. It is interesting that Josiah Quincy, in recalling his visit to Nauvoo in April 1844, took note of the work being done on the Mormon temple there. One workman at the temple site, according to Quincy, was "laboring on a huge sun" chiselled from solid stone, "the countenance was of the negro type . . . surrounded by the conventional rays." See his *Figures of the Past* (Boston, 1883), pp. 376-400.

72. *Times and Seasons,* 15 July 1845, 1 November 1845; Almon W. Babbitt to Brigham Young, 1 July 1850, Almon W. Babbitt Papers, LDS Church Archives.

73. Smith, *History of the Church,* 3: 294; *Times and Seasons,* October 1840; *Latter-day Saints Millennial Star,* August 1843. A spiritual identification with such people had been asserted during the 1830s. This was suggested in the patriarchal blessings given to apostles Wilford Woodruff and Erastus Snow during the 1830s. See journal of Wilford Woodruff, 25 April 1837, and journal of Erastus Snow, 3 December 1837, Woodruff and Snow Papers, LDS Church Archives. Also see *Doctrine and Covenants,* 64:36; *Latter Day Saints Messenger and Advocate,* February 1835, July 1837.

74. *Times and Seasons,* January 1840.

75. Orson Pratt, *The Kingdom of God* (Liverpool, England, 1848), p. 2.

76. *Times and Seasons,* October 1840; Parley P. Pratt to Elias Smith, 18 February 1845, Parley P. Pratt Papers, LDS Church Archives.

77. The designation of Winter Quarters as the "Camp of Israel" could convey a literal as well as a spiritual racial identification between the Saints and the Children of Israel.

78. *Latter-day Saint Millennial Star,* July 1841, August 1843; *Times and Seasons,* 1 September 1842, 1 July 1844.

79. This development was discussed in Chapter 1.

80. *Times and Seasons,* 15 November 1844.

81. Willard Richards, "Discourse given at a meeting of the Young and Richards family," 8 January 1845; Richards Papers; Journal of Wilford Woodruff, 3 May 1846, Woodruff Papers.

82. As recorded in Woodruff's journal, 16 February 1847, Woodruff Papers.

83. Winthrop Jordan, *White Over Black* (Chapel Hill, North Carolina, 1968), pp. 143-44.

84. Journal of Heber C. Kimball, 29 May 1847, Heber C. Kimball Papers, LDS Church Archives. This incident was also noted by the "Journal History," 29 May 1847, which drew a harsher analogy between the black man and the delinquent elders: "They will stoop and dance like nigers. I don't mean this debasing the nigers by any means." This account was corroborated by the observations of Howard R. Egan, *Pioneering the West* (Richmond, Utah 1917), p. 57; Wilford Woodruff in his journal, 29 May 1847, had Brigham Young denouncing the elders for "*Nigaring & Hobing* down all . . . " (italics in original).

85. Egan, *Pioneering the West,* pp. 58-61.

86. Journal of Joseph Smith, 30 December 1842, Joseph Smith Papers.

87. Klaus J. Hansen, "The Millennium, The West and Race in the Antebellum American Mind," *Western Historical Quarterly* 3 (October 1972): 386-7.

88. For a comparison of the black population of the Great Basin as contrasted with that of Nauvoo, see Appendix C, especially Tables 7 and 9.

89. Journal of Wilford Woodruff, 5 January 1852.

90. See "Constitution of the State of Deseret," Article 2, Section 5; Article 5, Section 10; Article 6, Section 1; Article 8, Section 1; "An Act to Establish a Territorial Government for Utah," Section 5: Chapter 35, 47, LDS Church Archives.

91. This development was discussed in Chapter 4.

6 | *Concurrent Antiabolitionist and Antislavery Rhetoric, 1852-1865*

> We are not by any means treasonists, secessionists, or abolition-
> ists . . . we are neither negro-drivers nor negro-worshippers. . . .
> Brigham Young, January 1862

> If I had had management [of the nation's affairs] . . . I would
> have hung up a number of Southern fire-eaters on one end of a
> rope and a lot of rabid Abolitionists on the other end, as ene-
> mies and traitors to their country.
> John Taylor, March 1865

Brigham Young's anger was showing on that March day in
1863 when he delivered a hard-hitting sermon to the throng of true believers assembled in the tabernacle. Young was upset by a national campaign
against Mormon polygamy. This campaign was launched in response to the
Mormons' public admission in 1852 that they were practicing polygamy and
considered it an essential feature of their religion. During the election campaign of 1860, the triumphant Republican party lashed out against Mormon polygamy, characterizing it and slavery "Twin relics of Barbarism,"
which must be eradicated. By 1863, Brigham Young's wrath was provoked
by two specific Republican antipolygamy actions. First, the Republican-
dominated Congress enacted the Morrill Anti-Bigamy Act of 1862, which
levied penalties against anyone practicing plural marriage. Second, in the
fall of 1862 President Lincoln dispatched the Third California Volunteers
to Utah, alleging concern about Confederate activity in nearby Colorado

and New Mexico. This armed force under the command of Patrick Edward Connor, a pugnacious Irish Catholic who had little love for Mormons, was stationed near Salt Lake City. Connor's force was assigned to protect overland mail and telegraph routes and keep a close eye on the polygamous Latter-day Saints.[1]

In response to these two actions Brigham Young berated "the rank, rabid abolitionists whom I call black-hearted Republicans." Young attacked his Republican tormentors not only for meddling in Mormon affairs but also for their role in bringing about the current state of national division and civil war. This conflict, which was reaching its bloody climax, prompted the Mormon leader to accuse the Republicans of setting "the whole national fabric on fire."

Young tempered his criticism of the Republicans by attacking also the South and its Peculiar Institution. Young was sensitive to the fact that Utah was subject to federal control. Utah had not seceded from the Union in 1861, despite strong Mormon dislike of the Republican party. In addition, Young probably felt intimidated by the presence of those California volunteers. The Mormon leader condemned the southern slaveholders "for their abuse of [the black] race," noting that white southerners would "be cursed, unless they repent." Young then summed up his overall position.

> I am no abolitionist, neither am I a pro-slavery man; I hate some of their principles and especially some of their conduct, as I do the gates of hell. The Southerners make the negroes, and the Northerners worship them; this is all the difference between slaveholders and abolitionists.[2]

Brigham Young's 1863 speech reflected two basic attitudes: first, a basic Mormon dislike for slavery and, second, a strong Latter-day Saint antipathy for antislavery advocates, who by the late antebellum period were primarily Republicans. The Saints had condemned both slavery and abolitionism from the earliest days of the Mormon movement, usually with an emphasis on one or the other. However, what was different during the 1850s was that church spokesmen manifested these two basic attitudes concurrently and with about equal force. Thus, Brigham Young, speaking on the general issue of slavery in 1856, declared both the "nigger drivers and nigger worshippers . . . decidedly wrong."[3] The Mormon-run *St. Louis Luminary* proclaimed the Saints "neither Abolitionist nor

pro-slavery. . . ."[4] In a similar fashion, Apostle John Taylor attacked
the proslavery and antislavery forces in "Bleeding Kansas." He questioned
the motives of both sides, noting, "If they tell the truth, it is by accident."[5]
The abolitionist and proslavery partisans in Kansas were also denounced
by both the *Western Standard*—a Latter-day Saint periodical published in
San Francisco—and the New York City-based *Mormon.* The latter publication characterized Kansas antislavery and proslavery elements as "a dis-
grace to the American Republic."[6] During the presidential campaign of
1856 the *Western Standard* decried the "unhappy divisions" caused by
"gas evolved by demagogues" on both sides of the slavery issue.[7]

In the wake of southern secession and the outbreak of civil war in
1861, Mormon attacks on abolitionism and slavery intensified. During
these troubled years Brigham Young emphasized that the Saints were
neither "secessionists or abolitionists. . . . We are," he continued, "neither
negro-drivers nor negro-worshippers."[8] Apostle John Taylor echoed these
same views in an 1863 Fourth of July speech denouncing the "intrigues"
and "sophism" of both the North and the South.[9]

Certain Latter-day Saints were particularly shrill in their denunciations
of both the North and the South during the Civil War. The pro-Mormon
Mountaineer suggested that the "extreme vindictive abolitionists" of the
North and the "leaders of the present insurrectionary movements in the
South should be penitentiaried or ignominiously executed."[10] In a similar
fashion, John Taylor stated that if it were in his power he would hang "up
a number of Southern fire-eaters on one end of a rope, and a lot of rabid
Abolitionists on the other end as enemies and traitors to their country."[11]

A Mormon willingness to publicly attack both abolitionism and slavery
was motivated by several factors. First, Mormon antislavery rhetoric
was rooted in a basic Mormon dislike of slavery. This dislike, evident since
the earliest days of the Mormon movement, was related to the fact that the
overwhelming majority of Latter-day Saints came from nonslaveholding
areas in the United States and after 1850 from abroad, particularly from
Great Britain and Scandinavia.[12] Even though the Saints continued to
give legal recognition to the enslavement of the few blacks in their midst
through "An Act in Relation to Service," the scope and intent of this institution was limited. Only a handful of Latter-day Saints held slaves
during the 1850s and early 1860s. In fact, the number of slaves held in
Utah apparently decreased during the 1850s if the United States Census

figures for 1860 are to be believed. According to these figures there
were only 29 black slaves held by twelve owners in the entire territory.[13]
The Saints, moreover, did not look upon this practice as slaveholding per
se. Rather, they considered it "benevolent servitude" beneficial to master and "black servant" alike. In addition, Brigham Young and other Mormons continued to rule out future slaveholding in Utah, once it became
a state. Thus, when Brigham Young was asked whether Utah would be
admitted to the Union as a free or a slave state, the answer was always
the same. Utah was not "slave country."[14] Young did not want "Slavery
entailed upon our young, vigorous, and thriving Territory."[15] He further
claimed "[N]either our climate, soil, productions, nor minds of the people
are congenial to African Slavery."[16] The Utah Saints had no "very decided
propensity in favor of slavery" because any large-scale slavery in the territory "would prove useless and unprofitable" and work against the basic
Mormon goal of "great moral and social reform."[17] In summary, Utah
would be admitted to the Union as a "free state."

Other Latter-day Saint spokesmen echoed the Free-Soil views of Brigham
Young. Utah territorial delegates William H. Hooper and John M. Bernhisel gave a vote of no confidence to the Peculiar Institution during Utah's
quest for statehood.[19] A lack of Mormon proslavery support was evident
in a Utah convention organized to draw up a proposed constitution for
Utah statehood. When certain Latter-day Saints proposed a provision
to make slavery constitutional, it was dropped when "few delegates" could
be found favoring it.[20] Likewise, Apostle John Taylor, travelling throughout the East to promote Mormon statehood, assured northerners that
"Utah shall not be admitted as a slave state."[21]

Various Saints also attacked slavery in more general terms. Brigham
Young, through his private exchanges, declared slavery "repugnant" and
"only productive of evil."[22] Young, in addition, expressed his dislike
for slavery in the South. While reading Hinton Rowan Helper's antislavery account, *The Impending Crisis of the South,* the Mormon president
advanced his view that slavery had been "the ruin of the South" even though
this region had "a beautiful climate and rich soil."[23] Young believed that if
southerners "would abolish slavery, and institute free labor they would be
much richer than they are."[24] The Saints also condemned slavery in other
quarters. Apostle Parley P. Pratt denounced the Catholic Church because it
held "slaves and souls of men."[25] Another Saint attacked the British for

attempting to reinstate slavery in a new form in the West Indies through the importation of Chinese laborers, while the *Millennial Star* condemned "slaveholders" in general.[26]

Though Mormon antislavery rhetoric was motivated by a basic Mormon repugnance toward the Peculiar Institution, concurrent antiabolitionist rhetoric was the by-product of Mormon efforts to defend their own "peculiar institution", polygamy, from non-Mormon attacks. These attacks intensified after 1852, following the official Mormon acknowledgement of polygamy's existence among the Saints. Mormon polygamy, as southern slavery, became a national political issue, generating debate and conflict both within and outside of the halls of Congress. Both the Democrats and after 1854 the newly formed Republican party attacked the Mormons' peculiar institution. The Republicans in their national party platforms of 1856 and 1860 labeled polygamy "a relic of barbarism" and called for its eradication. Not to be outdone, Democrat Stephen A. Douglas called the Mormon institution a "loathsome ulcer." President James A. Buchanan, another Democrat, aware of rising opposition to the polygamous Saints, dispatched United States armed forces to Utah in 1857.

These troops were stationed near Salt Lake City, where they remained until the outbreak of the Civil War in 1861. Following this removal, there was a short lull in federal action against the Saints. However, the passage of the Morrill Anti-Bigamy Act in 1862, coupled with the dispatch of those California Volunteers to Utah, were the opening shots in a renewed campaign against the Saints' peculiar institution. This crusade would continue nonstop until 1890, when the Saints, yielding to intense political and economic pressures, moved to end their practice of polygamy.[27] This antipolygamy campaign had support from non-Mormons in both the North and the South and from all political parties. The Republican party, already identified as ardently antislavery, led the charge against the Saints.

Thus Mormon antiabolitionist rhetoric was primarily a response to Republican attacks on Mormon polygamy. By the mid-1850s, the Mormons condemned their Republican tormentors as "abolitionists," "slave lovers," "nigger worshippers," and most often "Black Republicans" with a vehemence reminiscent of early Mormon anti-abolitionist rhetoric of the 1830s. In 1855 the *Deseret News* denounced Republican "abolitionists" for trying to interfere with the "domestic institutions of Utah."[28] The *Mormon* expressed particularly strong antiabolitionist views, berating the Republicans or "higher law advocates" for "throwing overboard both the Bible and Constitution" to attack Mormon polygamy.[29]

The tempo of Mormon antiabolitionism quickened as the Republicans attacked both the polygamous Saints and the slaveholding southerners during the presidential campaign of 1856. When Republicans adopted a presidential platform labeling polygamy and black slavery the "Twin Relics of Barbarism," the besieged Saints responded in kind, condemning the "Black Republicans" for their "disunion and treason."[30] Apostle John Taylor was particularly conspicuous in his assaults on the Republicans while editor of the New York *Mormon*. He accused the "Black Republicans" of using " '*Black Mail*' [in] coupling the cry of '*polygamy*' with that of 'slavery. . . .' "[31] On another occasion Taylor ridiculed "the insensate folly of the Abolitionists" for their "pledged hostility to polygamy."[32] Through an editorial in the *Mormon,* he accused "Black Republicanism" of threatening the Mormons "with sword, bayonets, and extermination." In conclusion, Taylor noted that he did not have "enough of the nigger worshipping propensities to adore [the Republicans'] colored diety."[33] Other Mormons, including Apostle George A. Smith, condemned the "Black Republican or Slave Lover Ticket" for attacking polygamy.[34] The *Western Standard* also hammered away at the Republicans, whom it labeled "political demagogues and abolition fanatics."[35]

Even though the Republicans did not prevail in 1856, Mormon antiabolitionist rhetoric continued unabated. Even in 1857, when President James Buchanan, a Democrat, launched his 1857 armed crusade against the Saints, culminating in the so-called Utah War, the Mormons found cause to blame the Republicans. The Saints accused the Republicans of goading Buchanan and other Democrats into action against the Saints with the ultimate Republican aim of making Utah a "base of their 'niggardly' operations."[36]

Three years later, during the election campaign of 1860, the Saints continued to denounce abolitionism, particularly when the Republican platform once more condemned Mormon polygamy and black slavery as the "Twin Relics of Barbarism." As the slaveholding South, the polygamous Saints expressed grave concern about the election of Abraham Lincoln.[37] In retrospect the pro-Mormon *Mountaineer* noted that "most" of the Saints "were opposed to" the election of Abraham Lincoln because of his "reported abolitionism."[38] Of more immediate Mormon concern were

Republican-led efforts in Congress to enact antipolygamy legislation in 1860. The editor of the *Millennial Star* sarcastically accused such antipolygamy Republicans of overlooking the equally serious problem of "Nigger Stealing."[39]

By the 1860s the Latter-day Saints were pulled in two different directions by the traumatic events of southern secession and civil war. On the one hand, the Utah Saints, despite their intense dislike for the antipolygamous Republicans, did not follow the slaveholding South out of the Union in response to Abraham Lincoln's election of 1860. This decision was based on the realities of Utah's northern geographic position—closer to Unionist centers of military strength than to those of the Confederacy—and the fact that the vast majority of Utah's Mormon citizens were from areas outside the slaveholding South. Brigham Young reflected these pro-Unionist sentiments in a telegram sent to J. H. Wade, president of the Pacific Telegraph Company. Young declared that Utah had "not seceded but is firm for the Constitution."[40] Utah's territorial delegate William H. Hooper was exceedingly careful to project the Mormons' pro-Unionist sympathies to a skeptical Republican-dominated Congress. He continued to push for Utah statehood in 1860 and 1862.[41] In doing so, Hooper called for the admission of Utah as a free state despite his own status as a Mormon slaveholder.[42] This of course conformed with Mormonism's basic antislavery position as expressed in public and in private throughout this period.

On the other hand, the Great Basin Saints remained basically antagonistic toward Republican officials in Washington, D.C. Although the Mormons were willing to stay in the Union and even see Utah become a free state, they refused to fight in the Civil War itself. Mormon antiabolitionist rhetoric, therefore, served to notify Republican officials of this Latter-day Saint refusal, especially as the Civil War evolved more and more into a crusade to abolish slavery.[43]

Also during the Civil War, Mormon millennialistic expectations encouraged Latter-day Saint attacks on both slavery and abolition.[44] These expectations were a mixture of hopeful optimism and fearful anxiety. As early as 1854, Apostle Jedediah M. Grant had reflected the hopeful optimistic side of these millennial expectations. He had looked forward to the elimination of both southern slaveholders and northern abolitionists as part of a cleansing action that would pave the way for ultimate Mormon control of

the earth through the millennium and the Second Coming.[45] By 1860
William H. Hooper, Utah's Territorial delegate, expressed this same optimism even in the face of secession and civil war. He declared "Utah's star"
to be "in the ascendancy," predicting that the Saints' "Mountain Home"
would serve as "an asylum for the honest from among all nations."[46] The
Deseret News viewed the outbreak of Civil War hostilities in a positive light,
labeling the war itself a "heaven ordained opportunity" to strike a "decisive
blow at the root of existing evils . . . the noxious fruits of nullification, disunion, and slavery agitation."[47] The millennium would mark an end to the
strife over slavery.[48]

At the same time, however, the Civil War generated Mormon fears and
anxieties about the apocalyptic violence that would precede this millennium.
Antiabolitionist rhetoric reflected a Mormon fear about the disorder and
violence that would accompany the elimination of the Peculiar Institution.
After all, slavery served as a bulwark of social control over a restive black
population. This bulwark seemed threatened even before the first shots
were fired at Fort Sumter. John Brown's 1859 raid on Harper's Ferry had,
in the words of Apostle George Q. Cannon, "engendered feelings of hatred"
between the North and the South that would never "be allayed."[49] Several
Mormons linked John Brown's raid to Joseph Smith's millennialistic apocalyptic 1832 prophecy that "after many days [the] slaves shall rise up
against their masters," triggering widespread bloodshed and disorder.[50]
The *Millennial Star* maintained that

> We look upon this negro insurrection as a type and foreshadowing
> of something to come; and in the meantime it may be considered
> as more than probable that this insurrection will greatly aggravate
> the cankering difficulties between the Northern and Southern States
> of the Union.[51]

There was every prospect, continued the *Star,* that the slaves would rise
en masse, "executing a horrid massacre upon their masters' wives and
children." Ultimately civil war would rage, "with such fury, and such
dreadful slaughter of life, and numerous fiendish horrors, as to form a
spectacle more fearful and hell-like than has ever been seen in the
experience of mankind."[52]

By 1861, following the southern secession and the commencement of hostilities, Mormon apocalyptic anxieties intensified. Brigham Young did not believe that northern war aims would be limited to preserving the Union. He feared that "The Abolitionists would let the negroes loose to massacre every white person."[53] This fear seemed on the verge of fulfillment when Abraham Lincoln announced his Emancipation Proclamation in 1862. The *Deseret News* predicted "upheavings among the dark myriads of the sons of Canaan" and retributions by "incensed blacks" for past wrongs, which would "convulse the land of their bondage and execration from its center to its circumference."[54] The Saints anticipated "all the indescribable horrors of a servile insurrection."[55] The future, reported the *Millennial Star,* appeared "as black as Erebus." America, once "the pride and boast of the world," was about to "sink into the darkest, blackest shades of oblivion."[56] There was not much the Mormons could do to reverse this gloomy prognosis. After all, the Saints expected the Emancipation Proclamation to "bring about a literal fulfillment of certain predictions of the prophets, recorded in the 'scriptures of truth,' concerning events that would transpire in the 'latter days.' "[57] The black slaves incited by this proclamation would fulfill Mormon prophecy and "after many days ... rise up against their masters."[58]

Mormon apocalyptic-millennialistic fears continued unabated for the remainder of the Civil War. The Saints viewed with alarm Abraham Lincoln's decision to utilize the "brawny arms" of the "Hamites ... in squelching the imperiousness of their masters." At the same time, this "marshalling ... of 100,000 slaves" was consistent with Mormon prophecy.[59] While "that portion of the [1832] prophecy referring to the slaves" had been literally fulfilled, the Mormons anticipated "a much more general and terrible accomplishment of the whole in the future."[60] Even the formal termination of sectional warfare in 1865 did not allay Mormon fears concerning the dreaded future role of blacks:

> Already have slaves risen against their masters, but we, like our predecessors, look for a far more general rising of the blood-thirsty African against their masters, and woe, woe unto the whites who may be so unfortunate as to fall into their pitliess hands, for, from experience we know the negro is a stranger to mercy when fully aroused, and the course that is being pursued

throughout the entire Union will shortly transform the now
seemingly tame and almost imbecile black, into a perfect demon.[61]

Throughout the Civil War, Mormon attacks on abolitionism and slavery
served two somewhat contrasting purposes for the millennialistic-minded
Saints. Mormon antiabolitionist rhetoric provided the anxiety-ridden
Saints hope that the institution of black slavery would somehow survive
the apocalyptic events preceding the millennium. Thus a restless and
"blood-thirsty" black slave population would be controlled. At the same
time, Mormon antislavery rhetoric reminded these same Saints that the
glorious millennium itself would usher in a perfect society in which the
institution of black slavery would no longer be necessary.

The Latter-day Saints were not unique in viewing the Civil War period
as a prelude to the impending millennium. Even before the 1860s the
"open espousal" of millennialistic expectations gained support in "respectable quarters." Harriet Beecher Stowe's famous work *Uncle Tom's Cabin*
was based on a strong belief in the approaching millennium.[62] Many
religious Americans interpreted the outbreak of the Civil War in a millennialistic light. They viewed this event as the beginning of the end, the
setting-off of a train of apocalyptic events culminating in the Second Coming and the establishment of the kingdom of God.[63]

A Mormon willingness to express publicly concurrent antiabolitionist
and antislavery rhetoric during the period from 1852 to 1865 stood in
sharp contrast to an earlier Mormon tendency to stand aloof and detached
from the whole slavery controversy. Mormon antiabolitionist expressions
were reminiscent of those assumed by the Saints during the 1830s, while
the Saints' antislavery declarations revived memories of the 1844 Mormon
crusade against slavery. In contrast to these earlier periods, the Saints did
not carry these feelings beyond the rhetorical level. There was no Mormon effort to enshrine antiabolitionist attitudes in Latter-day Saint scripture, as had been the case during the 1830s, or to actively promote Mormon antislavery views in the political arena, as the Saints had done during
the 1840s. However, simultaneous Latter-day Saint antislavery and especially antiabolitionist rhetoric did complement and, in fact, was reinforced by
concurrent Mormon efforts to publicize their racist concepts and practices,
particularly black priesthood denial. In turn, such publicity coupled with
antiabolitionist rhetoric helped to reinforce the subordinate status of blacks
within Mormonism.

NOTES

1. For a discussion of Mormon actions and responses during the Civil War, see: Gustive O. Larson, "Utah and the Civil War," *Utah Historical Quarterly* 33 (Winter 1965); George U. Hubbard, "Abraham Lincoln as Seen by the Mormons," *Utah Historical Quarterly* 31 (Spring 1963): 97-108; and Larry Schweikart, "The Mormon Connection: Lincoln, the Saints, and the Crisis of Equality," *Western Humanities Review* 34 (Winter 1980): 1-22.

2. *Journal of Discourses* (Liverpool, 1854-1886), Brigham Young, 10, 8 March 1863.

3. *Journal of Discourses,* Brigham Young, 4, 31 August 1856.

4. *St. Louis Luminary,* 26 May 1855.

5. *Journal of Discourses,* John Taylor, 5, 9 August 1857.

6. *Western Standard* (San Francisco), 20 September 1856; *Mormon* (New York City), 28 April 1855.

7. *Western Standard,* 30 August 1856.

8. *Journal of Discourses,* Brigham Young 9, 19 January 1862.

9. *Deseret News* (Salt Lake City), 10 July 1861.

10. *The Mountaineer* (Salt Lake City), 25 May 1861.

11. *Journal of Discourses,* John Taylor, 11, 5 March 1865. Also reprinted in *Deseret News,* 29 March 1865.

12. For a closer look at shifting Mormon sociogeographic origins during the 1850s see S. George Ellsworth, "A History of Mormon Missions in the United States and Canada" (Ph.D. diss., University of California, 1951), pp. 295-306; P. A. M. Taylor, *Expectations Westward* (Ithaca, N.Y., 1966); and William H. Mulder, *Homeward to Zion: The Mormon Migration from Scandinavia* (Minneapolis, Minnesota, 1957).

13. As indicated by a two-page compilation of Utah's black population in 1860 prepared from "1860 Federal Census, Utah Territory," by George Olin Zabriskie, copy in Library of Utah State Historical Society, Salt Lake City, Utah. These census figures are not complete, as indicated by Charles W. Nibley, *Reminiscences* (Salt Lake City, 1934), pp. 35-36, which describes two black slaves held by John Bankhead of Logan not included in the 1860 census.

14. *Journal of Discourses,* Heber C. Kimball, 2, 17 September 1854.

15. Young to Taylor, 8 September 1855, Young Papers, LDS Church Archives.

16. Young to Kane, 14 April 1856, Young Papers.

17. Horace Greeley, *An Overland Journey* ed. Charles T. Duncan (New York, 1964), p. 180. Young to Taylor, 8 September 1855, Young Papers.

In his discussions with Greeley, the Mormon leader expanded on his views concerning the limited economic feasibility of slavery for himself or among the Saints in general. "I regard it [slavery] generally a curse to the masters. I myself hire many laborers and pay them fair wages: I could not afford to own them. I can do better than subject myself to an obligation to feed and clothe their families, to provide and care for them in sickness and health. Utah is not adapted to slave labor."

18. Young to Taylor, 8 September 1855, 1 March 1856; Young to Willard Richards, 1 April 1856; Young to Bernhisel, 6 January 1858, Young Papers.

19. William H. Hooper to Brigham Young, 4 December 1861, William H. Hooper Papers, LDS Church Archives. John M. Bernhisel to Brigham Young, 19 February 1863, Bernhisel Papers, LDS Church Archives; *Mormon*, 15 December 1855.

20. *New York Daily Times,* 31 March 1856, as reprinted in *Mormon,* 14 June 1856.

21. Taylor to Young, 18 January 1856, Taylor Papers.

22. Young to Taylor, 8 September 1855, Young Papers.

23. Brigham Young's office journal, 4, 6, 7 May, 26 December 1860, Young Papers. Mormon interest in Helper's work is probably not too surprising. According to George Fredrickson, *The Black Image in the White Mind* (New York, 1971), pp. 68, 133, the writings of Helper were attractive to lower-middle-class Americans who were inclined toward Free-Soil sentiments.

24. Brigham Young's office journal, 5 July 1860.

25. Parley P. Pratt, "Repent! Ye People of California," January 1852, reprinted in Parker Pratt Robinson, *Writings of Parley Parker Pratt* (Salt Lake City, 1952), p. 153.

26. *Latter-day Saints Millennial Star* (Liverpool, England), 29 October 1853; *Deseret News,* 15 December 1853.

27. For a closer look at the developing Mormon-non-Mormon conflict over polygamy see Norman F. Furniss, *The Mormon Conflict, 1850-1859* (New Haven, Conn., 1960); and Larson, "Utah and the Civil War."

28. *Deseret News,* 8 February 1855.

29. *Mormon,* 17 November 1855.

30. George A. Smith to Wilford Woodruff, 8 July 1856, George A. Smith Papers, LDS Church Archives; *Deseret News,* 29 September 1857.

31. John Taylor to Brigham Young, 14 August 1856, John Taylor Papers, LDS Church Archives.

32. Ibid., 17 October 1856.

33. *Mormon,* 23 August 1856.

34. George A. Smith to Woodruff, 8 July 1856, George A. Smith Papers.

35. *Western Standard,* 11 October 1856.

36. *Mormon,* 8 June 1857.

37. *Deseret News,* 8, 25 April, 9 May 1860, *Latter-day Saints Millennial Star,* 8 September, 1 December 1860.

38. *Mountaineer,* 6 July 1860.

39. *Latter-day Saints Millennial Star,* 14 July 1860.

40. Gaylon L. Caldwell, " 'Utah Has Not Seceded': A Footnote to Local History," *Utah Historical Quarterly* 26 (1958): 172-75. For a recent work describing the activities of the Utah Mormons during the Civil War, see E. B. Long, *The Saints and the Union: Utah Territory During the Civil War* (Urbana, 1980).

41. *Deseret News,* 18 December 1861, 31 December 1862; *Latter-day Saints Millennial Star,* 8 February 1862; *Journal of Discourses,* Brigham Young, 9, 19 January 1862; Hooper to Young, 4, 11 December 1860, Hooper Papers.

42. *Mountaineer,* 25 May 1861.

43. Larson, "Utah and the Civil War."

44. For a comprehensive treatment of the relationship between the Civil War and Mormon millennialism, see Klaus J. Hansen, *Quest for Empire* (Ann Arbor, Michigan, 1961), pp. 17, 167; Boyd L. Eddins, "The Mormons and the Civil War" (M.A. thesis, Utah State University, 1966).

45. *Journal of Discourses,* Jedediah M. Grant, 2, 2 April 1854.

46. Hooper to Young, 23 November 1860, Hooper Papers.

47. *Deseret News,* 5 June 1861. Some of the Saints anticipated the destruction of the "black race" or at least the death of many slaves. According to Brigham Young, the Civil War would not only fail to free the black slave but "may kill . . . the black race . . . by thousands and tens of thousands" (*Journal of Discourses,* Brigham Young, 10, 6 October 1863). See also his discourses of 14 June 1863 in the same volume.

48. However, certain Saints did indicate a belief that a form of slavery or servitude would exist during the millennium. See Parley P. Pratt, *Key to the Science of Theology* (Liverpool, England, 1855), p. 134; *Journal of Discourses* Brigham Young, 3, 23 March 1856; Erastus Snow, 6, 29 November 1857.

49. *Journal of Discourses,* George Q. Cannon, 8, 9 September 1860. It is interesting that the initial report of Brown's raid was reported under the category of "nothing of special interest" or merely another escapade of "Ossawattamie Brown;" *Mountaineer,* 24 December 1859; *Deseret News,* 30 November 1859, 7 December 1859.

50. This "Revelation and Prophecy on War" was originally published in *Pearl of Great Price.*

51. *Latter-day Saints Millennial Star,* 12 November 1859.

52. Ibid., 28 January 1860.

53. *Journal of Discourses,* Brigham Young, 9, 28 July 1861.

54. *Deseret News,* 7, 28 January 1863.

55. *Latter-day Saints Millennial Star,* 14 February 1863.

56. Ibid., 31 January 1863.

57. *Deseret News,* 7 January 1863.

58. *Latter-day Saints Millennial Star,* 14 February 1863.

59. *Deseret News,* 16 September 1863, 4 February 1863; *Latter-day Saints Millennial Star,* 1 October 1864. As had been the case in the past, Mormon spokesmen used the terms "slave" and "Negro" interchangeably when describing the fulfillment of this portion of the 1832 prophecy. *The Millennial Star,* 25 March 1865, suggested a connection between the use of these two terms. It said that "upwards of 200,000 negroes—formerly slaves—engaged in its military service"; which showed that "many of the slaves formerly belonging to the southern states have been 'marshalled and disciplined for war.'"

60. *Latter-day Saints Millennial Star,* 25 March 1865. The *Star* on another occasion, 22 August 1863, warned that the South might be forced to follow in the footsteps of the North and adopt the "dreadful alternative" of black conscription.

61. Ibid., 28 October 1865.

62. Ernest Lee Tuveson, *Redeemer Nation* (Chicago, 1968), pp. 152, 191.

63. Ernest R. Santeen, *The Roots of Fundamentalism* (Chicago, 1971), p. 97; Tuveson, *Redeemer Nation,* p. 192. Also see: James H. Moorhead, *American Apocalypse: Yankee Protestants and the Civil War* (New Haven and London, 1978).

7 | *Black Priesthood Denial Publicized and Reinforced, 1852-1865*

[Blacks] cannot hold the preisthood [*sic*] . . . they cannot bear rule in any place until the curse is removed from them, they are a servant of servants. . . .

Brigham Young, January 23, 1852

If there never was a prophet or apostle of Jesus Christ spoke it before, I tell you, this people that are commonly called negroes are the children of old Cain. I know they are, I know that they cannot bear rule in the preisthood [*sic*], for the curse upon them was to remain upon them, until the resedue [*sic*] of the posterity of Michal [*sic*] and his wife receive the blessings. . . ."

Brigham Young, February 5, 1852

The year of 1852 was a year of decision for Brigham Young and the Utah Mormons. The federal government finally granted the Saints a degree of self-government. After four years of sectional debate and crisis, Congress created a territorial government for the Utah Saints as part of the Compromise of 1850. Under the compromise, Utah residents, along with those in New Mexico, were allowed through popular sovereignty to regulate the black slaveholding in their midst. This issue, along with the general question of monitoring all Utah blacks, came before Utah's first territorial legislature in 1852. This body was guided by the dictates of Brigham Young, acting in his capacity as Utah territorial governor. Young addressed the legislature on two different occasions, calling for legislation of black slavery in the territory. His comments represent the first Mormon effort to thoroughly publicize black priesthood denial. In the first of these addresses delivered before the upper house of the legislature on January 23, Young declared that since blacks could not "bear any . . . preisthood [sic] " they could not "bear rule in any place until the curse is removed from them."[1] In a second speech, delivered on February 5 before a joint session of the territorial legislature, Young went into greater detail concerning black priesthood proscriptions. He attributed black priesthood denial to the curse of Cain. According to Young, "a man who had the Affrican blood in him cannot hold one jot nor tittle of preisthood [sic]." The "Lord told Cain that he . . . nor his seed" could receive the priesthood "until the last of the posterity of Abel had received the preisthood; until the redemtion of the earth [sic]." This "curse" was to remain upon Cain's posterity "until the resedue of the posterity of Michal and his wife receive the blessings [sic]."[2]

Brigham Young's 1852 speeches before the territorial legislature were significant in that they represented the first Mormon effort to publicize the subordinate position of black people within Mormonism. Even though the church had inaugurated its practice of denying blacks the priesthood during the mid-1840s, the Saints did not publicize this practice until 1852. Throughout the remainder of the 1850s and into the early 1860s Young continued to assert publicly that blacks, as the "descendants of Cain" or "children of Ham," were not "entitled to the Priesthood." This denial or "curse,"[3] maintained Young, would remain on the black race until "All the other families [races] of the earth have received the ordinances" or "blessings" of the "true Gospel."[4] Apostle George A. Smith echoed the views of the Mormon president in a public discourse. He explained that blacks,

> in consequence of their corruptions, their murders, their wickedness, or the wickedness of their fathers, had the priesthood taken from them, and the curse that was upon them was decreed should descend upon their posterity after them, it was decreed that they should not bear rule [sic].[5]

The church press also gave extensive publicity to black priesthood denial. The *Deseret News,* the voice of the Utah Saints, led the way through an April

1852 editorial addressed "To the Saints." Blacks, according to the *News*, were "cursed . . . with a skin of blackness," which they "cannot cast off. . . once and immediately." Although blacks could "be baptised and receive the spirit of God" they could not "receive a fullness of the priesthood."[6] *The Seer*, edited by Apostle Orson Pratt in Washington, D.C., also publicized the subordinate position of blacks within Mormonism. Pratt hinted that the preexistent behavior of black people might be related to priesthood denial. In doing this Pratt expanded on Orson Hyde's 1845 preexistent theory that the current liabilities of black people resulted from unrighteous behavior during a premortal existence. According to Pratt,

> Some [pre-existent] spirits take bodies in the lineage of the chosen seed, through whom the Priesthood is transferred, others receive bodies among the African negroes, or in the lineage of Canaan, whose descendants were cursed, pertaining to the priesthood.[7]

An editorial in the New York *Mormon* referred to the Book of Abraham in discussing the "negro's deformity" of blackness and his "bondage." Building upon the preexistent theories previously presented by Apostles Hyde and Pratt, the *Mormon* noted that the "spirits" of blacks were obligated "to take bodies or tabernacles cursed with bondage and blackness." It added that "Ham and all his descendants were cursed as pertaining to . . . the Priesthood."[8] Other church periodicals including *The St. Louis Luminary* and the San Francisco *Western Standard* also publicized the prevailing Mormon view that blacks could not "receive the Holy Priesthood and govern the Kingdom of God."[9]

Several factors caused the Mormons to publicize their practice of black priesthood denial. First, this publicity was the product of Mormon efforts to justify the black servitude in their midst. This was certainly evident in both of Brigham Young's 1852 speeches before the territorial legislature. Young carefully linked black priesthood denial to the "natural" destiny of blacks to be servants. In his January 23 speech, Young declared that the black man was doomed to be "a servant of servants" because he could not "bear any share of the priesthood."[10] Young was equally emphatic in his February 5 speech, in which he emphasized the relationship between black priesthood denial and the degraded position of blacks as the "rightfull servants of the resedue of the children of Adam."[11] Young hammered away at this same relationship throughout the rest of the 1850s. In a sermon delivered to the Saints in the tabernacle, Young emphasized the correlation between black priesthood denial and the status of blacks as "servants of servants."[12] In another sermon delivered shortly before the Civil War, Young noted that blacks were "servants of servants" because they were prohibited from "the first ordinances of the priesthood."[13] Conversely, the continuing presence of slavery in Utah until 1862 provided an important justification for black priesthood denial. As blacks were actually "servants of servants," they were not entitled to the Mormon priesthood.

A second factor, the vigorous use of antiabolitionist rhetoric during the 1850s and early 1860s, caused the Saints to publicize and uphold the subordinate position of Mormon blacks. The Saints lashed out at their abolitionist-Republican tormentors for being oblivious to those righteous decrees that upheld the inferior status of blacks in both the secular and the ecclesiastical realms. For example, one Mormon periodical berated the Ohio abolitionist Joshua Giddings for his failure to see the relationship between the black curse of servitude and black priesthood denial.[14]

A third factor, the Mormon efforts to defend their own "peculiar institution" of polygamy, was even more important for publicizing and reinforcing black priesthood denial. The Saints were anxious to defend polygamy against increased outside attack after 1852, following the Saints' acknowledgement of its existence in their midst. Non-Mormon attacks frequently drew sharp parallels between the polygamous Latter-day Saints and black people, both in Africa and in America. According to one sarcastic critic, Brigham Young in his practice of polygamy was like the polygamous African King of Ashantee. Young, however, had a distinct advantage over his African counterpart in that he could have an unlimited number of wives while the African monarch was "limited" to a mere 5,333![15] Two non-Mormon British publications described parallels between polygamy as practiced by the Saints and that promoted by the African Kaffirs and Zulus.[16]

Within the United States other non-Mormon writers suggested a physical connection between the polygamous Saints and black people. With the Saints clearly in mind, the vitriolic anti-Mormon *Union Vedette* sneeringly observed that "the negro naturally inclines to polygamy."[17] During the presidential campaign of 1856, some Republicans insinuated an intimate black-polygamous Mormon relationship. At a pro-Republican parade in Indianapolis, one wagon drawn by oxen contained "Brigham Young, with his six wives [with] Brigham . . . making himself useful and interesting as possible among his white, black and piebald better-halves."[18] Writing from Utah, another non-Mormon newspaper reporter suggested that the Saints and blacks in that territory had close social contacts. He wrote that "Two Negro Balls" were

> given this week, at which I am informed by eye witnesses, some ten or a dozen white women attended and danced with the negroes with perfect freedom and familiarity. White men were also "mixed in," and were dancing with the negro wenches. In fact, it presented the most disgusting of spectacles—negro men and women, and Mormon men and women, all dancing on terms of perfect equality.[19]

Other non-Mormon critics saw a link between the polygamous Saints and the alleged ancestor of all black people, Cain. Polygamy, they claimed, had originated in a "direct line from Cain" through the "accursed race."[20] At least two rival Mormon groups, opposing the polygamous Utah Saints, alluded to polygamy's "accursed" racial origins. [21] One of these reported that

> the first polygamist that we have an account of was a descendant of Cain, whom God had cursed because he was a murderer. This descendant Lamech was also a murderer, showing that which has been verified in our day, that polygamy and murder are often twin crimes.[22]

Non-Mormon critics suggested that polygamy caused the Saints to assume "inferior" cultural and racial characteristics. According to one writer, polygamy "degrades all men to one miserable level of fanaticism and mental debasement."[23] Another non-Mormon critic theorized that as the female birthrate in "polygamic countries" exceeds that of males it was possible that "the male [Mormon] race in a few generations would become extinct." It wasn't possible, he concluded, for the Saints to "obtain the hardy bodies and sound minds of northern Saxons from the worst practices of effemite [*sic*] Asiatics."[24] The children of one polygamous family, according to another non-Mormon, resembled "young savages . . .

with faces unwashed, hair uncombed, and feet [with] the color and consistence of huge toads."[25]

On a more scientific level, Dr. Roberts Barthelow, an assistant surgeon attached to the United States Army force sent to Utah in 1857-58, suggested that Mormon polygamy was already producing an inferior race of people. In a report "On the Effects and Tendencies of Mormon Polygamy in the Territory of Utah," Barthelow notes,

> The yellow, sunken, cadaverous visage; the greenish-colored eye; the thick protuberant lips, the low forehead, the lank, angular person, constitute an appearance so characteristic of the new race, the production of polygamy, as to distinguish them at a glance.[26]

Barthelow theorized that the polygamous Saints "would eventually die out" as a people if they were solely dependent on natural increase for their members.[27] C. G. Forshey and Samuel A. Cartwright, two southerners interested in Barthelow's findings and the burgeoning science of ethnology, tended to agree with the army surgeon's hypothesis.[28] Forshey felt that the Mormons' peculiar institution ran counter to the "nature and . . . instincts" of the "white race;" while Cartwright argued that "polygamy is too injurious to the mind and body to be tolerated among a progressive and Christian people."[29]

Other hostile non-Mormons suggested that the Saints because of their alleged racial inferiority were like blacks or Indians in their inability to govern themselves. Thus the Saints, like a "savage tribe," lacked the "inherent capacity" for self-government. Because "the Constitution does not recognize in all races the inherent right of self-government," it was necessary to closely monitor the activities of the polygamous Saints.[30]

The Latter-day Saint affirmation of black priesthood denial, therefore, served as a bulwark against such allegations of Mormon racial inferiority and charges of polygamous Mormon-black interaction. The Saints refuted their non-Mormon critics in other ways. Apostle Heber C. Kimball responded to the charges of those non-Mormons who "never thought for a moment [the Mormons] were *white* men and women."[31] Kimball countered that, "the Saints were quite white."[32] The *Latter-day Saints Millennial Star* summed up the feelings of most churchmen on this question. When non-Mormons address themselves to the Saints they are not

> talking to an inferior race a thousand years behind them in science
> and intelligence; it is white men talking to white men; it is equal
> assuming to dictate to equal; and the "Mormons" will not willingly
> accept such instruction till the supposed superiority is proved.[33]

Indeed, the *Star* used racial analogies to show that the Saints were culturally
superior to non-Mormons. "We are certain that 'Mormon society' is as fair
compared with 'English society,' as is the face of the white man to that of
the swarthy son of Ethiopia."[34] The Saints also refuted charges of a link
between Mormon polygamy and the accursed seed of Cain by emphasizing
their literal descent from the chosen biblical figures of Abraham, Joseph,
and Ephraim. They claimed that "most," or at least nine-tenths of all of
the Saints, were "Ephraimish" in their origin or the "pure seed of Ephraim."[35]
Some Saints even outlined various ways that such descent could be proven.[36]
Brigham Young carried this idea of chosen lineage one step further. According to Young the chosen seed of Abraham and "the Anglo-Saxon race" were
one and the same.[37]

The Saints also refuted non-Mormon charges that racial amalgamation
followed naturally from Mormon polygamy by declaring their opposition
to all black-white racial intermixture. Mormon observers travelling in the
South condemned the numerous "negro mistresses" and "blue-eyed . . .
negro . . . children."[38] Apostle John Taylor characterized this "amalgamation process" as "niggerism in the South."[39]

Among the Saints, themselves, black-white racial intermixture was
against both secular and ecclesiastical laws. The 1852 "Act in Relation to
Service," specifically outlawed "sexual or carnal intercourse" between white
masters and their black slaves.[40] On an ecclesiastical plane, the *Deseret News*
proclaimed racial intermixture to be against the Lord's "righteous decree."
Those mingling "their seed with that of the negress" would be guilty of
"transferring the curse of Cain to their own posterity."[41] Brigham Young
himself was perhaps the most emphatic in his arguments against black-white
racial intermixture: "Shall I tell you the law of God in regard to the African race? If the white man who belongs to the chosen seed mixes his blood
with the seed of Cain, the penalty under the law of God, is death on the
spot. This will always be so."[42]

Defenders of Mormon polygamy claimed that there was much less racial
intermixture among the Saints than among non-Mormon monogamists in

both the North and the South. In Mormon polygamy white men had white wives "honorably given them according to the law of God." By contrast in "Southern Polygamy" white men often had "from one to twenty wives, and nineteen out of the twenty are BLACK."[43] In addition, the Saints felt that the same type of amalgamation existed among northern whites and freed blacks.[44]

There was little room, therefore, among the polygamous Saints for those individuals or groups, including blacks, considered inferior or degraded. Mormon statutes outlawing racial amalgamation were part of a general church effort to "purge out" all those elements, black and otherwise, considered "filthy." Black priesthood denial served this same purpose by excluding "impure" blacks from full fellowship within the church.

In fact, the Saints were anxious to "purge out . . . impure elements" not just from the larger Mormon community, but also from the bodies of individual church members. This could be done, Young said, "through the Holy Ghost," which could act upon individual Saints tainted with impure "Gentile blood." These impurities would actually be purged "out of their veins" and replaced with the pure blood of Abraham.[45] This process would remove impure "blood out" of the bodies of Mormons of varied ethnic backgrounds including those who had the "blood of Judah" and "Ishamaelitish blood."[46]

As for black people, they, of course, could not be cleansed of their impure or tainted blood. Any such effort would naturally be impaired by the physical reality of the blacks' dark skin, which in Mormon eyes was emblematic of their "tainted" blood as well as their accursed racial origins. Blacks therefore were denied full fellowship among the polygamous Mormons as the Saints built up their community of true believers. Mormon efforts to defend polygamy, therefore, encouraged the Saints to publicize black priesthood denial. At the same time, the existence of polygamy itself reinforced the Mormon need to perpetuate black priesthood denial into the indefinite future even after slavery, that other "relic of barbarism," was abolished in 1865.

A fourth factor, the limited Mormon missionary success among dark-skinned peoples, caused the Saints to reinforce and publicize black priesthood denial. At first, however, during the early 1850s, the Saints acted in the spirit of Christian universalism. They promoted Mormonism as a universal religion to be preached throughout the world and to all peoples.[47]

The Saints called upon those peoples who were "not Christian, but who worship the various Gods of India, China, Japan, or the Islands of the Pacific or Indian Oceans," to open their "ears" and "hearts" to "the apostles and elders of the church of the Saints."[48] By 1861 Mormon missionaries had "carried . . . the Gospel: "From Australia to Scandinavia, from Oceana to either India, through the length and breadth of the vast American continent in every nation of Europe, on Africa's wild and luxuriant land, and over the burning plains of Asia. . . ."[49] The Saints insisted their religion was for all peoples; "it mattered not what color or country, what nation or language, learned or unlearned, Hindoo, or anything else."[50] The "light" of Mormonism would "go forth" until it had penetrated "the darkest corners of the earth" and "searched out every creature under heaven."[51] All men, "rich or poor, bond or free, noble or ignoble" of every religious background would "embrace the Gospel and become associated with the Kingdom of God."[52]

However, such high expectations were not fulfilled. Latter-day Saint missionaries in Great Britain and in Scandinavia succeeded in attracting an impressive number of new converts and encouraging many of these to migrate to Mormonism's new Zion in the West, but missionary results in other parts of the world were less successful.[53] The limited geographic-ethnic appeal of Mormonism was dramatized by the negative results of Latter-day Saint efforts among three diverse groups of people—the inhabitants of Asia, particularly those on the Indian subcontinent; the South Africans; and finally the American Indians.

When Mormon missionaries first preached in Asia in 1852, the Saints had high expectations. In India one optimistic Saint declared:

> amongst India's swarthy sons, the word of the Lord still runs
> and is glorified, that their dark countenances are rapidly being
> lit up with the intelligence of heaven as it is borne to their midst
> by those who have received authority from on high.[54]

The conversion of an Indian polygamist caused one churchman to anticipate a gathering to Zion of this convert along with his "*nine wives* and *forty children*." In Utah this Indian polygamist could continue the "sacred . . . custom of plural marriage."[55]

Despite such expectations, church missionaries did not convert many Asian Indians. The Saints viewed the reluctant East Asians in an unfavorable light. Frustrated missionaries described the unreceptive Indians as mental "slaves bound with superstition's strong cords," who deserved to remain "a nation of servants."[56] The Saints looked for an excuse for the limited appeal of Mormonism in India. They seized upon the Indian's "inferior" ethnic racial composition. There was "little royal blood [of Abraham]" among these recalcitrant Indians. The Saints labeled these Indians "descendants from the Priests of 'Elkanah!"[57] In the face of this failure the church concluded that the time had not come to spread the Gospel among the natives of India.[58] Therefore, by the late 1850s the Saints terminated their missionary efforts on the Indian subcontinent. The "benighted" residents were left "to their dark and loathsome condition."[59]

Latter-day Saint missionaries encountered similar difficulties in other parts of Asia—Ceylon, Burma, and Hong Kong. As in India, frustrated Saints blamed their minimal missionary success not on themselves, but on the hesitant Asians. The Ceylonese were characterized as a "drunken and filthy" people, while the Burmese were pictured as a people "bound in the chains of superstition and ignorance."[60] Writing from Hong Kong another frustrated missionary clinically analyzed the cause of his failure: "From what I can discover of the character of the Chinese, I do not believe that much of the blood of Israel is among them."[61] He expressed his "Firm belief" that the "oriental nations will not receive the Gospel nor succumb to the Kingdom of God until they are obliged to do so. . . ."[62]

The Latter-day Saints confronted similar difficulties in South Africa. Although the Mormons directed most of their proselytizing efforts toward South Africans of British and Dutch descent, they also preached to certain non-European South Africans. Church missionaries hoped that South Africa's Malay-Mohammedan population would "receive the Gospel" even though racially they were "darker than the American Indian."[63] These "pure blooded" Malays, according to Mormon belief, were the "descendants of Abraham and his wife Hagar." The Saints at first hoped this racial-ethnic link would make the Malay-Mohammedans receptive to the true gospel.[64]

The Mormons, however, had little success in South Africa among either the dark-skinned Malays or the white Europeans. Although church missionaries deliberately avoided contact with the black native Kaffir and Fingoe populations, because they had "too much of the blood of Cain in them for the Gospel to have much effect on their dark spirits," frustrated Mormons nevertheless pointed to the mere presence of this overwhelming black native population as an impediment to missionary success.[65] "The African world" was "fast settling down in darken unbelief and hardness of heart," and "Darkness [held] reign through this land of Ham."[66] In the face of this failure the Saints terminated their missionary efforts in South Africa and withdrew with the "few scattered Saints . . . anxious to take their departure of this Hottentot country."[67]

Latter-day Saint missionaries did not fare much better among the American Indians. It made little difference that the Indian held a special status within Mormon theology. The *Book of Mormon* had outlined the special mission of the Saints to carry the true gospel to their red brothers.[68] In this spirit, the Saints initially expressed optimism about their probable success among the Native Americans. The Indians would become "enlightened" with the true gospel. At the same time they would literally shed their dark countenances and become a light-skinned people. Brigham Young expected "hundreds and thousands" of Indians to

> come and acknowledge the truth . . . and . . . begin to turn from their wickedness, forsake their folly and their loathsome degredation, wash themselves, and begin to live as men and women should, and to learn at the hands of the servants of God. They [the Indians] will go into the waters of baptism, confessing their sins, and taking upon them the new and everlasting covenant, by thousands, and it will not pass away [*sic*] before they become a white and delightsome people.[69]

The Indians, moreover, had a natural affinity for the "True Faith" because they were the "seed of Israel" and "house of Joseph."[70] According to Apostle Wilford Woodruff, the Indians would "embrace the Gospel" because "they are the seed of Abraham, and God has promised to bless the descendants of Abraham, and they will be saved with the house of Israel, for the Lord has spoken it, and made those promises unto them through their fathers."[71]

However, these hopes were dashed. "Missionaries of different orders" had "little or no success" among the Indians.[72] This lack of missionary success, according to Apostle Parley P. Pratt, resulted from the Indians' "disgusting deformity . . . dark features . . . filthy habits . . . idleness . . . cruelty . . . nakedness . . . misery, and ignorance."[73] Apostle George A. Smith theorized that "when the curse of the Almighty comes upon a people," whether it be upon Indians or blacks, it "certainly" takes "the work of generations to remove it."[74] In the short run the Saints could not "do a great deal for that people" other than "pray for them and treat them kindly."[75]

Because of limited Latter-day Saint missionary success among non-European, dark-skinned peoples, Mormonism became more and more a religion oriented to white people from an American or western European background. Thus, a white skinned individual from America or western Europe was a more probable convert to Mormonism than a darker-complexioned person of non-European origins. This racial-ethnic situation made it easier for the Saints to uphold and publicize black priesthood denial. The Saints saw little reason to confer the priesthood upon blacks when they, along with other nonwhite groups, were less than ideal candidates for the True Gospel.

An interesting corollary to the failure of the Saints to convert non-white, non-European ethnic groups were the predictions made by certain influential Mormons concerning those races most likely and those least likely to be converted to the true faith. The blacks, of course, would be the last converted en masse and gathered to Zion "to share the joys of the Kingdom of God." This would occur only after

> all the other children of Adam have had the privilege of receiving the Priesthood, and of coming into the Kingdom of God, and of being redeemed from the four quarters of the earth, and have received their resurrection from the dead. . . .[76]

Therefore, even though blacks could be baptised into the church and "enjoy many of the blessings which attend obedience to the first principles of the Gospel," they were destined to occupy a subordinate place within the Mormon kingdom for an indefinite period of time.[77]

The Jews were in a somewhat better position than blacks, because they were descended from Abraham. Nevertheless, Jews would be the "last" of this chosen lineage to receive the true gospel.[78] It was therefore impractical to preach among and try to convert Jews to Mormonism. The Jews' limited capacity for Mormonism was in fact compared with that of blacks. "Preaching would have no more effect" on the Jews, according to Brigham Young than "upon the color of the descendants of Cain."[79] Young carried this black-Jew analogy one step further.

> It is all folly to suppose that there are Jews in this Church: they will not believe the Gospel at present; they are in the same position as the

Cainites [blacks] are, they cannot come in until the rest of the [human] family come in and receive their blessings, then they can have an opportunity.[80]

The Jewish people, he predicted, would never "believe until Jesus comes again."[81]

American Indians were like the Jews in that they, according to Mormon belief, were descendants from Abraham. However, they would be converted ahead of the Jews even though they had been divinely cursed with a dark skin and had "had the priesthood driven from [their] midst."[82] At present, however, the Saints, according to Brigham Young, were concerned with converting and gathering white people from northern and western Europe who, like the Indians and Jews, were considered the "children of Abraham" or "Ephraim."[83] This ethnic group or "noble race" had received top priority because it possessed the "spirit of rule and dictation" and would thus provide leadership within the ever-growing Kingdom of God.[84]

The Mormons also believed in the idea of a stratified heaven based in part on race. Although practically every man and woman would be "crowned with glory and eternal life if faithful . . . , the quantity," Brigham Young cautioned, would not be the same for all people.[85] People of white European ethnic origins would, in all probability, have a higher place than other ethnic groups because they had been the leaders in the kingdom of God on earth.[86] By contrast, blacks who had been converted last and were servants on earth would probably occupy a similar position in heaven.[87]

Mormonism's secular environment also contributed to Latter-day Saint efforts to publicize and reinforce black priesthood denial. Starting in 1852, the Utah legislature enacted legislation discriminating against blacks and other nonwhites on both the territorial and the local level. Throughout the 1850s, moreover, Mormon municipal officials continued to enact legislation prohibiting blacks from voting and holding public office as new Great Basin regions were settled and incorporated.[88] Such antiblack proscriptions were also present in proposed state constitutions submitted to Congress by the Saints in 1856, 1860, and 1862.[89]

Such secular discrimination was also reflected in the condescending attitudes that certain Mormons took toward the blacks in their midst. These Saints pictured blacks as whimsical, childlike Sambos who took great delight

in performing for white folks.[90] At a Latter-day Saint "ward party" in Salt
Lake City, "A solo dance was . . . performed by a 'genuine Ethiopian' in a
style somewhat original and 'werry pecoolia.' "[91] A theatrical performance in
Salt Lake City, presenting "Sambo's Opinion of the World," was lauded as
"particularly good," eliciting "a rapturous *encore*."[92] During the Civil War
the local citizenry received enthusiastically the stage version of *Uncle Tom's
Cabin,* performed at the Salt Lake Theatre. This play presented several
black stereotypes. According to the *Deseret News,* these included: Uncle
Tom as "the praying, pious old colored individual represented in the book"
and Topsy as "a 'shiftless, heathenish-looking' being."[93] Latter-day Saint
periodicals, moreover, carried numerous "Sambo" stories, which undoubtedly helped to reinforce this black stereotype.[94] Latter-day Saint
spokesmen frequently utilized "Sambo" stories to convey a particular
point or lesson, thus giving further credence to this black image.[95]

The publicity given to Mormon-black priesthood denial helped to establish this practice as a firm fixture within Mormonism by 1865. Thus, even
though the Saints, after 1865, could no longer refer to black servitude in
their midst or use antiabolitionist rhetoric to uphold black priesthood denial,
the perpetuation of this practice was assured by other crucial developments
during this period, namely, Mormonism's vigorous defense of polygamy,
Latter-day Saint missionary failure among dark-skinned peoples, and the increased stratification of Mormonism along racial-ethnic lines.

NOTES

1. "Speach [*sic*] by Gov. Young in Counsel on a Bill relating to the
Affrican [*sic*] slavery," 23 January 1852, Brigham Young Papers, LDS
Church Archives.

2. Brigham Young, "Speech to the Joint Session of the Legislative
Assembly," 5 January 1852, Brigham Young Papers.

3. As always, it wasn't clear whether the "curse" of priesthood denial,
referred to by Young, was to stand by itself or in combination with slavery
and/or a black skin.

4. *Journal of Discourses* (Liverpool, 1854-1886), Brigham Young, 2,
3 December 1854, 18 February 1855; *Deseret News* (Salt Lake City),
1 March 1855, 26 October 1859, 15 October 1862; *Latter-day Saints Millennial Star* (Liverpool, England), 24 December 1859.

5. *Deseret News,* 10 October 1855; *Journal of Discourses,* George A.
Smith, 3, 23 September 1855.

6. *Deseret News,* 3 April 1852.

7. *Seer* (Washington, D.C.), April 1853.

8. *Mormon,* 12 September 1857. It is interesting that the author of this article was William L. Appleby, who some ten years before had questioned Brigham Young concerning the ordination of blacks to the priesthood. The subject of black priesthood denial was even expressed in Mormon poetry when one Saint rhythmically proclaimed "without the Priesthood they're condemned to be" (*Mormon,* 26 May 1855).

9. *St. Louis Luminary,* 24 March 1855; *The Western Standard* (San Francisco), 7 February 1857.

10. "Speach by Gov. Young in Counsel on a Bill relating to the Affrican Slavery," 23 January 1852.

11. Brigham Young, "Speech to the Joint Session of the Legislative Assembly," 5 January 1852.

12. *Journal of Discourses,* Brigham Young, 2, 18 February 1855.

13. Ibid., Brigham Young, 7, 9 October 1859.

14. *Mormon,* 12 September 1857.

15. Quoted from the *Springfield Republican* in the *Daily Union Vedette* (Utah), 20 May 1864.

16. *London Weekly Dispatch,* reprinted in the *Latter-day Saints Millennial Star,* 21 September 1861; *Letter to the Archbishop of Canterbury, by Dr. Colenso, Bishop of Natal,* reprinted in *Millennial Star,* 28 September 1861. The latter source suggested that the polygamous marital practices of Kaffirs and Zulus were "probably derived from the days of Abraham himself, through their Arab Descent."

17. Quoted from the New York *World* in *The Daily Union Vedette,* 29 November 1865.

18. Richard D. Poll, "The Mormon Question Enters National Politics, 1850-1856," *Utah Historical Quarterly,* 25 (April 1957), p. 131.

19. New York *Times,* 7 February 1859.

20. *Kirk Anderson's Valley Tan* (Salt Lake City), 25 January 1859; *Sacramento Union,* as reprinted in *The Union Vedette,* 18 December 1863, and *Daily Vedette,* 11 May 1864.

21. This had been done as early as 1847 by those Mormons who acknowledged the Latter-day Saint leadership claims of James J. Strang. See *Zion's Revelle,* 2 September 1847.

22. *The True Latter Day Saints' Herald,* April 1860.

23. John Hyde, Jr., *Mormonism: Its Leaders and Designs* (New York, 1857), p. 114.

24. Ibid., pp. 74-5, 79.

25. Maria Ward, *Female Life Among the Mormons* (New York, 1855), p. 82.

26. Roberts Barthelow, "On the Effects and Tendencies of Mormon Polygamy in the Territory of Utah," S.D. No. 52, 36th Cong., 1st Sess., 301-02 (1860).

27. Ibid. This "extinction" of the Mormon "race" according to Barthelow would be facilitated "by the preponderance of female births," a relatively high "mortality of infantile life," and the "sexual debility" and "genital weakness of the boys."

28. *De Bow's Review* (New Orleans) 30 (February 1861): 210-16.

29. Ibid., p. 216. Cartwright, who was noted for his polemic on pro-slavery and ethnic theories concluded, however, "that the facts adduced by Dr. Barthelow and Professor Forshey, of the debasing influences of Mormonism on the physical structure and stamina of the inhabitants of Utah, are less strong than that which might be brought in proof of the debasing influence of abolitionism on the moral principles and character of . . . the Northern people. . . ." This analysis of Barthelow's findings on the Mormons was not Cartwright's first exposure to the Saints and their teachings. Less than a year earlier, the southern ethnologist had commented favorably on the racial theories of Charles B. Thompson, a former follower of Joseph Smith who, after the death of the Mormon prophet, had formed his own schismatic group in opposition to Brigham Young. Cartwright, who utilized Thompson's biblical-ethnic theories in his efforts to prove the black man's inherent inferiority, described the former Mormon as "a Hebrew scholar of the first class." *DeBow's Review* (August 1860), p. 132. For a good historical overview of the theories of "Mormon physiology" as promoted by Barthelow, Forshey, Cartwright and others, see Lester E. Bush, Jr., "A Peculiar People: The Physiological Aspects of Mormonism," *Dialogue* 12 (Fall 1979): 61-83.

30. *National Intelligencer* as reprinted in *Kirk Anderson's Valley Tan*, 6 November 1858.

31. For a description of Kimball and his background see Orson F. Whitney, *Life of Heber C. Kimball* (Salt Lake City, 1888). The current president of the Church of Jesus Christ of Latter-day Saints (as of 1980) is Spencer W. Kimball, a direct descendant of this early Mormon leader.

32. *Journal of Discourses*, Heber C. Kimball, 2, 17 September 1854. Apostle John Taylor discounted non-Mormon "claims" that statehood for the Saints "would at once turn the entire population of the Union into Arabs, Hottentots or some other kind of heathens." See *The Mormon*, 19 July 1856.

33. *Latter-day Saints Millennial Star*, 28 October 1856. Both Heber C.

Kimball and John Taylor discussed the specific ethnic origins of the Saints—Puritan, Yankee with a "great many" Saints coming from England; *Journal of Discourses,* Heber C. Kimball, 2, 17 September 1854; *Mormon,* 19 July 1854.

34. *Latter-day Saints Millennial Star,* 11 July 1857.

35. Ibid., 26 September 1863; *Deseret News,* 15 October 1853.

36. One Saint suggested that the chosen seed could be detected through the use of a set of oracles known as the Urim and Thummin, while another felt that it could be determined by the science of phrenology or the study of the shape of one's head. A third suggested that the chosen "Children of Abraham" could make themselves known by simply "doing the work of Abraham." See *Latter-day Saints Millennial Star,* 20 June 1857, 16 July 1862, 1 July 1865.

37. *Journal of Discourses,* Brigham Young, 10, 31 May 1863. Such a tendency became increasingly evident in the period after 1865. See *Latter-day Saints Millennial Star,* 2, 9 September, 14, 21 October 1878.

38. *Deseret News,* 16 July 1856, 26 August 1857; *Mountaineer,* 5 May 1860. They also expressed revulsion that slaveholders would go so far as to work their "own black children."

39. *Deseret News,* 2 September 1857. According to the *News* such "revolting scenes" were not limited to the South, but it was "becoming quite common in some of the free states for white girls to marry negroes," suggesting that such girls "ought to be put in an insane asylum," *Deseret News,* 11 May 1859. Mormon missionaries also noted with some concern black-white racial intermixture in South Africa. See *Deseret News,* 15 December 1853.

40. "AN ACT in Relation to Service," *Acts, Resolutions and Memorials of the Legislative Assembly of the Territory of Utah* (Salt Lake City, 1855), p. 160.

41. *Deseret News,* 13 April 1859.

42. *Journal of Discourses,* Brigham Young, 10, 8 March 1863.

43. *Deseret News,* 26 August 1857.

44. *Mountaineer,* 5 May 1860.

45. *Journal of Discourses,* Brigham Young, 2, 8 April 1855. Young claimed that he was expressing and quoting the teachings of Joseph Smith. This writer has not uncovered any contemporary corroborating evidence. Young seemed to be suggesting that a definite racial transformation took place within the individual so treated and "the revolution and change in the system" was "so great" that he would have "spasms" with the appearance of "going into fits."

46. Ibid., Brigham Young, 2, 3 December 1854; *Latter-day Saints Millennial Star,* 29 November 1862.

47. S. George Ellsworth, "A History of Mormon Missions in the United States and Canada, 1830-1860" (Ph.D. diss., University of California, 1951), pp. 304-5. At the same time missionary work within the United States was severely curtailed in the wake of increased anti-Mormon activity.

48. Parley P. Pratt, "Proclamation! To the People of the Coasts and Islands of the Pacific: of Every Nation, Kindred and Tongue" (n.p., n.d.).

49. *Latter-day Saints Millennial Star,* 16 March 1861.

50. *Journal of Discourses,* John Taylor, 1, 12 June 1853; *Latter-day Saints Millennial Star,* 1 September 1860.

51. *Journal of Discourses,* Orson Pratt, 8, 8 April 1860.

52. *Latter-day Saints Millennial Star,* 14 July 1860.

53. See Appendix A for a brief discussion of Mormonism's limited ethnic-geographic appeal during the nineteenth and early twentieth centuries.

54. *Latter-day Saints Millennial Star,* 21 August 1852.

55. W. W. Phelps to James Morgan, 8 August 1855, W. W. Phelps Papers, LDS Church Archives.

56. *Latter-day Saints Millennial Star,* 24 September 1853, 16 August 1856. Although they were denounced for their "crouching servility," hope was expressed that these natives would eventually "lay down their shackles and produce their quota to swell the numbers of the redeemed of the Lord."

57. Ibid., 1 September 1855, 16 August 1856, 10 February 1855. The Hindus, in addition, were described as "a godforsaken race" and their neighbors, the Karen tribe, pronounced to be the descendants of Esau, "an idolatrous and a heathenish nation with no hopes of redemption this side of the 'Prison!'" The "Priests of Elkanah" are described in Mormon scripture, *Pearl of Great Price,* Abraham, 1:7-17, as idolatrous Egyptian priests who attempted to sacrifice the Prophet Abraham but were foiled in their attempt by divine intervention.

58. *Latter-day Saints Millennial Star,* 25 November 1854. It was also noted that it was "a waste of time to have anything to do with them [the natives]."

59. *Deseret News,* 5 December 1855. The missionaries as they departed from the country were called upon to "gather out the few Saints" who were there. However, Mormon missionaries were apparently still in the country as late as 1856. See R. Lanier Britsch, "The Latter-day Saint Mission to India," *B.Y.U. Studies* 12 (Spring 1972): 262-78.

60. *Latter-day Saints Millennial Star,* 29 October 1853, 8 September 1855.

61. Ibid., 27 September 1856.

62. Ibid.

63. Ibid., 17 May 1856. These accounts were also careful to point out that the Malay natives possessed "none of the Negro features."

64. Ibid., The fact that they, like the Saints, practiced polygamy was also considered a factor favorable to their conversion.

65. Ibid., 18 July 1863, 7 June 1856.

66. Ibid., 14 November 1863, 19 December 1863.

67. Ibid., 6 February 1864, 14 February 1863. The *Star* described these Saints as "tolerably well [off] when taking into consideration the gross darkness and opposition that surrounds them." It is interesting that one of the several companies of Saints migrating from South Africa included a Kaffir lad named "Goboao" who found his way to Utah, "Journal History," 13 September 1861.

68. *Book of Mormon,* 2 Nephi 30:6, 3 Nephi 2:15. Apostle George A. Smith recalled that during the early days of the church he and other missionaries had rejoiced "exceedingly in the things that were about to transpire when they would be permitted to go and preach the Gospel to the Lamnites," *Journal of Discourses,* George A. Smith, 3, 23 September 1855.

69. *Journal of Discourses,* Brigham Young, 4, 28 June 1857.

70. Ibid.

71. Ibid., Wilford Woodruff, 4, 22 February 1857.

72. Ibid., Wilford Woodruff, 2, 25 February 1855.

73. Parley Pratt, *Key to the Science of Theology,* (Liverpool, 1855), p. 25.

74. *Journal of Discourses,* George A. Smith, 3, 23 September 1855. In fact, Mormon missionaries took note of the literal ethnic relationship existing between the black man and certain members of the Cherokee and Creek tribes. The Cherokees were "mixed . . . to a great extent . . . with the Gentiles [non-Mormon whites] and to some degree with the negroes," while the Creeks were "less mixed with the Gentiles, but more with the negroes," thus decreasing the likelihood of their conversion to Mormonism. See "Journal History," 31 August 1860.

75. *Journal of Discourses,* Wilford Woodruff, 2, 25 February 1855.

76. Ibid., Brigham Young, 2, 3 December 1854.

77. *Deseret News,* 1 March 1855; *Journal of Discourses,* Brigham Young, 2, 18 February 1855. One Saint optimistically predicted that "in due time" the Lord would "feel after the Sable sons of Ham, and Ethiopia will stretch out her hands to God." See *Mormon,* 21 July 1855.

78. *Deseret News,* 8 February 1855.

79. *Latter-day Saints Millennial Star,* 3 June 1865. Apostle Wilford Woodruff was convinced of the impracticality of converting the Jewish people. "You cannot convert a Jew, you might as well try to convert this house of

solid walls as to convert them into the faith of Christ." *Journal of Discourses*, Wilford Woodruff, 4, 22 February 1857.

80. *Deseret News*, 15 October 1862; *Latter-day Saints Millennial Star*, 29 November 1862.

81. *Latter-day Saints Millennial Star*, 3 June 1865. Another group, the descendants of Ishmael or the Mohamedan people, were declared as "not particularly designed to hold the Keys of the Priesthood" or to rule in the Mormon Kingdom. See *Deseret News*, 2 March 1854.

82. *Journal of Discourses*, Brigham Young, 2, 3 December 1854; Brigham Young, 7, 8 October 1859; *Deseret News*, 3 February 1854. In a somewhat revealing tone, Young explained that he would "rather undertake to convert five thousand Lamanites [Indians], than to convert one of those poor, miserable creatures whose fathers killed the Savior."

83. *Deseret News*, 15 October 1862.

84. *Journal of Discourses*, Brigham Young, 10, 31 May 1863.

85. Ibid., Brigham Young, 7, 3 July 1859; Brigham Young, 10, 31 July 1864.

86. *Latter-day Saints Millennial Star*, 9 July 1859; *Journal of Discourses*, Brigham Young, 10, 31 July 1864.

87. Ibid., Brigham Young, 8, 6 April 1860; *Latter-day Saints Millennial Star*, 15 May 1858.

88. For examples of the various antiblack statutes enacted on both the territorial and local level during the early 1850s see *Acts, Resolutions, and Memorials of the Legislative Assembly of the Territory of Utah* (Great Salt Lake City, 1855), passim.

89. Copies of the constitution for the proposed State of Deseret were published in various Mormon and non-Mormon publications throughout the 1850s and 1860s.

90. The Mormons were not unique in their tendency to play up such "Sambos." See George M. Fredrickson, *The Black Image in the White Mind* (New York, 1971), pp. 102-3.

91. *Deseret News*, 2 March 1854.

92. *The Daily Union Vedette*, 25 February 1864 (italics in original).

93. *Deseret News*, 29 March 1865.

94. Such stories were reprinted in all Latter-day Saint sponsored periodicals throughout the period of 1852 to 1865.

95. For example, one of the most popular stories was the "fable of the pig and the puppy," often related by Brigham and other church leaders. In this story a slow-witted black servant has been instructed to deliver a pig, but on his way to perform this task and without his knowledge some mischievous whites divert his attention and exchange the pig for a puppy.

Upon arriving at the place of delivery the servant is chastized for bringing a puppy instead of the ordered pig. Baffled, the servant then proceeds to return to his master to try and find out what is going on but is once more stopped by the same prank-playing whites who then reexchange the puppy for the original pig. Still too dull-minded to figure out what is happening to him, the black servant arrives back at his master's and tries to explain his earlier difficulty at arriving at the delivery point with a dog, but is berated by his disgusted master for returning to his presence with the undelivered pig. See *Deseret News,* 3 September 1862; *Latter-day Saints Millennial Star,* 21 August 1852; *Journal of Discourses,* Brigham Young, 8, 11 May 1862.

8 | The Perpetuation of Black Priesthood Denial, 1865-1918

we learn . . . from the *Pearl of Great Price* . . . that the seed
of Ham was cursed as pertaining to the Priesthood [because]
. . . Ham's wife was . . . a descendant of Cain, who was cursed
for murdering his brother. . . .

Brigham H. Roberts, 1885

the Prophet Joseph Smith taught the doctrine in this day that
the seed of Cain would not receive the priesthood. . . .

Joseph F. Smith, 1904

It was an important meeting of church leaders at the home of
Abraham O. Smoot on that spring day in 1879. Brigham Young had been
dead for almost two years, and control of church affairs had temporarily
passed into the hands of the Quorum of Twelve Apostles. John Taylor, the
president of Quorum, and other church leaders were anxious to clarify the
Mormon position on a number of doctrinal matters. One of these, the precise origins of Mormon black priesthood denial, was the subject of that
spring 1879 meeting hosted by Smoot, a high church official and former
mayor of Salt Lake City. In attendance were Apostle Taylor, Brigham Young,
Jr., a church apostle and son of the recently deceased Mormon president, and
Zebedee Coltrin, a long-time member of the church. These leaders paid particular attention to the recollections of Smoot and Coltrin, which attempted
to link black priesthood denial to Mormonism's founder, Joseph Smith.[1]

The Smoot-Coltrin testimonies represented a sharp departure from the way that Brigham Young had viewed the origins of black priesthood denial during his lifetime. The dynamic, charismatic Young apparently felt no need to link the practice of black priesthood denial to Mormonism's founder. Indeed, Young seemed to suggest that he himself and not Smith had inaugurated black priesthood denial. In discussing the origins of black priesthood denial during the 1850s, Young had maintained that "if no other prophet ever spake it before I will say it now" that "any man having one drop of the seed of [Cain] . . . in him cannot hold the priesthood."[2] This all changed, however, by the time of that spring 1879 meeting. According to Zebedee Coltrin, the question of the black man's priesthood status had come up in 1834 while he was in Missouri and during the course of a discussion with another church member, J. P. Greene. Greene had argued that the black man had "a right to the priesthood," while Coltrin maintained that he had "no right." The debate became so heated that Green accused Coltrin of "preaching false doctrine" and threatened to report him to Joseph Smith once they returned to Ohio. Coltrin then recalled:

> And when we got to Kirtland, we both went to Brother Joseph's office together to make our returns, and Brother Green[e] was as good as his word and reported to Brother Joseph that I said the Negro could not hold the priesthood. Brother Joseph kind of dropped his head and rested it on his hand for a minute, and then said, "Brother Zebedee is right, for the spirit of the Lord saith the Negro has no right nor cannot hold the Priesthood." He made no reference to Scripture at all, but such was his decision.[3]

Smoot in his recollections asserted that the subject of black priesthood ordination had come up again in 1835 and later in 1836 as a consequence of Mormon missionary activity in the South.[4] According to Smoot, some "Negroes . . . made application for baptism, and the question arose with them whether Negroes were entitled to hold the Priesthood." Southern-based missionaries decided that the priesthood would not be conferred upon these blacks until Joseph Smith's opinion was solicited. "His decision," as Smoot "understood was, they [the Negroes] were not entitled to the Priesthood, nor yet to be baptized without the consent of their Masters."[5] More important, Smoot recalled that he had conferred personally with

Joseph Smith on this same subject two years later, following the movement of the church headquarters from Kirtland to Far West, Missouri, in 1838.

> I received from Brother Joseph substantially the same instructions. It was on my application to him, what should be done with the Negro in the South, as I was preaching to them. He said I could baptise them by consent of their masters, but not to confer the priesthood upon them.[6]

The Coltrin-Smoot testimonies represented the earliest known Mormon effort to attribute black priesthood denial to Joseph Smith.

The 1879 efforts by Zebedee Coltrin and Abraham O. Smoot to identify Joseph Smith as the originator of black priesthood denial dramatizes a basic Mormon desire to reinforce and perpetuate black priesthood denial during the post-Civil War period. A Mormon desire to cling to black priesthood denial stood in sharp contrast to the efforts of certain non-Mormon, post-Civil War reformers who were trying to "reconstruct" a better society for black Americans. The Saints, however, were like the vast majority of Americans, both North and South, anxious to maintain the subordinate status of black people despite the implementation of important pro-black legislation during the era of Reconstruction.

The Latter-day Saints reinforced their commitment to black priesthood denial in several ways. First, Mormon leaders moved to prohibit blacks from participating in certain sacred temple ordinances. Such prohibitions followed naturally from black priesthood denial and in turn reinforced proscriptions on black priesthood ordination. Any faithful Latter-day Saint male who wanted to participate in the temple endowment or sealing ceremonies, essential for exaltation in the Hereafter, had to be a Melchizedek priesthood holder. As for Latter-day Saint women, they were allowed to participate in such temple ceremonies by virtue of their husband's priesthood authority.[7] While these temple ordinances had been practiced during the Nauvoo period, they assumed an increasingly important place in Latter-day Saint life following the Mormon migration to the Great Basin. This importance was underscored by the completion of four Latter-day Saint temples during the late nineteenth century. These included the St. George Temple, opened in 1877, the Manti and Logan

Temples, which were dedicated during the 1880s, and finally the long-awaited Salt Lake Temple, which was opened for services in 1893. In addition, the church started construction on temples in Canada and Hawaii during the 1910s.[8]

Therefore, it is not surprising that the church moved to formalize a policy restricting black participation in temple ordinances. Elijah Abel, Mormonism's first known black priesthood holder, was apparently the first Mormon black to confront these restrictions. There is a certain irony in Elijah Abel's case. Abel had migrated from Cincinnati to Utah in 1853 with his wife, whom he had met and married in Ohio, and his three children. Soon after his arrival in the Great Basin, Abel, along with other devout Mormons, volunteered his labor to the construction of the Salt Lake Temple.[9] This service, however, did not help Abel when he "applied to President Young for his endowments . . . to have his wife and children sealed to him." The Mormon president "put him off" even though Abel held the Melchizedek Priesthood office of Seventy. Young, according to one account, "could not grant" Abel this "privilege" because of Abel's blackness. Abel renewed his application for these same ordinances to Young's successor, President John Taylor.[10] Again Abel's request was denied. Despite his failure to secure his temple ordinances, Abel remained active in the church.[11] In fact, Abel, after the death of his wife in 1878, agreed to go on a mission for the church in the Eastern United States and Canada, the setting of his earlier missionary activities during the 1830s. Abel, then an elderly man of seventy-three, was set apart and left for the East in 1883.[12] Abel's missionary activities, however, were cut short by ill health, and he returned to Utah in December 1884. He died two weeks later of "old age and debility."[13] Abel's motive for going on a mission at such an advanced age and at a time when his status as well as that of blacks in general had deteriorated is a mystery. Perhaps he was motivated by a desire to demonstrate his "full faith in the Gospel" and thereby obtain his long-sought temple endowments and sealings before he died.

The issue of black participation in temple ordinances was not settled with the death of Elijah Abel in 1884. The persistence of this issue was illustrated in the case of another black Mormon, Jane Manning James. This black Mormon woman had lived with her family in Nauvoo during the 1840s. Following the death of Joseph Smith, she cast her lot with Brigham Young and migrated west, arriving in the Great Basin with her husband

and family in 1847. Like so many Mormons in the Great Basin, the James family engaged in farming, achieving a fair degree of success. However, Jane and her husband Isaac had marital difficulties and separated by late 1869 or early 1870.[14] Possibly as a result of this separation, Jane James expressed concern about her future salvation. Realizing the importance of temple ordinances for future exaltation, she petitioned for the right to receive her sealings and endowments. She did this in a number of requests submitted to various Latter-day Saint leaders, including John Taylor and Joseph F. Smith, throughout the late nineteenth and early twentieth centuries.[15] In the most interesting of these requests, James asked to be "sealed" to Walker Lewis, the black Mormon elder who lived in Lowell, Massachusetts, during the 1840s. According to James, "Brother Lewis wished me to be sealed to Him."[16] This, along with her other requests, was rejected by church authorities.[17]

As church leaders confronted the problems created by Elijah Abel and Jane James, they moved to tighten up the rules limiting black participation in temple ordinances. Initially, there was some disagreement over the criteria that should be used in establishing such proscriptions. At a 1902 meeting of church leaders, Apostle John Henry Smith took a "liberal" position. He suggested that persons of mixed black-white ancestry "should not be barred from the Temple" if "the white blood predominated." However, Joseph F. Smith, the new church president, disagreed. He argued that "in all cases where the blood of Cain showed itself, however slight, the line should be drawn there. . . ." At the same time Smith suggested that where children of tainted [black] people were found to be pure Ephraimites, they might be admitted to the temple. He concluded that "This was only an opinion, however; the subject would no doubt be considered later."[18] Indeed it was. In 1907, the First Presidency and Twelve Apostles adopted a position more circumscribed than that of either Apostle Smith or President Joseph F. Smith. "[N]o one known to have in his veins Negro blood (it matters not how remote a degree)" could receive "the blessings of the Temple of God."[19] Essentially this became the formal church position on black participation in temple ordinances, which helped to reinforce the church practice of denying blacks the priesthood.

Mormon black priesthood denial was reinforced by the belief that Joseph Smith had inaugurated this practice. At first, this belief, as asserted through the 1879 Coltrin-Smoot testimonies, was questioned in a Council of the

Twelve meeting just four days after the May 31 gathering in Smoot's home. At the latter meeting Apostle Joseph F. Smith pointed out certain inconsistencies in the Coltrin-Smoot testimonies and seemed to question the whole idea that Joseph Smith had inaugurated black priesthood denial. Apostle Smith's skepticism was compounded by Elijah Abel's case. Apostle Smith, after carefully examining this case, concluded that Joseph Smith had recognized the priesthood authority of this black man. This was in direct contradiction to the views of Zebedee Coltrin and Abraham Smoot. Apostle Taylor tried to reconcile these conflicting views by suggesting that Abel had "been ordained before the word of the Lord was fully understood."[20]

Despite the questions raised by Apostle Joseph F. Smith, Mormon attempts to identify Joseph Smith as the originator of black priesthood denial intensified during the 1890s and early 1900s. At a "regular meeting of the First Presidency and Apostles held in the Salt Lake Temple" in 1895 and presided over by President Wilford Woodruff—installed as church president following the death of John Taylor in 1887—the question of blacks and their place in the church was again the topic under discussion. George Q. Cannon, a member of the First Presidency, "remarked that the Prophet Joseph Smith taught this doctrine: That the seed of Cain could not receive the priesthood nor act in any of the offices of the priesthood...."[21] Apostle Franklin D. Richards also expressed his belief that Joseph Smith had established special proscriptions on black people.[22] By 1904, even Joseph F. Smith, now church president, asserted that "the Prophet Joseph Smith taught the doctrine in his day that the seed of Cain would not receive the priesthood."[23] Four years later President Joseph F. Smith fully embraced this concept by abandoning his 1879 belief that the Mormon Prophet had recognized Elijah Abel's priesthood authority. Thus, President Smith explained that even though Abel had been "ordained a Seventy ... in the days of the Prophet Joseph ... this ordination was declared null and void by the Prophet himself" when he became aware of Abel's "blackness."[24] In 1909 George Q. Cannon "remarked ... that the Prophet Joseph Smith had said in substance that there would be a great wrong perpetuated if the seed of Cain were allowed to have the priesthood...."[25] By 1912, the Mormon belief that Joseph Smith had sanctioned black priesthood denial was formalized to the point that the First Presidency of the Church was able to unequivocally identify it as a teaching of the Prophet Joseph Smith.[26]

By the time that Joseph F. Smith died in 1918, there were no prominent

Latter-day Saints able to assert the opposite conclusion. All of those high church officials who had been contemporaries of Joseph Smith had died by this time with their places filled by a new generation of church leaders. The senior member of this younger group and new church president, Heber J. Grant, was born in 1857, thirteen years after the death of the Mormon Prophet.

The practice of black priesthood denial was further reinforced by Mormon canonization of the *Pearl of Great Price* in 1880, followed by its formal use as a scriptural instrument for upholding black priesthood denial. This work, containing the Books of Moses and Abraham written by Joseph Smith during the 1830s and early 1840s, had been initially published in book form in 1851, but did not have the same canonized status as Smith's earlier writings, the *Book of Mormon* and the *Doctrine and Covenants*. Nevertheless, many of its racist precepts, including those adversely affecting the status of blacks within Mormonism, had been incorporated into the superstructure of Latter-day Saint theology during the 1840s and 1850s. These included hints of a link between contemporary blacks and the alleged first murderer Cain, suggestions of black misbehavior during a premortal existence,[27] and an implied "curse" on blacks "as pertaining to the priesthood."[28] These racist precepts had been publicized within the church since the late 1840s. It was not until the 1880s that these ideas were given added legitimacy through the elevation of the *Pearl of Great Price* to the status of holy scripture and its sanctification on a par with the *Book of Mormon* and the *Doctrine and Covenants*.

At about this same time, church leaders started to use the *Pearl of Great Price* as an instrument for upholding the subordinate Mormon status of black people. As early as 1881, John Taylor, recently installed as church president, alluded to the *Pearl of Great Price* in describing the "curse that had been pronounced upon Cain [and] continued through Ham's wife."[29] In 1885 Brigham H. Roberts, a young, articulate spokesman from the post-Joseph Smith generation, quoted extensively from the *Pearl of Great Price* in upholding the inferior position of blacks within Mormonism. Roberts, writing in a church periodical, *The Contributor,* noted, "we learn . . . from the *Pearl of Great Price* . . . that the seed of Ham was cursed as pertaining to the priesthood" because Ham's wife Egyptus was a "descendant of Cain," who was cursed for murdering his brother. In addition, blacks were cursed because of their premortal behavior. They "were not valiant in the great rebellion in heaven."[30] Echoing the views of Roberts was Apostle George Q. Cannon, who also used the *Pearl of Great Price* as an instrument of black priesthood denial.[31] By the early 1900s a number of church periodicals, including the *Millennial Star* and *Liahona, The Elders' Journal,* were quoting chapter and verse from the *Pearl of Great Price* in upholding the inferior place of black people within Mormonism.[32] Church spokesmen were so willing to use the *Pearl of Great Price* as an instrument of black priesthood denial that by 1912 it "had become a foundation of church policy."[33] In that year a letter written by the church First Presidency in response to the question "what is the reason . . . a Negro cannot receive the priesthood?" declared,

> You are referred to the Pearl of Great Price, Book of Abraham, Chapter 1, Verses 26 and 27, going to show that the Seed of Ham was cursed as pertaining to the priesthood; and that by reason of this curse they have no right to it [*sic*].[34]

Therefore, by the time Joseph F. Smith died in 1918 and Heber J. Grant assumed leadership of the church, the *Pearl of Great Price* was well established as an instrument of black priesthood denial.

Black priesthood denial was reinforced by another development, the move by church leaders to formally discourage active Mormon missionary efforts among blacks. From Mormonism's earliest days the Latter-day Saints tended to avoid proselytizing among blacks. This was certainly the case prior to 1865 in the slaveholding South, where the Saints were anxious to avoid charges of "tampering with" the black slave population. At the same time Latter-day Saint missionaries in South Africa also avoided contact with the native black population. However, it was not until 1908 that the First Presidency and Council of the Twelve Apostles under the leadership of Joseph F. Smith formally instructed Latter-day Saint missionaries "not [to] take the initiative in proselyting among the Negro people . . . or [to] people tainted with Negro blood."[35] Two years later the church First Presidency gave scriptural legitimacy to this position by referring to the *Pearl of Great Price*. Quoting this work, these church leaders declared, "we learn that Enoch in his day called upon all the people to repent, save the people of Canaan, and it is for us to do likewise."[36] This policy of avoiding Mormon missionary contacts with blacks would remain in effect for the next fifty years.[37]

Why were the Saints so anxious to reinforce and perpetuate black priesthood denial? There are several possible explanations. First, the Mormons were upset at Republican, problack government officials attempting to abolish polygamy. These officials, encouraged by their earlier success in abolishing black slavery through the Thirteenth Amendment, now focused their attacks on that other "relic of barbarism," Mormon polygamy. These officials felt the time had come to "enforce the moral law in Utah."[38] Thus, the Republican-dominated Congress enacted a series of antipolygamy measures. These included the Cullom Bill of 1870, the Freylinghuysen Bill of 1873, the 1874 Poland Act, and Edmunds Act of 1882, and finally the 1887 Edmunds-Tucker Act. These acts severely limited the political and civil rights of the polygamous Saints. The Mormons were prohibited from voting and subject to imprisonment. The church as an organization was at first limited in the amount of property it could own and finally disincorporated altogether.[39]

Therefore, the perpetuation of black priesthood denial stood as a Mormon symbol of defiance against a hostile, radical Republican-dominated federal government attempting to deprive the polygamous Saints of their political and civil rights while extending these same privileges to blacks. In this spirit the *Deseret News* noted, "The Mexican greasers, barbarians of Russian America [Alaska] , Chinese, Indians, and Negroes, and all inferior races are to have the right of suffrage before white [Latter-day Saint] people."[40] The *Millennial Star* complained that unfavorable federal treatment had the effect of "thrusting" the Saints, "personages of royal birth and lineage . . . a long way below the negro." This represented an attempt to determine "whether crabs can progress backwards or not."[41]

The affirmation of black priesthood denial was encouraged by a second, related factor, a Mormon tendency to identify with the states of the former Confederacy. Both the polygamous Saints and white southerners found themselves under attack by radical Republicans such as Schuyler Colfax of Indiana and Benjamin F. Wade of Ohio. Such individuals alternately attacked the polygamous Saints and promoted legislation to guarantee newly emancipated southern blacks their political and civil rights. Therefore, the polygamous Saints and southern whites found themselves on the same side in assailing the Reconstruction policies of the federal government. The *Millennial Star* accused northern Republicans of attempting to reverse "the social, political, and civil relations of the blacks and whites" by placing "the white man's head under the nigger's heel."[42] Another *Millennial Star* article upheld the prerogatives of white southerners, describing blacks as "utterly unprepared, unfit, and incapable" of assuming any leadership positions in the South.[43] Brigham Young denounced the meddling tendencies of northern Republicans in establishing southern "schools for the freedman."[44] John Taylor, after his ascension to the church presidency, called upon northern Republicans to "strike off the fetters of the white men of the South, who have been ground under the heel of sectional injustice."[45] In a similar vein, Apostle Franklin D. Richards denounced northern Republicans for their "deprivations and arbitrary rule in the South," noting that "the people of the Southern States" had "been limited or deprived of some of their rights."[46]

Mormon attacks on the Reconstruction policies of radical Republicans were reciprocated by southern congressmen who spoke out against federal antipolygamy measures. The northern Republican-sponsored Cullom Bill of 1870 was defeated in large part thanks to the opposition of congressional Democrats, particularly those from the South.[47] Throughout the 1870s and 1880s southern Democrats tended to vote against other congressional antipolygamy acts. One group of southern congressmen denounced the "absolute congressional authority" of northern Republicans, which they claimed "had brought war and ruin to the South and promised to do the same for Utah."[48] Expressing Mormon gratitude, Apostle Franklin D. Richards praised the "few men . . . in Congress, from the Southern States" who had "had the manhood and the moral courage" to vote against pending antipolygamy legislation.[49]

In this spirit of mutual friendship, Latter-day Saint leaders in the period after 1865 moved to promote a vigorous missionary program in the states of the former Confederacy. Brigham Young hoped that "the late war and consequent misery that has attended it" would have the effect of "softening the hearts" of the vanquished southerners, causing them to "listen to the testimonies of the servants of God."[50] By 1869 the *Latter-day Saints Millennial Star* was pleased with initial Mormon efforts in this "excellent field," noting that there was a "great demand" for additional missionaries.[51] "All the decent people," or Mormon converts, observed a southern-based missionary, were migrating from the South to Utah "leaving [behind] only the Scallawags [sic]."[52] By the 1880s, it was estimated that one out of every three Latter-day Saint missionaries was being sent to the South, "where in recent years they have made many converts."[53]

At the same time, however, the bonds of identification between the polygamous Saints and white southerners were far from absolute. White southerners, despite their basic belief that a state or territory had the right to regulate its own institutions, found the institution of polygamy morally repugnant. In addition, southern-based Mormon missionaries labored under the additional difficulty of being outsiders at a time when white southerners looked upon all nonsouthern individuals and groups as meddlesome do-gooders or outside agitators. As a result, southern-based Mormons were subjected to violence, including the disruption of church gatherings, the burning of Mormon meeting houses, and even the beating and murdering of church missionaries throughout the late nineteenth and early twentieth centuries.[54] In fact, it could be argued that the affirmation of black priesthood denial represented a Mormon effort to show white southerners that the Saints were different from other outsiders. That is, the Saints were definitely not problack in their actions and attitudes.

The reinforcement and perpetuation of black priesthood denial was encouraged by a third factor, the increased influx of blacks into Utah. During the fifty-year period from 1860 to 1910, the number of blacks living in Utah increased nineteen-fold, from 59 to 1144. The vast majority of these blacks settled in or near Salt Lake City, the center of Latter-day Saint activity.[55] These blacks were attracted to the Great Basin during the post-Civil War period by opportunities in mining, ranching, and the military.[56] The latter was particularly significant because in 1869 Congress created two black infantry and two black cavalry regiments. Three of these four units—the Ninth Cavalry, the Twenty-Fourth Infantry and the Twenty-Fifth Infantry—were stationed at Fort Duchesne in eastern Utah and Fort Douglas in Salt Lake City. These black units were charged with controlling the Indian populations of eastern Utah, western Colorado, and southwestern Wyoming.[57] As a result of this black influx, the broad outlines of a Utah black community were evident by the 1890s. This was reflected in the publication of four black newspapers and the formation of an association of black Republicans. In addition two black Protestant denominations were formed during the 1890s, reflecting the shifting religious focus of Utah's black community from its pioneer Mormon origins to an increasingly Protestant orientation.[58]

While the affirmation of black priesthood denial represented one way in which the Mormons reacted to Utah's growing black population, other Saints acted in a more enlightened manner. Latter-day Saint lawmakers enacted some token problack measures in the spirit of Republican Reconstruction. Local and territorial Mormon officials abolished those statutory provisions that had prohibited blacks from voting and holding public office.[59] This same spirit was carried into an 1869 constitutional convention that drew up a constitution for the proposed Mormon state of Deseret. Brigham Young announced that the delegates in striking out the words "free, white male" reflected "our [Mormon] views on the Fifteenth Amendment."[60] In fact, the following year, Utah's territorial legislature went one bold step further, allowing all women, black as well as white, to vote in territorial elections![61] Utah's 1852 "Act in Relation to Service" was formally buried by an 1872 constitutional convention provision, which conceded that "Neither slavery nor involuntary servitude, unless for the punishment of crimes shall ever be tolerated in this state."[62]

However, the predominant Mormon mood toward Utah's ever-increasing black population was less enlightened. Certain Utah residents expressed strong opposition to the practice of racial intermixture or miscegenation. In 1866 Thomas Colburn, a former slave and later an employee of Brigham Young, was murdered in a remote part of Salt Lake City. He was found with his throat slit and a cryptic note pinned to his body.

> Notice to All Niggers!
> Warning!!
> Leave White Women Alone!!![63]

By 1888, Utah's territorial legislators enacted a statute outlawing black-white racial intermixture. Thus, "any marriage between a negro and a white person" was "prohibited and declared void."[64] Within the Mormon church, efforts were also made to discourage racial intermixture. In 1895, President Wilford Woodruff, in conjunction with the First Presidency and Twelve Apostles, rejected the application of a white woman for her temple ordinances because of her marriage to a black man. This was the case despite her earlier separation from this individual and present marriage to a white man.[65] Two years later, at another meeting of church leaders, Apostle George Q. Cannon declared it "improper" for a white man "who has a wife who is either black or is tainted with negro blood" to receive the priesthood.[66]

In other ways the Saints expressed their opposition to the increased influx of blacks into Utah. Apostle Amasa Lyman denounced the efforts of a hostile Republican-dominated federal government to encourage black migration to Utah in order to "correct" the "morals" of the Saints.[67] On a figurative level, Brigham Young felt that it would "be but a little while" before meddlesome pro-black Republican officials in Washington, D.C., would "determine the number of beans that . . . I have in [my] porridge, and whether they shall be white or black. I think, if some of them had their way, they would have them all black."[68]

By 1896, as increasing numbers of black soldiers were stationed in Utah, Senator Frank J. Cannon, the son of Apostle George Q. Cannon, did everything he could to convince officials in Washington, D.C., not to station black soldiers at Fort Douglas. Supporting Cannon was the Salt Lake *Tribune*, which questioned the character of the black soldiers and suggested that under the influence of liquor they might make advances toward white women.[69] Black priesthood denial served to allay Mormon fears and anxieties over the increased influx of blacks into Utah during the late nineteenth and early twentieth centuries.

The Utah Mormon affirmation of black priesthood denial along with its attendant racist concepts stood in contrast to the racial attitudes and practices of the rival Reorganized Church of Jesus Christ of Latter Day Saints. The Reorganized Church, headquartered in the Midwest, was made up, to a large extent, of Latter-day Saints who had been loyal to Joseph Smith during the Mormon sojourn at Nauvoo, Illinois, but had refused to accept the leadership claims of Brigham Young and the Twelve following the death of the Mormon Prophet. These dissenting Latter-day Saints were in agreement on two basic points throughout the 1850s; first, they opposed plural marriage, and second, they believed that Joseph Smith III, the oldest son of the slain Mormon prophet, was the rightful heir to Latter-day Saint authority. Out of this opposition emerged the Reorganized Church of Jesus Christ of Latter Day Saints. When this church was formally organized in 1860, "young Joseph" came forward and assumed his role as "Prophet, Seer and Revelator."[70] Although polygamy was the major divisive issue, the two Mormon groups also differed in the positions they assigned black people within their respective organizations. Although leaders and spokesmen within the Reorganized Church restricted the actions and behavior of individual black members, the Reorganization did not formally assign their blacks a subordinate position within their organization or theology.[71] Leaders of the Reorganization felt that no man should be "deprived of the right" to the priesthood simply because his "fathers in the Gentile world did not have the priesthood."[72] In this spirit the Reorganized Church's Quorum of the Twelve Apostles in May 1865 received through Joseph Smith III a "revelation expressing an "expedient" desire to "ordain priests unto men, of every race who receive the teachings of my law and become heirs according to the promise." These midwestern Saints then "*Resolved*, That the gospel make provision for the ordination of men of the Negro race who are received into the Church by obedience to its ordinances."[73] The Reorganized Church defended its decision allowing blacks to hold the priesthood,

> Now it would seem that inasmuch as the Negro embraces the gospel thereby becoming a child of God, and a "fellow citizen of the household of Faith," that he might, if "full of faith and the Holy Ghost," be called to participate in the work of preaching the glad tidings of redemption.[74]

In the wake of this decision the Reorganized Church ordained a number of blacks to various priesthood offices within both the Aaronic and the Melchizedek orders.[75]

Besides ordaining blacks to their priesthood, the Reorganized Church also promoted missionary activity among blacks. In 1865 a church conference resolution called for "the ... preaching [of] the gospel to the negro race."[76] Ten years later the Reorganized Church adopted a second resolution affirming "that the gospel is to be offered to all mankind irrespective of color, nationality, sex, or condition in life."[77] In this spirit the Reorganized Church announced that the only major objections that could be mustered "against the idea of preaching the gospel" to blacks is "founded in the prejudice of the white man."[78] This Mormon group preached among blacks in the former states of the Confederacy during the years immediately following the Civil War. Blacks as well as white RLDS missionaries were recruited for this purpose.[79] In addition, during the late nineteenth and early twentieth centuries, the Reorganized Church sent missionaries to preach among northern blacks living in urban centers such as Chicago.[80] Such RLDS missionary activity stood in sharp contrast to the Utah Mormon position formally discouraging missionary activity among blacks.

The Reorganized Church also differed with the Utah Mormons on their perceptions of Joseph Smith's involvement with the practice of black priesthood denial. In contrast to Utah Mormon efforts to ascribe black priesthood denial to Mormonism's founder, the Reorganized Church moved in the opposite direction. Although one RLDS spokesman confessed in 1868 that "It is said by someone that Joseph Smith has said that the Negro cannot enter into the congregation of the Lord until his third generation," he noted, "I cannot say whether he did so or not."[81] A second RLDS writer went further. He asserted that the practice of black priesthood denial had nothing to do with Joseph Smith but was instead "founded on teachings received from [errant Mormon] elders since 1844."[82]

These two Latter-day Saint Churches also differed in their feelings about the *Pearl of Great Price.* The Utah Saints had utilized the racist concepts contained in this work in developing their doctrinal rationale for denying blacks the priesthood. By contrast, the Reorganized Church discounted the scriptural significance of this work, particularly the Book of Abraham.[83] In this spirit W. W. Blair, an RLDS apostle, rejected the arguments of those who maintained that this work provided scriptural justification for black priesthood denial.[84]

The differing attitudes and practices assumed by the two Mormon groups toward blacks were clearly evident by the time Joseph Fielding Smith, the son of President Joseph F. Smith, wrote a 1909 tract rejecting the problack position of the Reorganized Church. According to Smith: "The Lord did not tell Abraham [in the *Pearl of Great Price*] that the children of Ham were cursed as pertaining to the Priesthood, and then command Joseph Smith [III] of the 'Reorganization' to . . . [ordain] them. . . ." Smith declared that the ordination of blacks within the Reorganized Church was "contrary to the word of God" and rejected the 1865 Revelation of Joseph Smith III as "spurious."[85]

The Mormon Church perpetuated their practice of black priesthood denial because of the Latter-day Saint acceptance of the historical myth that Joseph Smith had inaugurated this practice, coupled with the use of the Book of Abraham as a scriptural instrument justifying it. This effort was further aided by church leaders who actively discouraged missionary efforts among blacks in both the United States and abroad during the early twentieth century. Thus, with the ascension of Heber J. Grant to the presidency of the Church in 1918, black priesthood denial was an entrenched Mormon practice, a status that assured its perpetuation for the next sixty years.

NOTES

1. For a description of this meeting and the statements of Coltrin and Smoot, see L. John Nuttal, "Journal," 31 May 1879, L. John Nuttal Papers, LDS Church Archives.

2. Wilford Woodruff Journal, 16 January 1852, Woodruff Papers, LDS Church Archives.

3. Journal of L. John Nuttal, 31 May 1859, Nuttal Papers.

4. These included Apostles David W. Patten and Thomas Marsh, along with Warren Parrish.

5. Diary of L. John Nuttal, 31 May 1879, Nuttal Papers. In this Smoot was partially paraphrasing the 1835 church position concerning "bond servants." The 1835 statement, while declaring that the church did not "believe it right" to "neither preach the gospel to nor baptize them [bond servants] contrary to the will or wish of their masters," said nothing about ordination. See *Doctrine and Covenants,* 134:12.

6. Diary of L. John Nuttal, 31 May 1879, Nuttal Papers.

7. As for an LDS woman who did not marry, she could participate in these ceremonies by virtue of her father's priesthood authority.

8. For a description of these developments, see James B. Allen and Glen M. Leonard, *The Story of the Latter-day Saints* (Salt Lake City, 1976), pp. 370, 472.

9. "Salt Lake Temple Time Book," December 1853, June and July 1854, LDS Church Archives.

10. Council Meeting Minutes, 2 January 1902, George A. Smith Papers, University of Utah Library; Council Meeting Minutes, 12 August 1908, Adam S. Bennion Papers, Brigham Young University Library.

11. First Quorum of Seventies Minute Book, 6 June 1877, LDS Church Archives. According to this account Abel "was notified that he was still a member of the Third Quorum."

12. Missionary Records, 6176, Part 1, 1860-1906, p. 75, 1883, LDS Church Archives.

13. Andrew Jenson, *Latter-day Saint Biographical Encyclopedia* (Salt Lake City, 1920), 3: 557; *Deseret News* (Salt Lake City), 26 December 1884.

14. Henry J. Wolfinger, "A Test of Faith: Jane Elizabeth James and the Origins of the Utah Black Community," in Clark S. Knowton, ed., *Social Accommodation in Utah,* American West Occasional Papers (Salt Lake City, Utah, 1975), pp. 130-34.

15. See "Documents Relating to Jane E. James," as contained in Henry J. Wolfinger, "A Test of Faith," pp. 150-51.

16. See letter from Jane E. James to Joseph F. Smith, 7 February 1980, as reprinted in Wolfinger, "A Test of Faith," p. 149.

17. However, church officials allowed Jane James to "be adopted into the family of Joseph Smith as a servant" through a "special" temple ceremony prepared for that purpose. See Minutes of a Meeting of the Council of the Twelve Apostles, 2 January 1902, George A. Smith Papers, LDS Church Archives.

18. Council Meeting Minutes, 2 January 1902, Adam S. Bennion Papers.

19. Extract from George F. Richards Record of Decisions by the Council of the First Presidency and the Twelve Apostles, no. 3 (no date is given, but the next decision, no. 4, is dated 8 February 1907), George A. Smith Papers.

20. Council Meeting Minutes, 4 June 1879, Adam S. Bennion Papers.

21. Council Meeting Minutes, 22 August 1895, Adam S. Bennion Papers. See also "Journal History," 22 August 1895, LDS Church Archives.

22. "Journal History," 5 October 1896.

23. First Presidency letter to David O. McKay, 16 March 1904, as quoted in Lester E. Bush, Jr., "Mormonism's Negro Doctrine: An Historical Overview," *Dialogue* 8 (Spring 1973): 61.

24. Minutes of a Council Meeting, 26 August 1908, Adam S. Bennion Papers.

25. George F. Gibbs, secretary to the First Presidency to Bishop John M. Whitaker, 18 January 1909, John M. Whitaker Papers, University of Utah Library.

26. First Presidency letter from Joseph F. Smith, Anthon H. Lund, and Charles W. Penrose to Milton H. Knudson, 12 January 1913, Adam S. Bennion Papers.

27. Although in 1869 Brigham Young seemed to discount questions surrounding the black man's premortal existence as a cause of his current unfavorable situation. See "Journal History," 25 December 1869.

28. As previously indicated, church spokesmen had implicitly suggested a link between black priesthood denial and the writings of the *Pearl of*

Great Price by describing this concept as the "curse . . . as pertaining to the priesthood." It wasn't until after 1880 that this work was quoted chapter and verse in giving scriptural justification to such practices.

29. *Journal of Discourses* (Liverpool, 1854-1886), John Taylor, 22, 28 August 1881. Taylor also made a similar reference a year later. See *Journal of Discourses,* John Taylor, 23, 29 October 1882. Taylor also expanded on Joseph Smith's writings, maintaining that it was "necessary" for the "accursed [black] seed" to continue through the Flood so that the devil would "have representation upon the earth."

30. *The Contributor* (Salt Lake City) 6 (1885): 296-7.

31. *Journal of Discourses,* George Q. Cannon, 23, 20 November 1881; George Q. Cannon, 26, 18 October 1884; *Juvenile Instructor,* 15 October 1891.

32. *Latter-day Saints Millennial Star* (Liverpool, England), 3 December 1903; *Liahona, The Elders' Journal,* 18 April 1908.

33. Bush, "Mormonism's Negro Doctrine," p. 35.

34. Joseph F. Smith, Anthon H. Lund, and Charles W. Penrose to Milton H. Knudson, 13 January 1912, Adam S. Bennion Papers.

35. Council Meeting, 26 August 1908, George A. Smith Papers.

36. Joseph F. Smith and Anthon H. Lund to Rudger Clawson, 18 November 1910, Adam S. Bennion Papers.

37. Bush, "Mormonism's Negro Doctrine," p. 39.

38. *Chicago Tribune,* as reprinted in the *Latter-day Saints Millennial Star,* 5 September 1868; and W. Hepworth Dixon, *New America,* as reprinted in the *Star,* 11 May 1867. Also see *Star,* 10 April 1870.

39. For the best discussion of federal antipolygamy efforts after the Civil War see Gustive O. Larson, *The "Americanization" of Utah for Statehood* (San Marino, California, 1971).

40. From the *Deseret News,* as reprinted in the *Latter-day Saints Millennial Star,* 31 October 1868.

41. *Latter-day Saints Millennial Star,* 1 February 1870.

42. New York *Herald,* reprinted in the *Latter-day Saints Millennial Star,* 29 February 1868.

43. New York *Herald,* reprinted in the *Latter-day Saints Millennial Star,* 7 November 1868. According to this article, the radical Republicans "in making the Black man think he is equal of White [*sic*] unleashed his savage and crual [*sic*] nature, hence trouble in the South. This is a violation of the laws of nature."

44. *Journal of Discourses,* Brigham Young, 11, 8 April 1867.

45. Ibid., John Taylor, 23, 9 April 1882.

46. Ibid., Franklin D. Richards, 8 April 1882; Franklin D. Richards, 26, 18 January 1885.

47. Richard D. Poll, "The Political Reconstruction of Utah Territory, 1866-1890," *Pacific Historical Review,* 27 (May 1958), p. 115.

48. Ibid., p. 119.

49. *Journal of Discourses,* Franklin D. Richards, 23, 8 April 1882.

50. *Latter-day Saints Millennial Star,* 8 June 1867.

51. Ibid., 29 September 1869, 3 November 1869.

52. Ibid., 12 June 1876.

53. According to the non-Mormon observer Ellen E. Dickinson, *New Light on Mormonism* (New York, 1885), p. 187. The Church-owned *Latter-day Saints Millennial Star,* 8 October 1880, also noted the importance of southern missionary activity, explaining that Mormon efforts had expanded to the point that as many missionaries were being sent to this region as to the British Isles.

54. For an interesting analysis of Mormon problems in the South see Gene A. Sessions, "Myth, Mormonism, and Murder in the South," *South Atlantic Quarterly* 75 (Spring 1976): 212-25. Also see William Whiteridge Hatch, *There Is No Law: A History of Mormon Civil Relations in the Southern States, 1865-1905* (New York, 1965).

55. See Appendix C for census figures on Utah's black population during this period.

56. Ronald G. Coleman, "Blacks in Utah History: An Unknown Legacy" in *The Peoples of Utah,* ed. Helen Z. Papanikolas (Salt Lake City, 1976). Also see Coleman, "Utah's Black Pioneers, 1847-1869," *UMOJA: A Scholarly Journal of Black Studies,* N.S., 2 (Summer 1978): 95-110; and Coleman, "A History of Blacks in Utah, 1825-1910" (Ph.D. diss., University of Utah, 1980).

57. Thomas G. Alexander and Leonard J. Arrington, "The Utah Military Frontier, 1872-1912: Forts Cameron, Thornburgh and Duchesne," *Utah Historical Quarterly* 32 (1964): 346-53; Michael J. Clark, "Improbable Ambassadors: Black Soldiers at Fort Douglas, 1896-99," *Utah Historical Quarterly* 46 (Summer 1978): 282-301; Ronald G. Coleman, "The Buffalo Soldiers: Guardians of the Unita Frontier 1886-1901," *Utah Historical Quarterly* 47 (Fall 1979): 421-39.

58. Henry J. Wolfinger, "A Test of Faith," p. 144; Ronald G. Coleman, "Blacks in Utah History," p. 134.

59. See for example, "An Ordinance to Incorporate the City of Payson," *Acts, Resolutions and Memorials of the Legislative Assembly of the Territory of Utah* (Salt Lake City, 1866).

60. Brigham Young to Thomas L. Kane, 29 October 1869, Brigham

Young Papers, LDS Church Archives.

61. "Civil Practice Act," *Acts, Resolutions and Memorials of the Legislative Assembly of the Territory of Utah* (Salt Lake City, 1876).

62. *Latter-day Saints Millennial Star*, 16 April 1872. In this the Saints were merely assenting to the legal abolition of slavery, which had been implemented through the congressional territorial Statute of 1862 and re-enforced by the Thirteenth Amendment in 1865.

63. Harold Schindler, *Orrin Porter Rockwell* (Salt Lake City, 1966), pp. 341-42. However, at the same time, certain writers maintained that Colburn's death resulted from factors in addition to his alleged improprieties toward white women. This black man's cooperation with federal officials in supplying important evidence concerning certain unsolved crimes against federal authorities and Utah non-Mormons ("Gentiles") has been cited as contributing to his demise. See Schindler, p. 341; and Charles Kelly and Hoffman Birney, *Holy Murder: The Story of Porter Rockwell* (New York, 1934), pp. 230-32.

64. *Compiled Laws of Utah,* Section 2, 584 (Salt Lake City, 1888).

65. Meeting of First Presidency and Apostles, 22 August 1895, Adam S. Bennion Papers.

66. Council Meeting, 16 December 1897, Adam S. Bennion Papers.

67. *Journal of Discourses,* Amasa Lyman, 11, 5 April 1866.

68. Ibid., Brigham Young, 11, 8 April 1867.

69. Ronald G. Coleman, "Blacks in Utah History," p. 31; Jack D. Foner, *Blacks and the Military in American History* (New York, 1974), pp. 70-71.

70. For a description of the events surrounding the emergence of the Reorganized Church see Robert B. Flanders, "The Mormons Who Did Not Go West" (M.A. thesis, University of Wisconsin, 1954); and Richard P. Howard, "The Reorganized Church in Illinois, 1852-82; Search for Identity," *Dialogue* 5 (Spring 1970): 63.

71. William D. Russell, "A Priestly Role for a Prophetic Church: The RLDS Church and Black Americans," *Dialogue* 12 (Summer 1979): 37-49.

72. *The True Latter Day Saints Herald*, February 1860.

73. Ibid., 1 June 1865. At the 1878 Conference of the RLDS Church this revelation was made "binding" on members of the church and became section 116 in their *Doctrine and Covenants*.

74. *The True Latter Day Saints Herald* (Cincinnati, Ohio), 1 August 1867 (italics in original).

75. Ibid., 1 October 1867; Joseph Smith III and Heman C. Smith, eds., *The History of the Reorganized Church of Jesus Christ of Latter Day*

Saints, vol. 4 (Lamoni, Iowa, 1903), entry for 7 October 1889; F. Harry Edwards, *The History of the Reorganized Church of Jesus Christ of Latter Day Saints,* vol. 5 (Independence, Missouri, 1969), p. 180.

76. Smith and Smith, eds., *The History of the Reorganized Church,* vol. 3, entry for 4 May 1865, p. 495.

77. Ibid., vol. 3, entry for June 1875, p. 101.

78. *The True Latter Day Saints Herald,* 1 May 1868.

79. Ibid., 1 July 1866, 1 November 1866, 1 October 1867; Smith and Smith, eds., *The History of the Reorganized Church,* vol. 4, entries for 29 June 1880, p. 314; 2 August 1880, p. 318; 1 April 1881, p. 351.

80. F. Edwards, *The History of the Reorganized Church,* pp. 451, 507, 585.

81. *The True Latter Day Saints Herald,* 15 March 1868.

82. Ibid., 1 August 1867.

83. See Howard, "The Reorganized Church in Illinois," pp. 62-75. Also see his "The 'Book of Abraham' in the Light of History and Egyptology," *Courage* (pilot issue, April 1970): 33-48, which outlines the current RLDS position on the Book of Abraham.

84. *True Latter Day Saints Herald,* 1 August 1867.

85. Joseph Fielding Smith, *Origin of the "Reorganized" Church* (Salt Lake City, Utah, 1909), p. 116.

9 | Segregation, Civil Rights, and Black Priesthood Denial, 1918-1978

The attitude of the Church with reference to Negroes remains as it has always stood. It is not a matter of the declaration of a policy but of direct commandment from the Lord, on which is founded the doctrine of the Church from the days of its organization, to the effect that Negroes may become members of the Church but that they are not entitled to the priesthood at the present time.

LDS Church First Presidency, August 17, 1949

From the beginning of this dispensation, Joseph Smith and all succeeding presidents of the Church have taught that Negroes, while spirit children of a common Father, and the progeny of our earthly parents Adam and Eve, were not yet to receive the priesthood, for reasons which we believe are known to God, but which He has not made fully known to men.

LDS Church First Presidency, December 15, 1969

On August 17, 1949, the Church of Jesus Christ of Latter-day Saints issued an official statement affirming its long-standing practice of denying blacks offices within its priesthood. This statement, signed by President George Albert Smith and his two counselors, proclaimed black priesthood denial to be a "direct commandment from the Lord . . . founded on the doctrine of the Church from the days of its organization." This statement referred to "the conduct of spirits in the premortal existence" as having a "determining effect" in upholding black priesthood denial. At the same time, however, this declaration quoted Brigham Young in promising that "the day will come" when all blacks "will be redeemed and possess all the blessings which we now have," including the priesthood.[1]

The 1949 First Presidency statement—the first official Mormon declaration affirming and justifying black priesthood denial—came at the end of a decade during which a large number of blacks migrated to Utah. In the ten-year period from 1940 to 1950, Utah's black population more than doubled, from 1,235 to 2,729, which was double the rate of increase of the state's white population.[2] The concentration of these blacks was most evident in the urban centers of Salt Lake and Ogden, also the two largest centers of Mormon church members in the state. These newly settled Utah blacks, like other black migrants, were drawn to the North and West by increased economic opportunities during World War II.[3] The migration of all these blacks undermined Mormon efforts to avoid contacts with blacks in both the secular and ecclesiastical realms, a long-standing Latter-day Saint objective.

This increased influx of blacks into Utah came at a time when the American civil rights movement was gathering force and momentum. The seeds of this movement were planted in the soil of rising black expectations and cultivated by the profound social changes during and after World War I. These changes included the mass migration of blacks into northern cities, the "Harlem Renaissance," and the rise of the "New Negro." Throughout the 1920s and 1930s, black activists and their sympathetic white allies assailed long-standing discriminatory practices, particularly the racial segregation of public and private accommodations. During the 1940s, the struggle for black equality gained the active support of federal officials in the Roosevelt and Truman administrations, who abolished discriminatory practices in various federal government agencies and departments.[4]

The movement for black civil rights, moreover, gained the support of the leaders of various religious denominations. By the 1940s concerned Catholic, Jewish, and Protestant spokesmen enrolled in the struggle for black equality. Several of these denominations officially endorsed the civil rights movement.[5] Latter-day Saint leaders, however, held back, shunning these developments. Thus, the 1949 affirmation of black priesthood denial by Mormon officials represented a reaction against the burgeoning American civil rights movement and stood as a barrier against all of those blacks migrating to Utah during this period.

As important as it was, the Official Church First Presidency Pronouncement upholding black priesthood denial was just one aspect of a basic Mormon effort to remain aloof from blacks in general and avoid what Mormon leaders believed to be the excesses of the civil rights movement during the sixty years following President Joseph F. Smith's death in 1918. A Mormon refusal to promote missionary activity among black people was part of this effort. According to one Mormon mission president, those missionaries under his jurisdiction avoided missionary activity in those areas "where it is known that color does actually exist. . . ."[6] By 1947 the First Presidency of the church was able to state that "No special effort has ever been made to proselyte among the Negro race."[7] Such a policy continued into the 1950s and early 1960s. Elder Bruce R. McConkie stated that "The gospel message of salvation is not carried affirmatively to black people."[8] In 1961 President Joseph Fielding Smith instructed the president of one particular Mormon mission to avoid seeking "out the Negros."[9]

Mormon efforts to avoid contact with black people was also reflected in the way individual Latter-day Saints treated the few blacks who came in contact with the church. In 1936 the members of a Mormon branch in Cincinnati, Ohio, were "extremely prejudiced against" the Len Hope family, a black family that recently joined this branch. These white Mormons told the branch president or presiding officer that the Hope family "must leave the branch or they as a group "would all leave." Bending to white pressure, the branch president "ruled that Brother Hope and his family could not come to church meetings."[10] A similar situation developed a few years later in the Washington, D.C., stake. In 1942 white members of this stake objected to the presence of "two colored sisters" who were "faithful members of the Church." The Church First Presidency resolved this problem by suggesting that if the "colored sisters were discreetly approached, they would be happy to sit at one side in the rear or somewhere where they would not wound the sensibilities of the complaining sisters."[11] A basic Mormon desire for separation between white and black Mormons was also evident in the 1956 remarks of Apostle Mark E. Peterson. He explained that if, by chance, a sufficient number of blacks joined the church, Mormon leaders would "build them a chapel of their own where they could worship to themselves."[12] Fifteen years later, in 1971, Mormon leaders authorized the formation of the Genesis Group, an organization exclusively for the 200 black members of the church living in the Salt Lake Valley. This group held its own Relief Society (women's auxiliary) and Primary and Mutual Improvement Association (youth organization) meetings.[13]

Actions by individual Latter-day Saints also reflected a basic Mormon desire to avoid black-white interaction in the secular realm. In 1939, the

Mormon-dominated Utah State legislature extended its antimiscegenation statute to prohibit a "white" from marrying not just a "negro" but also a "Mongolian, a member of the Malay race or a mulatto, quadroon, or octoroon. . . ."[14] In the same year, Sheldon R. Brewster, a Mormon Bishop and real estate developer, expressed alarm over the increasing influx of blacks into Salt Lake City by calling upon the Salt Lake City Commission to set aside an area in the "Northwest Section" of the city, "by the railroad tracks, to be zoned as a Negro District."[15] During World War II, Dr. Ralph Bunch and Marian Anderson experienced discrimination in trying to secure accommodations in the Mormon-owned Hotel Utah.[16]

Such antiblack practices in Utah were noted by concerned individuals both within and outside the state. A report written by Wallace R. Bennett and published in the *Utah Law Review* in 1953 noted that Utah blacks were barred from "practically all night clubs, bowling alleys . . . [and] most of the better restaurants." This report also found Utah blacks "restricted to balconies in the theaters." In addition, the "leading hotels of the state" were "notorious for their color-line policies."[17] In that same year, W. Miller Barbour, a field director for the National Urban League, reported that "In large areas of Utah . . . and in most of the smaller towns, [anti-black] discrimination is almost as severe as in the South."[18] Five years later, Albert B. Fritz, president of the Salt Lake chapter of the NAACP noted the "Segregation in employment."[19] Charles Nabors, another Salt Lake NAACP official, went so far as to declare in 1963 that Utah had "potentially the worst race problem in the United States."[20] Three years later, in 1966, this same NAACP chapter saw the Mormon Church as a factor in the unfavorable civil rights situation of Utah blacks. The NAACP adopted a resolution that accused the Mormon church of maintaining "a rigid and continuous segregation stand." The church was also assailed for its indifference to "widespread discriminatory practices in education, in housing, in employment, and other areas of life."[21]

Such observations concerning Utah's unfavorable civil rights situation came at a time when certain Mormons were making statements unfavorable to the burgeoning civil rights movement. As early as 1921, the Mormon-owned *Deseret News* warned that black demands "for full, and presumably immediate social equality . . . will do nothing more than intensify race antagonisms."[22] In 1946, J. Reuben Clark, a church apostle and member of the First Presidency, expressed reservations about the civil rights movement. He warned that "at the end of the road" of the struggle "to break down all race prejudice . . . is intermarriage. This is what it finally comes to." But at the same time Clark was careful to point out that "every man and every woman, no matter what the color of his or her skin may be" should be given "full civil rights."[23] Other Mormon spokesmen were not so charitable. Apostle Mark E. Peterson, speaking in 1954, lashed out against the civil rights movement. Blacks were not simply after equal economic, social, and political rights. According to Peterson "the Negro seeks absorption with the white race. He will not be satisfied until he achieves it by intermarriage. That is his objective and we must fact it." He defended segregation as a divinely sanctioned institution.

> I think the Lord segregated the Negro and who is man to change that segregation? It reminds me of the scripture on marriage, "what God hath joined together, let not man put asunder." Only here we have the reverse of the thing—what God hath separated let not man bring together again. . . .[24]

Two years later, in 1964, Joseph Fielding Smith, president of the church's elite ruling body, the Council of Twelve Apostles, expressed alarm about the "wave of 'non segregation'" sweeping the country. He feared that "the doctrine of social equality" would lead to racial intermarriage or amalgamation "enforced by the justices of the Supreme Court of the United States."[25]

In addition to the specter of racial intermixture, the civil rights movement posed a basic threat to American institutions, according to other concerned Latter-day Saints. The *Deseret News*, in 1948, saw a link between the struggle for black equality and the threat of Communist subversion. According to the *News*, "Many Negro organizations" were "signing petitions, introducing resolutions, sending protests and joining delegations on matters that have been put up to them by the Communists in their midst. . . ."[26] Ezra Taft Benson, a Mormon apostle, expressed the greatest fear over the civil rights movement and communism. Benson's views, expressed throughout the 1960s, drew national attention by virtue of his earlier service as secretary of agriculture under President Eisenhower during the 1950s. According to Benson, speaking in 1963, "the Civil Rights movement in the South had been 'fomented almost entirely by the communists.'"[27] A year later, Benson hammered away at this same theme at the April 1965 Latter-day Saints' General Conference. He

warned that "Communists were using the Civil Rights movement to promote revolution and eventual takeover of this country." He admonished
the gathered Saints to respond to this threat.

> When are we going to wake up? What do you know about the
> dangerous Civil Rights agitation in Mississippi? Do you fear the
> destruction of all vestiges of state government?
>
> Now, brethren, the Lord never promised there would be traitors
> in the Church. We have the ignorant, the sleepy and the deceived
> who provide temptations and avenues of apostacy for the unwary
> and the unfaithful. But we have a prophet at our head and he has
> spoken. Now what are we going to do about it?
>
> Brethren, if we had done our homework and were faithful we could
> step forward at this time and help save this country.[28]

On at least one other occasion, at the October 1967 General Conference,
Benson again warned church members about the menace of communism
within the civil rights movement. "The planning, direction, and leadership
... of today's Civil Rights agitation," according to Benson, came "from
the Communists." He called for an authorized legislative investigation to
"study and expose the degree to which secret Communists have penetrated
into the Civil Rights movement."[29]

   The practice of denying blacks the priesthood served as a bulwark against
the real and perceived threats posed by the civil rights movement, while at
the same time serving as an effective barrier between the Saints and Utah's
small but growing black population. President Heber J. Grant affirmed his
support for black priesthood denial early in his tenure as church president.
Like his predecessors in that office, he utilized the Book of Abraham as a
scriptural instrument affirming this practice.[30]
   The foremost church spokesman identified with the practice of black
priesthood denial was Apostle Joseph Fielding Smith, the son of Joseph
F. Smith and grandson of Hyrum Smith, the brother of the slain Mormon
prophet Joseph Smith. Because of his distinguished family background and
high church position Smith's ideas carried great weight within the church
from the 1920s to the 1960s. As early as 1924, Smith, through *The Improvement Era*—an official church magazine—defended black priesthood denial,

alleging that his great-uncle Joseph Smith "taught this doctrine." Smith, like Heber J. Grant, utilized the Book of Abraham as a scriptural instrument upholding this practice.[31] Seven years later, Smith wrote *The Way to Perfection,* a work containing Mormonism's most extensive and elaborate doctrinal defense of black priesthood denial. In addition to identifying this practice with "the teachings of Joseph Smith" and the Book of Abraham, Smith further developed and gave prominent publicity to the preexistence hypothesis," that is, the concept that the black man's inability to hold the priesthood was a consequence of his behavior during a premortal existence. Blacks, during a premortal war between the forces of God and Satan, "did not stand valiantly" with the forces of "Righteousness" and "were indifferent" or "sympathized with Lucifer. . . ."[32] Smith's arguments as presented in *The Way to Perfection* provided a theological framework utilized by other church spokesmen upholding black priesthood denial.[33]

Smith continued to uphold and defend black priesthood denial into the 1960s, even as this practice came under increased outside attack during this turbulent decade. He admitted that "the work of the [Mormon] ministry is given to other people [non-blacks]." He went on the offensive, asking, "Why should the so-called Christian denominations complain? How many Negroes have been placed as ministers over white congregations in the so-called Christian denominations?"[34] A year later Smith, through the pages of *Look* magazine, again defended black priesthood denial but went on to say, "I would not want you to believe that we bear animosity toward the Negro. 'Darkies' are wonderful people, and they have their place in our Church."[35] In 1964, Smith once more upheld black priesthood denial as a practice established by "the Lord!"[36]

Other Mormon spokesmen affirmed their support for black priesthood denial. David O. McKay, who served as church president from 1951 until 1970, defended this practice both in public and private. In 1947, four years before becoming church president, McKay in a private letter pointed out that this practice had a "scriptural basis" through "one verse in the Book of Abraham (1:26)." In addition, McKay suggested that this practice could be attributed to the situation of blacks during their "preexistent life."[37] McKay reaffirmed his support for black priesthood denial in 1964 when questioned by a news reporter at the dedication of a Mormon Temple in Oakland, California. McKay was asked "When will the Negroes receive the Priesthood?" He replied "Not in my lifetime . . . nor yours."[38] Near the end of McKay's tenure as church president, the Church First Presidency

issued an official statement upholding black priesthood denial. This statement, issued in 1969, was similar to the one issued some twenty years
earlier in that it upheld black priesthood denial as a practice "taught" by
"Joseph Smith and all succeeding presidents of the Church." According
to this statement, blacks "were not yet to receive the priesthood for reasons we believe are known to God, but which He has not made fully known
to man." This practice "is not something which originated with man, but
goes back into the beginning with God. . . ." Finally, it quoted McKay in
promising that "Sometime in God's eternal plan, the Negro will be given
the right to hold the priesthood."[39]

The Mormon practice of black priesthood denial had apparent strong
support from rank-and-file Latter-day Saints, at least from those living in
the State of Utah. A 1972 Louis Harris Poll found that 70 percent of all
Utah-based Mormons opposed granting blacks the right "to hold the priesthood in the Mormon Church."[40] In fact, this same poll found that a significant number of Latter-day Saints believed that the growing agitation
and controversy over the Mormon practice of black priesthood denial was
part of a "black conspiracy" to destroy the church.[41]

Individual Latter-day Saints, acting on their own, defended black priesthood denial in a number of privately published works. The best-known of
these was written in 1960 by John J. Stewart, a Utah State University
journalism professor, and William E. Berrett, a historian and Vice President
of Brigham Young University. In their *Mormonism and the Negro,* Stewart
and Berrett defended black priesthood denial as an essential feature of basic
Mormon doctrine and theology. Stewart and Berrett found black priesthood denial rooted in the historical realities of the Mormon past.[42] Seven
years later, John L. Lund, a Latter-day Saint Seminary teacher in Olympia,
Washington, presented an even more elaborate historical-theological defense
of black priesthood denial in his *The Church and the Negro.* Lund, like
Stewart and Berrett, emphasized the importance of doctrinal-historical
trends and practices in the development of black priesthood denial.[43]

Writing from a somewhat different perspective, a couple of black Mormons—part of that tiny Mormon minority actually affected by black priesthood denial—defended this unique Mormon practice. Alan Gerald Cherry,
in *It's You and Me Lord!*, affirmed his own subordinate position. Cherry
admitted that his own ineligibility for the priesthood was "sometimes . . .
frustrating," but concluded that "in the end the important thing in God's
kingdom will not be who leads us there, but simply who gets there."[44] In

a similar spirit, Wynetta Willis Martin, another black Mormon, articulated her acceptance of a subordinate Mormon position in *A Black Mormon Tells Her Story*. Martin discounted her concern that blacks could not hold the priesthood and in fact defended the church against the charges of fellow blacks who asked her why she joined a church that was "prejudiced." Her answer was that the "Gospel [or church] is not prejudiced." Martin underscored her acceptance of black priesthood denial by her willingness to include in her book an elaborate theological defense of black priesthood denial written by John D. Hawkes, the publisher of her work.[45]

Armand L. Mauss, a professor of sociology at Washington State University, also expressed an interest in the status of blacks within Mormonism, but Mauss did not try to defend the practice of black priesthood denial per se. Instead he carefully examined the sociological ramifications of this practice, using the tools and techniques of modern sociology. In a 1966 *Pacific Sociological Review* article, Mauss concluded that the Mormons, despite their practice of black priesthood denial, held basically the same "secular attitudes" towards black people as "moderate" Protestant denominations, such as the Presbyterian, Congregational, and Episcopalian.[46] Mauss elaborated on these findings in two later articles published in *Dialogue* in 1967 and 1972. He concluded that Church policy toward blacks did not significantly influence "Mormons in their everyday relations with blacks outside the Church realm" and felt that the Mormons lacked "any *unique* or *distinctive* prejudice toward blacks in matters of stereotypes, job opportunities, educational opportunities and the like."[47] Based on these findings, Mauss issued a "plea . . . to Civil Rights organizations and to all the critics of the Mormon Church" to "get off our backs!"[48] Mauss' findings, by discounting any relationship between black priesthood denial and official Mormon avoidance of the civil rights movement, possibly made it easier for rank-and-file Mormon civil rights proponents (such as Mauss) to go along, albeit reluctantly, with black priesthood denial.

Thus, in light of continuing grass-roots support from rank-and-file Latter-day Saints, it is not surprising that the Mormon leaders who followed David O. McKay into the office of church president during the early 1970s continued to uphold black priesthood denial. Joseph Fielding Smith, who became church president in 1970, was well known to Latter-day Saints for his numerous writings and statements justifying "the church policy of limiting Negro participation."[49] Harold B. Lee, who became church president following the death of Smith in 1972, reaffirmed the Mormon "decision with respect to black minorities." Before becoming church president he had expressed strong support for the theological and doctrinal arguments underlying black priesthood denial and saw it as a bulwark against racial intermarriage.[50] On another occasion he characterized those who questioned this practice as "smart boys" or "enemies."[51] Lee, who died suddenly and unexpectedly in 1973, was succeeded as church president by Spencer W. Kimball, who upon becoming president asserted his belief that black priesthood denial had been and was still sanctioned by God.[52]

Throughout the sixty-year period from 1918 to 1978, various church leaders and spokesmen affirmed their support for black priesthood denial. This practice served as a barrier against what certain Latter-day Saints perceived as the excesses of the civil rights movement and Utah's small but growing black population, which made itself felt during the years following World War II. More important, black priesthood denial had deep historical roots planted in the rich soil of Mormon doctrine and nurtured by long practice. After all, this practice had been upheld and defended by every Mormon president from Brigham Young on. Therefore, the decision by Latter-day Saint leaders to abandon black priesthood denial in June 1978 came as a great surprise and indeed a shock to individuals both within and outside the Church of Jesus Christ of Latter-day Saints.

NOTES

1. "Church First Presidency Statement," 17 August 1949, as reprinted in Lester E. Bush, Jr., "Unpublished Compilations on the Negro in Mormonism," LDS Church Archives.

2. See Appendix C, table 15.

3. Margaret Judy Maag, "Discrimination Against the Negro in Utah and Institutional Efforts to Eliminate It" (M.S. thesis, University of Utah, 1971), pp. 26-28.

4. For one discussion of the struggle for black rights in the twentieth century, see C. Vann Woodward, *The Strange Career of Jim Crow* (New York, 1955).

5. Frank S. Loescher, *The Protestant Church and the Negro* (Philadelphia, 1948), pp. 28-50; Robert Moats Miller, *American Protestantism and Social Issues, 1919-1939* (Chapel Hill, North Carolina, 1958).

6. Don Mack Dalton to Heber J. Grant, Adam S. Bennion Papers, Harold B. Lee Library, Brigham Young University.

7. Letter from Church First Presidency to President Virgil H. Sponberg, Adam S. Bennion Papers.

8. Bruce R. McConkie, *Mormon Doctrine* (Salt Lake City, 1958), p. 477.

9. "The Negroes," pamphlet, mimeographed, Andes Mission, n.d., LDS Church Archives.

10. Mark E. Peterson, "Race Problems—As They Affect the Church" (Speech delivered at Brigham Young University, 27 August 1957), reprinted in Jerald and Sandra Tanner, *Mormons and Negroes* (Salt Lake City, 1970).

11. Church First Presidency Letter to President Ezra T. Benson, 23 June 1942, Adam S. Bennion Papers.

12. David H. Oliver, *A Negro on Mormonism* (Salt Lake City, 1963), p. 12.

13. *Deseret News* (Salt Lake City), 23 October 1971. See also *San Francisco Sunday Examiner and Chronicle*, 24 October 1971; *New York Times*, 6 April 1972.

14. *Compiled Laws of Utah*, Section 2,584 (Salt Lake City, 21 February 1939).

15. Oliver, *A Negro on Mormonism*, pp. 25-6.

16. Ibid., p. 23.

17. Wallace R. Bennett, "The Negro in Utah," *Utah Law Review*, (Spring 1953). Also see Harmon O. Cole, "The Status of the Negro in Utah," in *Utah Law Review* (Spring 1953).

18. W. Miller Barbour, "Breaking the Barriers: Anti-Negro Prejudice Lessens in Western Hotels," *Frontier*, November 1954.

19. *Deseret News*, 23 April 1959.

20. *Indianapolis Star*, 6 November 1963.

21. *Deseret News*, 3 May 1966.

22. Ibid., 24 November 1921.

23. *The Improvement Era* 49 (August 1946).

24. Mark E. Peterson, "Race Problems—As They Affect the Church."

25. As quoted in Wallace Turner, *The Mormon Establishment* (New York, 1965), pp. 230-31.

26. *Deseret News*, 28 April 1948.

27. Ibid., 14 December 1963.

28. *Salt Lake Tribune*, 7 April 1965.

29. *The Improvement Era* (December 1967).

30. "Journal History," 28 January 1828, LDS Church Archives.

31. *The Improvement Era* 27 (April 1924).

32. Joseph Fielding Smith, *The Way to Perfection* (Salt Lake City, 1931), pp. 43-44, 97-111.

33. See for example, Church First Presidency to Francis W. Brown, 13 January 1947, Adam S. Bennion Papers; Mark E. Peterson's, "Race Problems—As They Affect the Church"; McConkie, *Mormon Doctrine*; Alvin R. Dyer, "For What Purpose"(Speech given to LDS Missionaries at Oslo, Norway, 18 March 1961).

34. *Church News* (Salt Lake City), 14 July 1962, Supplement to *Deseret News* for same date.

35. *Look*, 22 October 1963.

36. As quoted by Wallace Turner in *The Mormon Establishment*, pp. 230-31.

37. As quoted in John J. Stewart and William E. Berrett, *Mormonism and the Negro* (Oram, Utah, 1960), pp. 16-23.

38. John L. Lund, *The Church and the Negro* (Salt Lake City, 1967), p. 45. Quoted in somewhat different form in Turner, *The Mormon Establishment*, p. 262.

39. Church First Presidency Statement to General Authorities, Regional Representatives of the Twelve, Stake Presidents, Mission Presidents and Bishops," 15 December 1969, reprinted in *Deseret News*, 10 January 1970.

40. This was in contrast to only 16 percent of the Utah Saints who felt blacks should be ordained and 14 percent who were not sure. *New York Times*, 16 April 1972. It should be stressed that this survey was made only among the Saints living in Utah, and as suggested by the findings of Armand L. Mauss in "Moderation in All Things: Political and Social Outlooks of Modern Urban Mormons," *Dialogue* 7 (Spring 1972): 64, Utah Mormons were probably more conservative with regard to black priesthood ordination than Latter-day Saints living elsewhere.

41. One-third of the Latter-day Saints living in Utah felt this to be the case. See *New York Times*, 6 April 1972. Along these same lines, at least two writers felt that Latter-day Saint support for black priesthood denial was bolstered by an intense Mormon fear of black-white racial intermixture. See Thomas F. O'Dea, "Strains in Mormon History Reconsidered," in Marvin S. Hill and James B. Allen, eds., *Mormonism and American Culture* (New York, 1972), p. 162. David L. Brewer, "The Mormons," in Donald R. Cutler and Thomas F. O'Dea, eds., *The Religious Situation: 1968* (Boston, 1968), p. 524.

42. Stewart and Berrett, *Mormonism and the Negro*.

43. Lund, *The Church and the Negro*.

44. Alan Gerald Cherry, *It's You and Me Lord!* (Provo, Utah, 1970), pp. 63-64.

45. Wynetta Willis Martin, *Black Mormon Tells Her Story* (Salt Lake City, 1972).

46. Armand L. Mauss, "Mormon and Secular Attitudes Toward Negroes," *Pacific Sociological Review* 9 (Fall 1966): 91-99.

47. Mauss, "Moderation in All Things," pp. 64-66; Mauss, "Mormonism and the Negro: Faith, Folklore and Civil Rights," *Dialogue* 4 (Winter 1967): 18-39.

48. Mauss, "Mormonism and the Negro," p. 38.

49. As quoted in *Christianity Today*, 13 February 1970. Also see *New York Times*, 25 January 1970. However it should be pointed out that Smith's statements on this question as church president were more "low-keyed" and temperate than those made prior to his becoming church president.

50. Harold B. Lee, "Youth of a Noble Birthright" (Radio address given on 6 May 1945), unpublished, LDS Church Archives; "Youth and the Church," typescript collection, LDS Church Archives, pp. 3-12.

51. "Record of Conference of French East Mission of LDS Church," Geneva, Switzerland, 30 October 1961. For an example of Lee's position after becoming church president, see *Sacramento Bee*, 8 July 1972.

52. *Newsweek*, 14 January 1974; *Time*, 14 January 1974.

Epilogue:
The Abandonment
of Black
Priesthood Denial

the Lord ... has heard our prayers, and by revelation has confirmed that the long-promised day has come when every faithful, worthy man in the Church may receive the priesthood,
with power to exercise its divine authority, and enjoy with his
loved ones every blessing that flows therefrom, including the
blessings of the temple.

LDS Church First Presidency, June 8, 1978

What started out as just another Friday morning in early June
of 1978 took on an air of anticipation and rumor when members of the
press and electronic news media were summoned to the world headquarters
of the Church of Jesus Christ of Latter-day Saints. Jerry Cahill, spokesman
for the Mormon church, made public a startling directive issued by the
Church First Presidency and addressed "To All General and Local Priesthood
Officers of the Church ... Throughout the World." It instructed that henceforth "all worthy male members of the church may be ordained to the priesthood without regard for race or color." This directive "confirmed ... by
revelation" meant that the long-standing church ban on black priesthood
ordination was no longer in effect. Henceforth black Mormon males, along
with "every faithful, worthy man in the Church, may receive the holy priesthood, with the power to exercise its divine authority, and enjoy with his
loved ones every blessing that flows therefrom, including the blessings of
the Temple."[1] The repeal of black priesthood denial was hailed by observers

both within and outside of the Mormon movement. Indeed, this repeal represented the most significant doctrinal change since the Manifesto of 1890, which had terminated the church sanctioning of plural marriages.

As dramatic as it was, the Mormon decision to reclassify "a whole segment of humanity"[2] did not occur in a sociohistorical vacuum. There were a number of forces and pressures, increasingly evident during the years after World War II, that made Mormon black priesthood denial and related racist attitudes increasingly difficult to maintain and defend. Black priesthood denial was undermined by the civil rights movement, which started to make itself felt in American society generally and in Utah in particular by the late 1930s.

Initially Utah civil rights advocates were not concerned about Mormon black priesthood denial per se. They were upset about the discrimination that Utah blacks encountered outside the church, that is, in housing, employment practices, use of recreational facilities, and legal prohibitions on black-white intermarriage. Though such antiblack practices reflected the prejudices of Utah's dominant Latter-day Saint population, they also fit into the norm of an American society that basically treated blacks as second-class citizens.[3]

As early as the 1930s, Utah civil rights advocates reacted against these antiblack statutes and practices. The Salt Lake chapter of the National Association for the Advancement of Colored People pushed for the enactment in 1935 of a public accommodations bill by the Utah State Legislature.[4] In 1939 members of the Salt Lake NAACP, along with other black citizens in the city, successfully turned back the efforts of white citizens, led by Sheldon Brewster, to "ghettoize" the city's black population into a specifically designated residential area.[5] In 1945, the NAACP once more tried to get the Utah State Legislature to consider civil rights legislation. Although the desired legislation was not passed, this effort led to the formation of a special committee of the Utah State Senate in 1947 to investigate the employment practices of Utah businesses. The resultant study found evidence of widespread discrimination against blacks and called for the elimination of such practices through the enactment of an equal opportunity law. The NAACP and a new civil rights organization, the Council for Civil Unity, tried unsuccessfully to get the Utah State legislature to enact civil rights legislation in 1947 and again in 1949.[6] Despite these failures, Utah civil rights advocates did score one concrete victory when the Utah State Supreme Court in 1948 declared unconstitutional a Utah real estate provision that prohibited buyers of property from transferring it "to any person not of the Caucasian race."[7]

During the 1950s, two different groups concerned with civil rights examined, in depth, the problem of Utah's black community. The first group, the Utah Academy of Sciences, Arts, and Letters, was concerned with "The Legal Status of the Negro in Utah." The academy found that while Utah blacks "enjoyed . . . near-equality . . . in the field of Education," they faced "certain discriminations" in recreational facilities, including theaters, dance halls, swimming pools, bowling alleys, and restaurants. The report also noted the restrictions on interracial marriages upheld by Utah's "anti-miscegenation statute." The academy's report suggested a possible relationship between these discriminatory practices and Mormon black priesthood denial and related racist concepts.[8] A second investigation, initiated by the Utah State Advisory Committee on Civil Rights, decried the difficulties faced by Utah blacks in employment, housing, and restaurant-hotel service. These difficulties, the report suggested, were linked to the Latter-day Saint interpretation of scripture and Mormon concepts of white racial superiority.[9]

By the early 1960s, Utah civil rights advocates, as those throughout the country, became much more militant in their tactics. These activists were no longer content to limit their efforts to investigating discriminatory practices and legislative lobbying. Instead, they started to protest against and to boycott various businesses, recreational facilities, and public institutions they found engaged in discriminatory practices. In 1960 and again in 1963, the Salt Lake chapter of the NAACP organized boycotts against the local Woolworth department store. Also during the early 1960s, the Salt Lake NAACP led demonstrations against a local bowling alley and skating rink accused of antiblack practices. Finally, the same organization investigated the alleged segregation practices of public schools in Salt Lake City and Ogden.[10]

By the mid-1960s Utah civil rights activists started to demonstrate against the Mormon church itself, in their efforts to secure favorable civil rights legislation. At first, these activists tried to avoid a direct confrontation with Mormon church leaders. Instead they demonstrated in front of the state capitol in an effort to urge the legislature, a body consisting of a majority of Mormons, to pass appropriate civil rights legislation. At the same time, these proponents urged Governor George D. Clyde to take the lead in this effort.[11] The Utah legislature did repeal the state's long-standing antimiscegenation law, but failed to enact other desired legislation. In response, the

NAACP decided to organize a protest against Mormon church leaders, whom they perceived as blocking civil rights measures in the state legislature. NAACP leaders had some cause for concern, as church leaders had failed to make known the church's position on civil rights. The Salt Lake NAACP chapter made tentative plans to picket Temple Square during the LDS General Conference in the fall of 1963. In addition, NAACP chapters across the country announced plans to picket local Mormon mission headquarters in support of the Salt Lake chapter.[12] The threatened NAACP demonstrations, however, were averted when Apostle Hugh B. Brown of the Church First Presidency released a statement outlining the "position of the Church of Jesus Christ of Latter-day Saints on the matter of civil rights." This statement let it "be known that there is in this Church no doctrine, belief, or practice that is intended to deny the enjoyment of full civil rights by any person regardless of race, color, or creed."[13] The church's 1963 pro-civil rights statement was followed by a relatively tranquil period from October 1963 until the early spring of 1965, during which time civil rights protestors did not confront the Mormon church.[14]

This all changed, however, in early March, 1965, when the NAACP charged the Mormon church with "working behind the scenes" to prevent the passage of civil rights legislation pending before the Utah state legislature.[15] After the church-owned *Deseret News* refused to endorse pending legislation calling for fair employment and fair housing, the NAACP organized a series of three marches on the church administration building.[16] In the wake of these demonstrations, the *Deseret News* reaffirmed the church's 1963 pro-civil rights statement, labeling it "A Clear Civil Rights Stand."[17] The state legislature enacted both a public accommodations act and a fair employment practices act.[18] Subsequently demonstrations against the church tapered off, at least temporarily.[19]

By the late 1960s, however, the Mormon church faced new difficulties as advocates of black rights focused their attacks on Mormon black priesthood denial itself. This direct assault on black priesthood denial reflected a general shift in the American civil rights movement during the 1960s. Civil rights activists looked beyond discriminatory practices per se. They attacked what they felt to be the roots of such discriminatory practices, namely, fundamental racist concepts or doctrines. In the case of the Mormons, the target was the doctrine of black priesthood denial. In lashing out at black priesthood denial these advocates initially concentrated their fire on the church-owned Brigham Young University. Militant black and

white protesters demonstrated during athletic contests between Brigham
Young and other colleges and universities. In the spring of 1968, eight
members of the University of Texas-El Paso track team refused to compete against Brigham Young University because of their belief that the
Mormons considered "blacks . . . inferior and . . . disciples of the devil."[20]
In October 1968, militant demonstrators from San Jose State College
assailed Brigham Young University during a football contest between the
two schools. This contest was marked by student violence and the refusal
of black athletes to participate. Finally a bomb threat was made against
the hotel in which the B.Y.U. team was housed. Later that same year black
San Jose State basketball players refused to play against B.Y.U.[21]

Anti-B.Y.U. protests similar to those at the University of Texas-El Paso
and San Jose State continued throughout 1969 and into early 1970. Pickets
and off-field strife greeted B.Y.U. athletes during their contests with virtually all colleges and universities in the trans-Mississippi West, including Arizona,
New Mexico, Washington, Colorado State, and Cal Poly at San Luis Obispo.[22]
A particularly noteworthy incident involved fourteen black members of
Wyoming University's football team. When these athletes wore black arm
bands "to protest Mormon racial beliefs" prior to a football game with
B.Y.U., the Wyoming coach summarily dismissed them from the team. This
dismissal of the "Wyoming 14" stimulated further black protests against
B.Y.U.[23] More serious for the Mormon school, however, was the refusal
of Stanford University, the University of Washington, and San Jose State
to participate in any further athletic contests with B.Y.U. "because of alleged racial discrimination by the Mormon Church."[24] By January 1970,
Sports Illustrated observed that "the protests [against B.Y.U.] have grown
in intensity to the point where they have almost transcended all else."[25]

The year 1970 brought an end to the militant demonstrations against
B.Y.U., but this did not mean an end to non-Mormon protests against
Latter-day Saint black priesthood denial and related attitudes. Such protests, however, were less strident, reflecting the more tranquil atmosphere
of the 1970s. In October 1972 the Mormon black issue came up in connection with the proposed Mormon construction of a 38-story luxury apart-
ment building in New York City near Lincoln Center. Black members of
the New York City Planning Commission opposed this structure because
it would be a visual reminder to blacks visiting Lincoln Center of "the
poisonous myth of their alleged racial inferiority." Even though the planning commission granted approval for this Mormon structure, actual construction was threatened two months later when black residents living

near the construction site tried to get the planning commission to rescind its approval. These residents found the proposed presence of this Mormon structure an "affront" to the integrated neighborhood in which it was to be built. They also claimed that the Mormon church was engaged in "racial discrimination at the site." However, a short time later, black residents withdrew their objections to construction. In return, the church compensated a black resident living near the site for his property and became more sensitive to the problems of other nearby black residents.[26]

Two years later, in July 1974, Latter-day Saint racial practices were once more the object of non-Mormon criticism. The controversy involved the Boy Scouts of America and the church's long-time nemesis, the National Association for the Advancement of Colored People. The NAACP objected to the leadership structure in Mormon-sponsored Boy Scout troops, which it alleged discriminated against black members of these troups. According to Mormon practice, the senior patrol leader of each Mormon-sponsored troop had to be the president of the Deacon's Quorum in the particular ward to which he belonged. Quite obviously, black members of such Mormon-sponsored Boy Scout troops were not eligible for the position of senior patrol leader. In response, the NAACP filed a suit against the Boy Scouts of America and subpoenaed the president of the Mormon church "to reveal all church policies and practices" concerning the role and place of blacks within the church. The controversy surrounding this particular issue diminished when the Mormons reversed their policy and made black members of Mormon-sponsored Boy Scout troops eligible for the position of senior patrol leader.[27]

During 1974-75, advocates for black rights attacked black priesthood denial and related attitudes from two other directions. The Mormon Tabernacle Choir had to cancel a New England appearance in the fall of 1974 because of objections by black clergymen.[28] In early 1975, Willie Wise, a black professional basketball player with the now defunct American Basketball Association Utah Stars, quit the team, "citing religious attitudes of Mormons toward blacks" as a primary reason for doing so. Wise said he could "never again bring himself to live in Salt Lake City because of . . . the Mormons' attitudes."[29]

In addition to continuing attacks from civil rights activists, black priesthood denial was undermined by criticism from individuals within the church. An early Mormon critic was Dr. Lowry Nelson, a prominent Mormon sociologist who expressed his objection to Mormon antiblack practices in 1947. In a letter to the Church First Presidency, Nelson complained that "the attitude of the Church in regard to the Negro makes me very sad. . . . I do not believe that God is a racist."[30] Five years later Nelson "went public" with his criticisms in an essay published in the *Nation* in 1952. Nelson characterized black priesthood denial an "unfortunate policy" and "a source of embarrassment and humiliation to thousands of" Mormons. Nelson wrote his article "in a spirit of constructive criticism," hoping that the open discussion of the Mormon-black issue within the church would lead to a Mormon environment that would render the offensive practice intolerable.[31] Nelson was significant in that he was the first liberal Mormon critic to come out against Mormon black priesthood denial.

A more prominent Latter-day Saint critic was Sterling M. McMurrin. A professor of philosophy and administrator at the University of Utah, McMurrin served as United States Commissioner of Education during the administration of John F. Kennedy. McMurrin expressed his criticism of Mormon racial practices within the context of the growing civil rights movement throughout the 1960s. Appropriately, McMurrin on several occasions used the Salt Lake chapter of the NAACP as a forum from which to blast Mormon attitudes and practices. McMurrin gave the first of his NAACP speeches in 1960 and followed it up with a second speech three years later, as friction was growing between the Mormon church and the NAACP.[32] By 1965, a critical year for the black civil rights movement in Utah, McMurrin addressed the NAACP a third time. He declared that "time is running out on the Mormon Church to exert any influence or leadership on . . . the greatest moral struggle of our time—civil rights."[33] In 1968 McMurrin delivered what was undoubtedly the most widely publicized of all of his NAACP speeches. He "personally deplore[d] . . . the position of the Church . . . in denying full fellowship to its Negro members" and "the failure of the Church to engage responsibility in the move toward full civil rights for Negroes." As for black priesthood denial, it, according to McMurrin, had "no official status in Mormon Church doctrine."[34] McMurrin warned his fellow Saints that unless the Mormon church "comes to grips" with the race issue it could "completely lose tens of thousands of its members."[35] McMurrin's critical comments were carried by newspapers across the country, calling national attention to Mormon anti-black attitudes and practices.[36]

With the publication of the independent Mormon journal *Dialogue* starting in the spring of 1966, Nelson and McMurrin were joined by other liberal Latter-day Saints critical of prevailing Mormon racial attitudes and practices. One concerned Mormon, writing in *Dialogue*, condemned Los Angeles Mormons for their silence and apparent indifference during the Watts racial disturbances of 1965.[37] In 1968, another Latter-day Saint used *Dialogue* to criticize the limited attention given by church authorities to Martin Luthur King's assassination.[38] Speaking in more general terms, other Mormons condemned what they perceived as a general lack of Mormon concern for civil rights or the problems of black people generally.[39]

By the 1970s there emerged within the church certain dissidents—more militant than Nelson, McMurrin, or the Mormon liberals writing in *Dialogue*— who resorted to confrontation tactics in their efforts to force the church to abandon black priesthood denial. Douglas A. Wallace, a Mormon High Priest and Vancouver, Washington, attorney, was one such individual. In April 1976, Wallace, acting on his own, ordained a black man, Larry Lester, to the Mormon priesthood. While Wallace conceded that he was "stepping outside the bounds of the church" in his action, he said that he hoped that it would "force the issue" of black priesthood denial before the Mormon General Conference meeting in Salt Lake City the following week.[40] At the conference Wallace tried to confront Mormon President Spencer W. Kimball with his complaints. However, Wallace and his two companions were swiftly ejected from the Tabernacle.[41] A few days later, Wallace was excommunicated from the church for "open and deliberate disobedience of the rules and regulations of the church in violation of the outlines of the church."[42] As for the ordination of Larry Lester, it was declared null and void by church officials in Salt Lake City.[43] This did not stop Wallace's actions against the church. Immediately following his excommunication, Wallace sought a rehearing on his ouster, and in October he tried once more to bring the black issue before the Mormon General Conference. Wallace's latter action was deferred by a court order prohibiting him from attending Mormon church conferences. Undaunted, Wallace then filed a counterclaim against the church asking for $200,000 damages.[44] In April 1977, Wallace made a third attempt to appear at the Mormon General Conference in order to protest Mormon antiblack practices. Again, attorneys for the church obtained a temporary restraining order.[45] Wallace promised further protests and legal actions against the Mormon church.[46]

Another militant Mormon dissident who directly confronted the church on the Mormon-black issue was Byron Marchant, a Latter-day Saint Boy Scout leader. Marchant was the scoutmaster of the Mormon Boy Scout troop that was the focal point of the 1974 NAACP controversy over the eligibility of blacks for leadership positions in Mormon-sponsored troops. Even though this issue was settled, Marchant continued to express his opposition to the general practice of Mormon black priesthood denial. Marchant did this by casting a dissenting vote against sustaining Spencer W. Kimball as church president during the Mormon General Conference in October 1977. A few days later Marchant was excommunicated from the church for his conference behavior and open opposition to Mormon racial practices.[47] Despite his excommunication, Marchant staged another protest on Temple Square during the Mormon General Conference in April 1978. Even though Marchant was arrested for trespassing on church property, he filed a civil suit against Spencer W. Kimball and promised to organize and stage a protest march on Temple Square during the next Mormon General Conference in October 1978.[48]

While dissidents within the church called attention to Mormon black priesthood denial, the emergence of several Latter-day Saints as national political figures helped to further publicize this practice, thus tarnishing an otherwise favorable image that the church had within the larger non-Mormon American society.[49] George Romney, an active and devout Latter-day Saint, was well aware of the perils fraught in the Mormon-black issue at the time he decided to seek the governorship of Michigan in 1962. These perils were bound up in the realities of Michigan's large black constituency. Romney was afraid that the Mormon-black issue would damage his own chances for election. At the same time he did not want to see his candidacy "put intense heat on his church's racial practices."[50] In order to avoid these two possibilities, Romney declared his "political independence" from Mormon racial practices and made it clear that "Mormonism's anti-Negro bias would not alter" his own pro-civil rights attitudes.[51] Romney was successful in his election. During his three terms as governor, Romney assumed a strong pro-civil rights position that enabled him to "neutralize" the fact that he belonged to a church that discriminated against its black members. In fact, Romney managed to pick up an increasing percentage of Michigan's black vote in each of his three gubernatorial campaigns.[52]

Romney, however, was less successful in minimizing the impact of the Mormon-black issue as he emerged as a Republican presidential possibility during the period from 1963 to 1968. The national media tended to overlook his favorable civil rights record in Michigan and, instead, focused on the antiblack practices of his church. Magazines such as *Time, Newsweek,* The *Nation,* and *Look* featured articles on the Mormon black priesthood question throughout this five-year period.[53] As early as 1964, Romney found himself under fire for the position of his church on the race issue.[54] By the time that Romney emerged as a leading Republican contender in late 1967 and early 1968, he was forced more and more to answer for his church's practice of denying blacks the priesthood.[55] According to *Look,* Romney's critics "narrowed their darts at Mormon attitudes on Negroes."[56] Although the Mormon-black issue has generally been discounted as a factor in the collapse of the Michigan governor's presidential campaign, Romney's emergence as a national political figure nevertheless exposed this controversial issue to an ever larger number of Americans.[57]

In addition to Romney, the emergence of the Udall brothers, Stewart and Morris, as national political figures, helped to further publicize the Mormon-black issue. Although the Udalls were descended from a pioneer Arizona Mormon family, they were not active, practicing Latter-day Saints. Nevertheless, they were identified with the Latter-day Saints and their racial practices. In fact, Stewart Udall himself brought the issue of Mormon black priesthood denial into the national spotlight in 1967 during his tenure as secretary of interior under Lyndon Johnson. Writing as a concerned Mormon in *Dialogue*, Udall condemned Mormon black priesthood denial as "a social and institutional practice having no real sanction in essential Mormon thought." Udall explained that the "church teaches that the day will come when the Negro will be given full fellowship." "Surely," concluded Udall, "that day has come."[58] Udall's comments were widely publicized, but were also criticized by practicing Mormons who felt that Udall as a lapsed or "Jack Mormon" had no right to criticize Latter-day Saint racial practices.[59] In addition, certain backers of George Romney's 1968 presidential bid felt that the remarks of Udall, a Democrat, were designed to undercut the candidacy of Romney, a Republican.[60]

Nine years later, the presidential candidacy of Morris Udall, Stewart's younger brother, brought the Mormon-black issue once more into the national political arena. Ironically, the setting was George Romney's home state of Michigan. This took place during the 1976 Michigan Democratic presidential primary, which pitted Udall against Jimmy Carter. One of Carter's black Michigan backers, Mayor Coleman A. Young of Detroit, linked Udall's Latter-day Saint affiliation, nominal as it was, to Mormon black priesthood denial. Before a group of black Baptist ministers, Young characterized Udall as a man belonging to a church that "won't even let you in the back door."[61] Young's attempt to exploit the Mormon-black issue to Udall's disadvantage probably did not make much difference one way or the other in Udall's floundering efforts to secure the Democratic presidential nomination.[62] However, the projection of this issue, once more into the national political arena, took away from the generally positive image that the public relations-minded Saints were trying to project before non-Mormon Americans during the 1970s.

Of crucial importance in undermining Mormon black priesthood denial was the dramatic growth of Mormonism abroad, particularly in the non-white regions of Asia, the South Pacific, and especially Latin America. By the late 1970s the total church membership of Asia and the South Pacific equaled that of the British Isles and Europe, the former strongholds of Mormon missionary success during the nineteenth century. More important, church membership totals for Latin America were double those of the British Isles and Europe.[63] This diversification of Mormonism's racial-ethnic composition helped to undermine those traditional Mormon white ethnocentric ideas and concepts that had been used not only to justify black priesthood denial but also to rationalize the earlier failure of Mormon missionary success among nonwhite peoples during the nineteenth and early twentieth centuries.

As Mormonism expanded into these nonwhite regions, the church confronted two Mormon-black problems that ultimately helped to undermine black priesthood denial. These included (1) the status of those Mormons of mixed-African ancestry, e.g., eligibility for the priesthood and for temple ordinances, and (2) the question of whether or not to send church missionaries to preach among people of known black African ancestry.

Mormon Church officials in the South Pacific confronted both of these problems during the 1930s and 1940s. In Hawaii, it was disclosed in 1932 that a man of African descent had been ordained to the priesthood and had, in fact, "presided for some time over a branch of the church until it was discovered he was a Negro instead of a dark-skinned Hawaiian."[64] Four years later, Hawaii was again the scene of a similar problem. Two Mormon priesthood holders were found to be "one-eighth negro." This situation was further complicated because these two individuals had performed "some baptisms and other ordinances." They were apparently told to stop exercising their priesthood authority. Apostle George Albert Smith was then sent to

Hawaii to determine the number of people involved in the oridnances performed by these black priesthood holders and the action to be taken.[65] In
1947, the president of the New Zealand mission noted a similar problem
where in "an instance or two . . . men with a trace of Negro blood were ordained to the priesthood." He asked church leaders what should be done
about these individuals and whether a person with "colored blood in his
veins may receive the Priesthood." The New Zealand mission president was
told that no one "known to have Negro blood in his veins . . . should be ordained to the Priesthood." Also those Mormons of African descent mis-
takenly ordained were "instructed not to attempt to use the Priesthood in
any other ordinations."[66] A year later, another facet of the Mormon-black
issue in the South Pacific came up in conjunction with the problem of "de-
ciding who was to be admitted" into the Hawaiian temple from that region's
"melting pot population." Church leaders were afraid that this problem
would "increase" in Hawaii and also affect the church in New Zealand,
once the temple in that country was completed.[67]

Latter-day Saint leaders considered carrying the message of Mormonism
to the residents of black Africa, during the post-World War II period. The
initiative for Mormon missionary activity in this region originated not in
Salt Lake City, but in Nigeria. A Nigerian citizen, one O. J. Umordak of the
Uyo District, somehow heard about Mormonism. In 1946 he wrote the
president of the LDS South African mission asking that Mormon literature
and missionaries be sent. The church leadership in Salt Lake City delayed
their response until they could "give the matter further consideration."
Undaunted, Umordak renewed his request the following year. Again, church
leaders decided to postpone their answer until the question received further
study.[68] Finally, in 1959, Utah Mormon leaders dispatched the requested
Mormon tracts along with a duly appointed church representative from
Salt Lake City.[69] Four years later, after further study, the church decided
"to open missionary work" in this black African nation. Five missionaries
under the leadership of Elder LaMar S. Williams were set apart for this
purpose.[70] In administering this mission, the church made tentative plans
to set up a large number of Sunday schools headed by Nigerians. White missionaries would travel from congregation to congregation to teach and ad-
minister the sacrament. In addition, Mormon Church officials planned to
build churches, schools, and small hospitals.[71] The 1963 decision to establish a black Nigerian mission represented a revolutionary departure from

the long-established church practice of avoiding active proselytising among black people.

The Mormons, however, never had the opportunity to establish this black African mission. In March 1963, the Nigerian government, through a strongly worded editorial in the *Nigerian Outlook,* became aware of black priesthood denial and related racist concepts.[72] As a result, the Nigerian government denied resident visas to the Mormon missionaries. Despite repeated Mormon efforts, over the next three years, the Nigerians remained firm in their refusal to grant resident visas to the Utah Saints.[73] In addition, the possibility of any further Mormon activity in Nigeria was effectively precluded by the outbreak of civil war in Biafra during the late 1960s. In summary, the Nigerian experience, besides being a dramatic departure from established Mormon missionary practices, represented a lost opportunity for the missionary-minded Saints. "Some five thousand [Nigerian people] applied for baptism" into Mormonism according to Apostle Hugh B. Brown.[74] But because of Mormon black priesthood denial the church lost out on this opportunity to capitalize on widespread Nigerian interest in Mormonism.

More important than the lost Nigerian opportunity was the expansion of Mormonism into Latin America, a development that further eroded the narrow white ethnic basis for Mormon black priesthood denial. During the mid-1940s, Latter-day Saint officials looked into the possibility of beginning missionary work in Cuba. Church officials were concerned about reports of widespread racial intermixture between the white, black African, and native Indian population. They commissioned Lowry Nelson, a noted sociologist and Mormon, to investigate this situation. Nelson was instructed to find out if there were "groups [with] pure white blood in the rural sections." Nelson's investigations disclosed that in rural Cuban communities "there was no segregation of the races" and therefore it was "difficult to find . . . groups of pure white people."[75] As a result, church leaders decided not to pursue missionary activity in Cuba.

The Mormons followed a different path in Brazil, another Latin American nation with a high degree of racial intermixture. At first the church focused its missionary efforts on Brazil's large German immigrant population. This changed after World War II, as the church attracted a large number of new converts from Brazil's Portuguese-speaking native population. This shifting missionary focus sparked a 1947 Church First Presidency investigation which found "the races . . . badly mixed" because "no color line is drawn among the mass of the people." It concluded that "a great part of the population of Brazil is colored."[76] Later that same year J. Reuben Clark, a member of the Church First Presidency, referred again to the Brazilian situation, noting that "it is very difficult if not impossible to tell who has negro blood and who has not." He admitted," if we are baptizing Brazilians, we are almost certainly baptizing people of negro blood, and that if the Priesthood is conferred upon them, which no doubt it is, we are facing a very serious problem."[77]

Unlike in Cuba, missionary work in Brazil was not aborted. In fact the conversion of Brazilians to Mormonism increased dramatically during the 1950s and 1960s even though church members of mixed-black ethnic origins were apparently being ordained to the priesthood.[78] The Brazilian situation took on added significance during the mid-1970s, when the church unveiled plans to build a new temple in São Paulo, Brazil. The expected completion of the Brazilian Temple in the fall of 1978 brought to a head the "major problem" and "often impossible" task of determining which Brazilian "Church members have black ancestry" and which do not.[79]

Although the evolution of Mormonism into a worldwide, multiethnic religion was of crucial importance in eroding the narrow white ethnic basis of Mormon black priesthood denial, other developments also helped to undermine this offensive practice. One of these involved the scholarly examination of the historical roots of black priesthood denial and related racist concepts in light of the so-called new Mormon History. This new scholarship produced by writers both within and outside the Latter-day Saint faith, represented an effort to carefully reexamine the Mormon past in a scholarly and nonpolemical manner, utilizing the latest historical techniques. It differed from traditional Mormon history in that most of its practitioners tried to avoid taking either a definite "pro" or "anti" position in interpreting events in the Latter-day Saint past.[80]

This "new Mormon History" was utilized in a number of studies that examined the origins of Mormon black priesthood denial and related racist attitudes. As early as 1954 L. H. Kirkpatrick, the director of the University of Utah library, maintained in a pioneering article that the origins of Mormon black priesthood denial could be traced to Mormon-anti-Mormon conflicts in the slave state of Missouri during the 1830s.[81] Kirkpatrick's "Missouri thesis" suggested that those Latter-day Saints who had migrated to this slaveholding state from the nonslave states of Ohio, New York, and

New England were anxious to prevent further misunderstanding on the issues of race and slavery and therefore adopted a proslavery and antiblack position, including black priesthood denial.[82] Other scholars tending to subscribe to this "Missouri thesis" included Jan Shipps, Naomi Woodbury, Stephen L. Taggart, and Dennis L. Lythgoe.[83] Woodbury's work was particularly interesting in that she argued that Mormon antiblack practices and attitudes during the 1830s were primarily the product of general antiblack and proslavery rhetoric that was so much a part of antebellum American thought.[84] However, the most prominent work linking black Mormon priesthood denial to church difficulties in Missouri during the 1830s was Taggart's *Mormonism's Negro Policy: Social and Historical Origins,* a work currently in its third printing.[85] All of these works utilizing the "Missouri thesis" were significant in that they related the origins of Mormon black priesthood denial to the larger sociohistorical environment in which Mormonism developed. In doing this, these works helped to strip away the religious myth and mystery surrounding this practice, thus undermining its doctrinal legitimacy.

The historical justification for black priesthood denial was dealt an even more telling blow by two seminal articles written by Lester E. Bush, Jr., for *Dialogue* during the early 1970s.[86] Bush, like those scholars subscribing to the "Missouri thesis," felt that the origins of Mormon black priesthood denial could be explained by considering Mormonism within the sociohistorical context of nineteenth-century American society. Unlike the "Missouri thesis" proponents, however, Bush's landmark articles rejected outright the view that black priesthood denial was a response to Mormon Missouri difficulties during the 1830s. In fact, Bush presented carefully documented evidence indicating that church officials did not even implement black priesthood denial until the late 1840s, following the death of Joseph Smith. Bush's convincing dismissal of Smith as the initiator of black priesthood denial was significant in that it demolished a historical myth that most Mormons had accepted since the 1870s, and thus further undermined the historical justification for this practice.[87] In addition, Bush's 1973 *Dialogue* article, by tracing the often contradictory twists and turns that Mormon black priesthood denial and related racist concepts took from the days of Brigham Young until the 1970s, brought into question not only the historical roots but also the ethical and moral basis upon which Mormon black priesthood denial rested.[88]

Mormon black priesthood denial was further undermined by the work of a second group of scholars, who questioned the legitimacy of the scriptural writings upon which this practice was based. The *Pearl of Great Price*, particularly the book of Abraham, had been utilized as a scriptural instrument to justify Mormon antiblack practices during the late nineteenth and early twentieth centuries. However, by the late 1960s certain scholars questioned the authenticity of the Book of Abraham as an ancient document. In 1968, fragments of the Egyptian papyri from which Joseph Smith had allegedly translated the Book of Abraham were rediscovered after being lost for over a century. These rediscovered papyri were then deciphered by Egyptologists who found that they did not even remotely resemble the Book of Abraham.[89] This discrepancy distressed certain Egyptologists within the church. One such individual was Dee Jay Nelson, who was asked by church officials to translate the papyri. When Nelson's translation did not square with the Book of Abraham, church officials apparently tried to supress his findings. This so distressed Nelson that he left the church.[90] Richard P. Howard, Church historian for the rival Reorganized Church, concluded that the Book of Abraham was "simply the product of Joseph Smith Jr.'s imagination."[91] While such findings failed to shake the beliefs of most Latter-day Saints in the scriptural legitimacy of the Book of Abraham, these findings apparently influenced Mormon leaders speaking in an "official" capacity on the Mormon black issue. These church spokesmen moved away from earlier practices of using the Book of Abraham as a scriptural instrument justifying black priesthood denial.[92] As a result, by the 1970s the practice of black priesthood denial no longer rested on the scriptural foundation of the Book of Abraham, which had provided the initial theological basis and later scriptural justification for this practice during the nineteenth and early twentieth centuries.

In light of the findings of Egyptologists, the "new Mormon history," the emergence of Mormon politicians seeking national office, critics within the church, the growing civil rights movement, and most important, the international expansion of Mormonism into nonwhite regions, it is not surprising that the church became more and more flexible in its policies and practices toward black people. This flexibility, which increased in tempo during the thirty-year period following World War II, ultimately resulted in the abandonment of black priesthood denial in June 1978. During the

mid-1960s Latter-day Saint leaders as well as most of the rank-and-file
membership accepted the basic concept of full civil rights for blacks within the United States. Abroad, the church demonstrated flexibility in its
willingness to overlook or ignore the possibility of black racial intermixture among its Brazilian members. The proposed Nigerian mission, despite
its failure to get off the ground, dramatized a Mormon willingness to abandon the long-established church practice of avoiding missionary contact
with people of African descent. In the South Pacific during the mid-1950s
the church initiated missionary work among the dark-skinned, "African-
like" Melanesians of Fiji.[93] In fact, in 1963 rumors circulated that the
"top leadership" of the church was "seriously considering abandonment
of its historic policy of discriminating against Negroes."[94] According to
Apostle Hugh B. Brown, the church was in the midst of a survey "looking
toward the possibility of admitting Negroes" to the Mormon priesthood.[95]

Even though these rumors proved premature, Mormon leaders continued
to demonstrate flexibility on various matters affecting black people. In
1965, the *Christian Century* suggested that the Saints were engaged in
"somewhat of a campaign to get some Negroes into the church."[96] By 1971,
room was made in the famed Mormon Tabernacle Choir for three blacks.[97]
Also, in that same year, Latter-day Saint leaders formulated the "Genesis
group." This organization or "special meeting" was designed to serve the
needs of the estimated two hundred black Latter-day Saints living in and
around Salt Lake City.[98] At the same time Latter-day Saint leaders organized a special committee consisting of three apostles, headed by Gordon
B. Hinkley, "charged with dealing with the Church's Negro problem."[99]

The Mormon church-owned Brigham Young University also demon-
strated flexibility in its racial policies and practices during the early to middle
1970s. Hoping to defuse the anti-Mormon, problack athletic protests that
had plagued the school during the late 1960s, B.Y.U. students, under the
leadership of Brian Walton, student body president, established communica-
tions and dialogue with black representatives from other schools with whom
B.Y.U. had athletic relations.[100] B.Y.U. also launched a campaign to recruit
blacks for their athletic teams and by 1974 had acquired the services of
blacks on both their football and basketball teams.[101] B.Y.U. also placed
a black woman, Wynetta Martin, on its College of Nursing faculty to teach
students about "the culture of the Negro."[102] In 1976, B.Y.U. students
elected a black man, Robert Lee Stevenson, to be their student body vice

president. This development was cited by the *New York Times* as "evidence of changing attitudes at B.Y.U. and among Mormons generally."[103]

The doctrinal basis of black priesthood denial was undermined by Mormon church leaders, who avoided using the *Pearl of Great Price* as a scriptural instrument to justify this practice. This doctrinal basis was further eroded by the public disclosure in late 1969 and early 1970 of a private conversation some years before between President David O. McKay and Sterling M. McMurrin. During the course of this conversation McKay deemphasized the theological basis of black priesthood denial, explaining, "We believe that we have scriptural precedent for withholding the priesthood from the Negro, it is a practice, not a doctrine, and the practice will someday be changed. And that is all there is to it."[104] At about the same time, Apostle Hugh B. Brown expected the Mormon ban on priesthood ordination to ease.[105] Even the official 1969 church affirmation of black priesthood denial betrayed signs of Mormon flexibility. This statement, while declaring that blacks "were not yet to receive the priesthood," promised that "sometime in God's eternal plan" blacks would "be given the right to hold the priesthood."[106]

One additional development, the emergence of Spencer W. Kimball as president of the Mormon church, provided the final catalyst for the abolition of black priesthood denial. Long before he was installed as church president in late 1973, Kimball had been concerned about the Mormon practice of denying blacks the priesthood. As an apostle during the 1950s Kimball had had the opportunity to travel throughout Latin America, monitoring Mormon activity in this region. Thus, he was aware of the problems and restrictions created by black priesthood denial. This practice was at variance with Kimball's basic desire to have the message of Mormonism carried to all races, colors, and creeds. While the ascension of Kimball to the church presidency did not in and of itself make the repeal of black priesthood denial inevitable, the emergence of this missionary-minded leader during a time when Mormonism was rapidly growing as a worldwide religion helped to make the abandonment of this restrictive practice a logical development.[107]

The abandonment of black priesthood denial marked the end of one era of Mormon-black relations and the beginning of another. It is obviously much too early to assess the relative impact of this decision. However, on an immediate basis, Spencer W. Kimball and other Mormon leaders have done several things to assure blacks the same status as all other ethnic groups within Mormonism. First, those relatively few blacks who presently belong to the church have been integrated into the mainstream of Mormon church activity. Just two days after the historic announcement lifting the ban on black priesthood ordination, Joseph Freeman, Jr., became the "first" Mormon of African descent to receive the Mormon priesthood. Numerous other black Mormons have been ordained since that date.[108] By September 1978, the church had started to call upon blacks to serve in the church's ever expanding missionary program; and by December of that same year the first black was called to serve in a stake presidency. Helvecio Martins was sustained as a second counselor in the Rio de Janeiro, Brazil, Niteroi Stake.[109] In addition, President Kimball announced in June 1978 that the church would extend its missionary work into the black "inner cities" of the United States and into black Africa.[110] By October 1978, church officials announced the appointment of two couples to serve as representatives of the church's international mission in Nigeria.[111] A year later church leaders noted the extent to which Mormonism had spread in both Nigeria and Ghana.[112] Also in 1979, President Kimball extolled the general appeal of Mormonism to blacks living both in America and abroad.[113]

By 1980, as the Mormons celebrated their 150th anniversary, it was evident that they had come full circle in their basic attitudes and treatment of blacks and other nonwhite ethnic groups. During the 1830s, the early Saints had manifested a universalistic desire to carry the message of Mormonism to all peoples. According to the *Book of Mormon,* the Lord "denieth none that came unto him, black and white, bond and free, male and female; and he remembereth the heathen: and all are alike unto God, both Jews and Gentile."[114] By the mid-nineteenth century this had all changed as church leaders became more Old Testament-like and particularistic in their attitudes and practices. As a result, the church focused its missionary efforts almost exclusively on those individuals of white European ancestry. At the same time, nonwhites of non-European ancestry were shunned and considered less than worthy candidates for the true faith, with blacks considered the least worthy. Today, Latter-day Saint leaders are once more promoting Mormonism as a universalistic religion designed for *all* races, colors, and nationalities. There are, however, a number of questions remaining, which only time will answer. What will be the long-range impact of this decision on blacks, both within and outside the church? More specifically, how will this decision affect the status of Utah's small but growing black population? Outside of Utah, how will white middle-class American Mormons interact with lower-class blacks as Mormonism attempts to expand into America's "inner cities"? Abroad, how will South African and Rhodesian (Zimbabwe) Mormons of European descent get along with Mormons from black Africa as Mormonism expands into these regions? These and other questions will make this new era of Mormon black relations a most interesting one to follow in the years to come.

NOTES

1. The official directive was actually dated 8 June, but was not made public to the news media until the following day. Its contents were printed in the *Deseret News* (Salt Lake City), 9 June 1978, and *Salt Lake Tribune*, 10 June 1978. See Appendix D for the complete text of this directive.

2. A term used by Mario S. De Pillis in the *New York Times,* 11 June 1978.

3. See Ronald G. Coleman, "Blacks in Utah History: An Unknown Legacy" in *The Peoples of Utah* (Salt Lake City, 1976), ed. Helen Papanikolas, pp. 135-40, for a description of the unfavorable situation of blacks in Utah during this period; and Gerald D. Nash, *The American West in the Twentieth Century* (Englewood Cliffs, New Jersey, 1973), pp. 220, 286-88, for a brief description of the situation of blacks in the West generally.

4. Margaret Judy Maag, "Discrimination Against the Negro in Utah and Institutional Efforts to Eliminate It" (M.S. thesis, University of Utah, 1971), p. 64.

5. Coleman, "Blacks in Utah History," p. 138.

6. Maag, "Discrimination Against the Negro in Utah . . . ," pp. 42,72.

7. Coleman, "Blacks in Utah History," p. 138.

8. This according to Margaret J. Maag, "Discrimination Against the Negro in Utah," pp. 29, 58. These findings were similar to those earlier outlined in Wallace R. Bennett, "The Negro in Utah," *Utah Law Review* 3 (1953): 340-48.

9. *Time* 13 April 1959.

10. Maag, "Discrimination Against the Negro in Utah. . . ," 66; *Salt Lake Tribune*, 13 March, 1 April 1960; 3 April, 6 May 1962.

11. *Salt Lake Tribune,* 10, 12 March, 24 April 1963.

12. *Christian Century,* 29 September 1965; *New York Times,* 6 October 1963.

13. *New York Times,* 1, 7 October 1963; *Salt Lake Tribune,* 4, 5, 6 October 1963; *Deseret News,* 6 October 1963. See Sterling M. McMurrin, "A Note on the 1963 Civil Rights Statement," *Dialogue* 12 (Summer 1979): 60-63. According to Lester E. Bush, Jr., McMurrin himself wrote the 1963 Civil Rights Statement. (Lester E. Bush, Jr. to Newell G. Bringhurst, 17 May 1980, original in possession of author).

14. Although the NAACP condemned Governor Clyde, a practicing Mormon, for his inaction in civil rights in December 1963. See *Salt Lake Tribune,* 5 December 1963.

15. *Christian Century,* 29 September 1965.

16. *Salt Lake Tribune,* 7, 8, 9, 10 March 1965; *New York Times,* 10 March 1965.

17. *Deseret News,* 9 March 1965.

18. *Christian Century,* 29 September 1965.

19. However, civil rights criticisms continued on a rhetorical level from 1966 to 1968. See *Deseret News,* 3 May 1966; *Salt Lake Tribune,* 4 May, 14 July 1966; 11 May 1968.

20. *New York Times,* 13 April, 1968; *Fort Myers* (Florida) *News Press,* 14 April 1968; *Arizona Daily Star,* 14 April 1968.

21. *New York Times,* 1, 6, December 1968.

22. *Salt Lake Tribune,* 30 November 1969; 4, 6, 16, 27, February 1970; 7 March 1970.

23. Ibid., 25 October 1969; *New York Times,* 15 November 1969.

24. *Salt Lake Tribune,* 13 November 1969; *Deseret News,* 9, 10 March 1970.

25. *Sports Illustrated,* 26 January 1970.

26. *New York Times,* 12 October 1972; 15, 21 December 1972.

27. Ibid., 28 July, 3, 29 August, 24 October 1974; *Christianity Today,* 22 November 1974.

28. *Christianity Today,* 22 November 1974.

29. *San Jose Morning News,* 26 January 1975; *San Francisco Chronicle,* 21 January 1975. Such a view should be "balanced off" against the less pessimistic position of another black living in Utah. See Sandra Haggerty, "Mormons and Black Folks," a syndicated article from the *Los Angeles Times* reprinted in the *Pacific Stars & Stripes,* 8 July 1974.

30. Lowry Nelson to Church First Presidency, 26 June 1947, as reprinted in Jerald and Sandra Tanner, *Mormons and Negroes* (Salt Lake City, 1970), 28.

31. *Nation,* 24 May 1952.

32. *Salt Lake Tribune,* 13 March 1960, 21 January 1963.

33. *Chicago Sun-Times,* 5 April 1965.

34. Sterling M. McMurrin, "The Negroes Among the Mormons," speech given 21 June 1968. Reprinted by Salt Lake Chapter of the NAACP, 1968. For a good analysis of this speech and the publicity surrounding it, see Douglas M. Trank, "The Negro and the Mormons: A Church in Conflict," *Western Speech* 35 (Fall 1971): 220-30.

35. Ibid., pp. 223-25.

36. For a list of the various newspapers covering the speech see Trank, "The Negro and the Mormons," pp. 226-27.

37. *Dialogue* 1 (Spring 1966): 162.

38. Ibid., 3 (Summer 1968): 5-7.

39. Ibid., 1 (Summer 1966): 6-7, 72-79.

40. *Oregonian*, 3 April 1976; *Idaho Statesman*, 3 April 1976; *Salt Lake Tribune*, 3 April 1976.

41. *Deseret News*, 6 April 1976; *Idaho Statesman*, 10 April 1976.

42. *Deseret News*, 12 April 1976; *Idaho Statesman*, 13 April 1976.

43. *Deseret News*, 3 April 1976.

44. *Idaho Statesman*, 20 April, 6 October 1976.

45. *Salt Lake Tribune*, 5 April 1978.

46. Ibid., 17 September 1977, 18 January 1978.

47. *Indianapolis Star*, 16 October 1977.

48. See Byron Marchant, "A Delayed Invitation," 1978 handout (copy in LDS Church Historical Department); *Salt Lake Tribune*, 3 April 1978, 10 June 1978.

49. For a discussion of the image of the Saints as perceived by non-Mormons see Dennis L. Lythgoe, "The Changing Image of Mormonism," *Dialogue* 3 (Winter 1968): 45-58.

50. *New York Times*, 27 November 1967. According to the *Times*, Romney traveled to Utah in order to warn LDS church leaders of this fact. At least one church leader, Joseph Fielding Smith, had reservations about Romney's decision to enter politics, warning that the "enemies" of the church would "play up the Negro question to the very limit," *Deseret News*, 14 July 1962, reprinted in *Look*, 22 October 1963.

51. *New York Times*, 26 November 1967; *Nation*, 6 April 1963.

52. According to one account, Romney's percentage of the black vote in Michigan had increased to 35 percent by the time of his third race for governor. See Dennis L. Lythgoe, "The 1968 Presidential Decline of George Romney; Mormonism or Politics?" *Brigham Young University Studies* 11 (Spring 1971): 232. Also see T. George Harris, *Romney's Way: A Man and an Idea* (New York, 1967), pp. 6, 9; Clark R. Mollenhoff, *George Romney: Mormon in Politics* (New York, 1968), pp. 186, 189; Richard C. Fuller, *George Romney and Michigan* (New York, 1966), pp. 69-74, 112-13.

53. *Time*, 18 October 1963; *Newsweek*, 17 June 1963, 6 March 1967; *Nation*, 6 April 1963; *Look*, 22 October 1963; 7 February 1967.

54. *Salt Lake Tribune*, 7, 8 January 1964.

55. *New York Times*, 24 January 1967, 21 February 1967, 19 May 1967, 26 September 1967, 1 October 1967. Even Romney's wife was called to account for Mormon antiblack practices. See *New York Times*, 24 January 1967, 19 May 1967.

56. *Look*, 7 February 1967.

57. See Dennis L. Lythgoe, "The 1968 Presidential Decline of George Romney," pp. 219-40. Two other scholars who discussed Romney and his role in the 1968 campaign did not even mention the Mormon-black issue as a factor in Romney's declining fortunes. See Theodore H. White, *The Making of the President 1968* (New York, 1969), pp. 36-41, 54-61; Lewis Chester, Godfey Hodgson, and Brice Page, *An American Melodrama: The Presidential Campaign of 1968*, (New York, 1969), pp. 91, 98, 112-14.

58. *Dialogue* 2 (Summer 1967): 5-7.

59. *Dialogue* 3 (Fall 1967): 7-9; (Winter): 5-7.

60. *New York Times*, 19 May 1967.

61. *Boise Statesman*, 16, 18 May 1976; *Las Vegas Sun*, 28 May 1976.

62. As pointed out in Jules Witcover, *Marathon: The Pursuit of the Presidency 1972-1976* (New York, 1977).

63. See "Summary of Church Membership as of January 1, 1976," *1978 Church Almanac* (Salt Lake City, 1978), pp. 242-44.

64. Postscript to a letter addressed to Bishop John Wells, 28 January 1932, Adam S. Bennion Papers, Harold B. Lee Library, Brigham Young University.

65. Council Meeting, 29 October 1936, Adam S. Bennion Papers.

66. Council Meeting minutes, 30 January 1947, Adam S. Bennion Papers.

67. "Interview with FB," 21 August 1966, Lester E. Bush, "Compilation on the Negro in Mormonism," unpublished, LDS Church Archives.

68. Council Meeting, 24 October 1946, Council Meeting minutes, 9 October 1947, Adam S. Bennion Papers.

69. *Time*, 18 June 1965.

70. *Deseret News*, 11 January 1963.

71. Account of Lamar S. Williams given to Lester E. Bush, Jr., 26 November 1968, contained in Bush, "Compilation on the Negro in Mormonism," pp. 365-66.

72. *Nigerian Outlook*, 5 March 1963.

73. *Time*, 18 June 1965. For a good collection of source materials dealing with the Nigerian Mission see Lester E. Bush, Jr., "Compilation on the Negro in Mormonism," pp. 360-68.

74. Bush, "Compilation on the Negro in Mormonism," pp. 366-67.

75. Unnamed Mission President to Lowry Nelson, 20 June 1947, as quoted in Jerald and Sandra Tanner, *Mormons and Negroes,* pp. 27-28.

76. First Presidency to Francis W. Brown, 13 January 1947, Adam S. Bennion Papers.

77. Council Meeting minutes, 9 October 1947, Adam S. Bennion Papers.

78. *Dialogue* 2 (Autumn 1967): 8; Wallace Turner, *The Mormon Establishment* (New York, 1966), p. 261.

79. *Deseret News,* 10 June 1978.

80. For a discussion of this development see: Robert Flanders, "Some Reflections on the New Mormon History," *Dialogue* 9 (Spring 1974): 34-41.

81. L. H. Kirkpatrick, "The Negro and the L.D.S. Church," *Pen* (1954): 12-13, 29. It should be pointed out, however, that Fawn M. Brodie postulated this concept as early as 1944 in her *No Man Knows My History* 2d ed. (New York, 1971), and Sterling M. McMurrin gave it further publicity during the 1950s and 1960s.

82. L. H. Kirkpatrick, "The Negro and the L.D.S. Church," pp. 12-13, 29.

83. Jan Shipps, "Second Class Saints," *Colorado Quarterly* 11 (1962-63): 183-90; Naomi Woodbury, "A Legacy of Intolerance: Nineteenth Century Pro-Slavery Propaganda and the Mormon Church Today" (M.A. thesis, University of California, Los Angeles, 1966); Stephen L. Taggart, *Mormonism's Negro Policy: Social and Historical Origins* (Salt Lake City, 1970). Dennis L. Lythgoe could also be included in the category of those scholars subscribing to the "Missouri Thesis" in light of his "Negro Slavery and Mormon Doctrine" article, which was published in 1967. However, by the time he wrote "Negro Slavery in Utah" in 1971, he seemed to have moved toward an acceptance of the idea that the Utah experience, more than the Missouri difficulties, was crucial in shaping Mormon antiblack attitudes.

84. Woodbury, "A Legacy of Intolerance."

85. Taggart, *Mormonism's Negro Policy.*

86. See his "A Commentary on Stephen G. Taggart's *Mormonism's Negro Policy: Social and Historical Origins,"* *Dialogue* 4 (Winter 1969) and his "Mormonism's Negro Doctrine: An Historical Overview," *Dialogue* 8 (Spring 1973).

87. Although Ronald K. Esplin in "Brigham Young and Priesthood Denial to the Blacks: An Alternative View," *Brigham Young University Studies* 19 (Spring 1979): 394-402, adheres to the traditional view that Joseph Smith probably implemented black priesthood denial.

88. Bush, "Mormonism's Negro Doctrine."

89. For a discussion of and responses to the findings of these Egyptologists see John A. Wilson, Richard A. Parker, Richard P. Howard, et al., "The Joseph Smith Egyptian Papyri: Translations and Interpretations" a series of articles published in *Dialogue* 3 (Summer 1968), and Klaus Baer, "The Breathing Permit of Hor: A Translation of the Apparent Source of the Book of Abraham" *Dialogue* 3 (Fall 1968).

90. See Dee Jay Nelson, "An Open Letter," 1976 (copy in the LDS Church Historical Library).

91. *New York Times*, 3 May 1970. For the complete text of Howard's critique see his "The 'Book of Abraham' in the light of History and Egyptology," *Courage*, (pilot issue April 1970): 33-47.

92. For a convincing discussion of this development see Lester E. Bush, Jr. "Mormonism's Negro Doctrine," pp. 44-49. Further undermining the scriptural legitimacy of black priesthood denial were the suggestions of Armand L. Mauss that the justification for this practice was strongly rooted in Mormon folklore. See his "Mormonism and the Negro: Faith, Folklore, and Civil Rights," *Dialogue* 4 (Winter 1967).

93. It is interesting to note that during the nineteenth century the Mormons considered the "Figi [*sic*] Islanders" along with the New Zealanders a problem because they were "greatly mixed . . . with the Negroes." See *Juvenile Instructor,* October 1868.

94. *New York Times*, 7 June 1963; *Newsweek*, 17 June 1963. According to the *New York Times*, 28 December 1965, the church as early as 1962 was contemplating a possible change in policy. In fact, as early as 1940, Apostle J. Ruben Clark, Jr., recommended the appointment of a subcommittee to the Council of Twelve to carefully study the black question, "and make some ruling or re-affirm whatever ruling that has been made on this question in the past as to whether or not one drop of negro blood deprives a man of the right to receive the priesthood." See "Council Meeting," 25 January 1940, George Albert Smith Papers, LDS Church Archives.

95. *New York Times*, 7 June 1963. The origins of such rumors are discussed by Wallace Turner in *The Mormon Establishment* (New York, 1965), pp. 218-45.

96. *Christian Century,* 9 June 1965.

97. One of these, Wynetta Willis Martin, discussed her experiences and conversion to Mormonism in her autobiography, *Black Mormon Tells Her Story* (Salt Lake City, 1972).

98. *Deseret News,* 23 October 1971. See also *San Francisco Sunday Examiner and Chronicle,* 24 October 1971; *New York Times,* 6 April 1972. It is interesting to note that the formation of this group received

minimal coverage in the Utah and California newspapers (near large concentrations of Latter-day Saints) while the article in the *Times* was much more extensive and detailed.

99. *New York Times,* 6 April 1972. Included on this committee was Harold B. Lee, who was to become church president in less than a year.

100. For a discussion of this development see Brian Walton "A University's Dilemma: B.Y.U. and Blacks," *Dialogue* 6 (Spring 1971): 31-36. Also see the *Daily Universe* (Provo, Utah), 22 September, 5, 6, 9, 19, 22 October 1970.

101. *Salt Lake Tribune,* 3 February 1970; *The Daily Herald* (Provo, Utah), 16 February 1970; *San Francisco Chronicle,* 17 December 1974.

102. *Daily Universe,* 4 December 1970.

103. *New York Times,* 4 April 1976.

104. *Salt Lake Tribune,* 25 December 1969, reprinted in *New York Times,* 15 January 1970; *Christianity Today,* 13 February 1970.

105. *Salt Lake Tribune,* 25 December 1969.

106. Church First Presidency Statement "to General Authorities, Regional Representatives of the Twelve, Stake Presidents, Mission Presidents, and Bishops," 15 December 1969. For copy of complete text, see Appendix D.

107. The importance of Kimball's personal attitudes and his desire to make Mormonism's expansion a truly universalistic religion through the expansion of Mormon missionary activity throughout the world has been noted by Sterling M. McMurrin. See his comments in the *New York Times,* 18 June 1978. See also Edward L. Kimball and Andrew E. Kimball, Jr., *Spencer W. Kimball* (Salt Lake City, 1978).

108. *Deseret News,* 17 June 1978.

109. Ibid., 16 September, 16 December 1978.

110. Ibid., 13 June 1978.

111. Ibid., 28 October 1978.

112. *Ensign,* March 1980. For two views of recent Mormon activity in black Africa, see: Spencer J. Palmer, "Mormons in West Africa: New Terrain for the Sesquicentennial Church" (Annual Religion Faculty Lecture, Brigham Young University, September 27, 1979); and Newell G. Bringhurst, "Mormonism amongst Blacks in Sub-Sahara Africa: An Historical Overview of Changing Attitudes and Practices, 1830-1981," *Sunstone* 6 (May-June 1981).

113. *New York Times,* 9 June 1979.

114. *Book of Mormon,* 2 Nephi 26:25.

APPENDIX A

Membership Totals and the Shifting Geographic-Ethnic Focus of the Latter-day Saint Movement, 1830-1980

The Mormon church has experienced a number of significant changes in its total membership and its geographic-ethnic focus, which have influenced its shifting attitudes and practices towards black people during the 150 years since its founding in 1830. The church grew in its total membership from six, when it was founded in 1830, to over 4 million by the time of its sesquicentennial in 1980. Despite this impressive growth, the Mormons were, and continue to be, a small minority within American society at large (see table 1). Historically, the Latter-day Saints constituted a minority in those areas where they were most active prior to 1846. For example, during the early 1830s the Mormons in Jackson County, Missouri, constituted 1,200 of the county's total population of 5,500. This situation encouraged Mormon spokesmen to mute their basic antislavery attitudes and become increasingly antiabolitionist during the 1830s. The Mormons continued to be a minority after their 1839 expulsion from Missouri into Illinois and thus felt compelled to adapt to the predominant antislavery attitudes in that nonslaveholding state during the 1840s.

However, following the Mormon migration west after 1846, the Mormons' minority-majority situation was reversed, and by 1870, 95 percent of Utah's total population were Latter-day Saints. Thus, Mormon leaders had greater flexibility in asserting their own unique racist practices, as reflected in a Mormon willingness to legalize their own form of black slavery in 1852. At the same time, the Mormons' relative geographic isolation made it easier for them to cling to certain racist practices and attitudes even as Americans elsewhere were eschewing such practices.

The emergence of Mormonism as a major American religious denomination during the past fifty years (see table 2), however, has made it increasingly difficult for the church to uphold and support its racist ideas and practices, particularly that of black priesthood denial.

Changing Mormon racial attitudes and practices have also been influenced by the shifting geographic-ethnic focus of Mormon missionary activity and church membership. There have been three major shifts during the 150-year period of Mormonism's existence. Initially, Mormon activity was focused in the New England-New York area. The Mormons drew most of their converts from middle-sized communities in New York and New England during the years from 1830 to 1850. Eastern Pennsylvania, Canada, and settled areas in Illinois and the Ohio Valley generally were of significant secondary importance. By contrast, the Saints attracted few converts from the large eastern cities despite vigorous missionary efforts in and near Boston, Philadelphia, and New York City. In addition, the Saints had only limited success in western "frontier" areas and in the South, drawing only a fraction of their membership from these regions. This northern geographic focus of Mormonism made it easier for the Saints to embrace attitudes that were both antislavery and antiabolitionist, both dominant views in the antebellum North.

After 1846, the ethnic-geographic focus of Mormonism entered a second phase as the Saints drastically scaled down their missionary activities within the United States following the Mormon migration west to the Great Basin. In the words of S. George Ellsworth, the "Mormons practically neglected the United States and Canada," concentrating their missionary efforts abroad. The Saints drew the bulk of their new converts from Great Britain and Scandinavia after 1850. Even before this time, the Mormons had converted an impressive number of Englishmen and encouraged a significant number of them to migrate to Nauvoo. The 4,000 Englishmen who settled there contributed to the growth and ethnic composition of this Mormon center. There was an even larger British migration after 1850. With the influx of additional converts from Denmark, Sweden, and Norway, the influence of immigrants on Mormonism became even more pronounced during the next 50 to 60 years (see tables 3 and 4). Therefore, Utah's Mormon population, according to William Mulder, assumed a "decidedly Anglo-Scandinavian" or "Nordic cast." This increased European immigrant thrust of Mormonism after 1840 was dramatized by the fact that the proportion of foreign-born Latter-day Saints was "consistently ahead" of the United States as a whole during the late nineteenth century. According to various estimates, between 9 and 15 percent of America's total population was born abroad during these years. At the same time the percentage of foreign-born Latter-day Saints was between 20 and 35 percent. This strong immigrant orientation tended to influence Latter-day Saint racial attitudes. Like other recently arrived immigrant groups, Saints found themselves questioned as to their basic cultural and ethnic fitness within American society. As a result, the Saints, as other immigrants, were anxious to emphasize their basic white ethnocentrism, while "playing up" the negative racial characteristics of dark-skinned peoples, especially blacks.

Since World War II, Mormonism's ethnic-geographic focus has entered a third phase, as Latter-day Saint missionaries have experienced success in drawing converts from nonwhite, non-European parts of the world. The Mormons have been particularly successful in Latin America, Asia, and the South Pacific. These new converts eclipse those coming from the British Isles, Scandinavia, and Northern Europe, the former centers of Mormon missionary activity (see table 5). Mormon missionary success in these non-European, nonwhite regions made black priesthood denial difficult to maintain and increasingly irrelevant to the Mormon experience.

TABLE 1

Membership of the Church of Jesus Christ of Latter-day Saints Contrasted with American Population at Large, 1830-1980

Year	Total Church Membership[1]	Total American Population
1830	62[2]	12,866,020
1840	30,000	17,069,453
1850	60,000	23,191,876
1860	80,000	31,443,321
1870	110,000	39,818,449
1880	160,000	50,155,783
1890	205,000	62,947,714
1900	268,331	75,994,575
1910	393,437	91,972,266
1920	526,032	105,710,620
1930	627,488	122,775,046
1940	862,664	131,669,275
1950	1,111,314	150,697,361
1960	1,693,180	178,464,236
1970	2,930,810	204,765,770
1980	4,439,000	223,889,000

Sources: Deseret News 1980 Church Almanac (Salt Lake City, 1980), pp. 245-46; S. George Ellsworth, "A History of Mormon Missions in the United States and Canada, 1830-1860 (Ph.D. diss., University of California, 1951), p. 86.

[1] These totals include those Saints abroad as well as within the United States.

[2] Total Church membership by September of that year. By the summer of 1831, between 600 and 800 had joined the new faith.

TABLE 2

**Growth of the Church of Jesus Christ of Latter-day Saints
Compared with Other American Religious Denominations,
1830-1980**
(in thousands)

Group	1830	1880	1930	1980
Catholic	330	5,900	21,000	48,881
Baptist	330	2,350	9,000	26,615
Methodist	500	3,250	7,900	12,755
Lutheran	90	640	4,200	8,247
LATTER-DAY SAINTS*	.062	160	627	4,439
Presbyterian	210	940	2,600	3,810
Episcopalian	40	330	1,200	2,858
United Church of Christ (Congregationalist)	130	380	900	1,801
Christian Church (Disciples of Christ)	25	600	1,500	1,279

Sources: Deseret News 1981 Church Almanac (Salt Lake City, 1981),
pp. 224-26; Edwin Scott Gaustead, *Historical Atlas of
Religion in America* (New York, 1962), pp. 52-53, 110.

*These totals include those Latter-day Saints both within the United
States and abroad.

TABLE 3

British Membership and the Number of British Church Members
Who Migrated to the United States, 1837-1929

Years	Total Number of Baptisms	Emigration to the United States
1837-39	1,517	——
1840-49	34,299	5,784*
1850-59	43,304	12,355
1860-69	16,112	9,924
1870-79	6,295	6,913
1880-89	6,061	8,219
1890-99	3,742	4,849
1900-09	7,587	3,195
1910-19	3,911	892
1920-29	2,349	256

Source: Richard L. Evans, *A Century of Mormonism in Great Britain,* (Salt Lake City, 1937) Appendix, pp. 244-45.

*P.A.M. Taylor in *Expectations Westward: The Mormons and the Emigration of Their British Converts in the Nineteenth Century* (Edinburgh and London, 1965) has estimated that 4,000 British Mormon converts migrated to Nauvoo during the Mormon sojourn there from 1839 to 1846.

TABLE 4

**Scandinavian Membership and the Number of Scandinavian
Saints Who Migrated to the United States, 1850-1904**

Years	Total Number of Baptisms	Emigration to the United States
1850-59	9,117	3,386
1860-69	12,886	8,055
1870-79	9,532	7,021
1880-89	7,878	7,613
1890-99	4,780	3,079
1900-04	2,304	1,289

Source: William Mulder, "Mormons from Scandinavia, 1850-1904"
(Ph.D. diss., Harvard University), p. 214.

TABLE 5

**Latter-day Saints Church Membership outside the
United States (as of January 1, 1980)**

Country or Region	Total Membership
Great Britain	90,854
Scandinavia	19,476
Other Europe	76,803
Canada	82,769
Mexico	231,266
Central America	50,018
South America	316,983
Asia	115,152
South Pacific	133,195
Africa	8,606
Foreign Country Total	1,125,122

Source: "Summary of Church Membership," *Deseret News 1981
Church Almanac* (Salt Lake City, 1981), pp. 229-32.

A Brief Essay on Mormon Socioeconomic Origins and Their Possible Relationship to Latter-day Saint Racial Attitudes

Although a definitive study of Mormon socioeconomic origins would require at least one if not several volumes, I wish here to briefly evaluate a number of existing studies and offer my own tentative views on how Mormon socioeconomic origin influenced Latter-day Saint racial attitudes.

While the geographic-ethnic origins of individual Latter-day Saints can be determined with some degree of precision (as suggested by Appendix A), the same is not true for Mormonism's socioeconomic origins. Since the founding of the Latter-day Saint movement, there have been conflicting views concerning the socioeconomic status of those who joined the church. This conflict started with Joseph Smith himself. Non-Mormons and those negatively disposed toward the Saints maintained that Smith and his family were economically deprived and "marginal" members of society. They suggested that Smith and his family looked to the writing and publication of the *Book of Mormon* as a means to improve their socioeconomic status. On the other hand, Latter-day Saint spokesmen and sympathizers countered that Smith and his family were of average economic means and were socially acceptable members of their community.[1]

The dialogue centering on the socioeconimic status of the Smith family has been expanded into a historical debate over the socioeconomic origins of all those individuals who embraced Mormonism. S. George Ellsworth, a Latter-day Saint and professional historian, in his 1951 study, "A History of Mormon Missions in the United States and Canada 1830-1860," concluded that "in education and occupation the majority of converts were average people of average communities," representing "a fair cross section of American society." Furthermore, he felt that "there was no economic class consciousness in the [Latter-day Saint] movement."[2] Laurence M. Yorgason examined the social and geographical origins of early Mormon converts between 1830 and 1845, and agreed with Ellsworth. According to Yorgason, also a Latter-day Saint, "Mormonism had its roots in the average and unobtrusive segments of society."[3] Yorgason concluded that generally "the wealthy did not flock to Mormonism's message, neither did the very poor nor the transients of society."[4] Mario De Pillis, a non-Mormon scholar also interested in the socioeconomic origins of Latter-day Saint converts, subscribed to a somewhat different view. "All early Mormon converts," explained De Pillis, "came from the lower but not the lowest classes, whether rural or urban in their origins."[5] Concentrating his study on those converts in the United States who joined the church during Mormonism's formative years, De Pillis found that "prospective converts almost always lived under unstable local social, economic, or religious conditions, usually in a newly settled, value disoriented society."[6] De Pillis expanded his analysis to those areas outside of the United States and concluded that in England, Wales, and Scandinavia, "a socially disoriented, evangelical population" was "quite ready to hear the new gospel."[7]

P. A. M. Taylor and William Mulder also dealt with the growth of Mormonism abroad, particularly in Great Britain and Scandinavia. They agreed in certain respects with both the "average" social origin interpretation of Ellsworth and Yorgason and with parts of the "poorer, social dislocation" hypothesis of De Pillis.[8] According to Taylor, the Latter-day Saints scored their greatest success in Great Britain during a time of "great" social and "economic turbulence."[9] The majority of the British converts who first migrated to Mormonism's gathering place during the 1840s and early 1850s were "relatively prosperous," i.e., "the middle-class element and the more substantial working-class converts." But after the mid-1850s, when the church started to provide financial aid to emigrating converts, a larger portion of "poorer" immigrants found their way to Utah.[10] Although William Mulder in his study of Scandinavian Saints did not attempt a systematic analysis of Mormon socioeconimic origins, he found that the majority of those Saints emigrating to America during the 1850s were "small farmers

... freeholders, tenants, or simple journeyman hands."[11] By the 1860s the number of farmers decreased as an increasing number of laborers, plus "artisans, who outnumbered ... unskilled laborers," migrated.[12] According to Mulder, these converts came from those areas in Denmark, Sweden, and Norway where economic and social dissatisfaction were prevalent.[13] Mulder has quoted various contemporary observers both within and outside the church who note Mormonism's appeal "among the poor and most downtrodden classes of mankind."[14] Mulder concludes, "It was precisely the poor and humble the Mormons were after. Poverty and ignorance were ills for which America itself was the remedy, an assurance that was one of Mormonism's enthusiasms."[15]

If all these works were taken collectively, it appears that Mormonism appealed mainly to individuals from middle-class and lower-middle-class social origins and held very little attraction for the upper elements of American or European society. If the findings of De Pillis, Taylor, and Mulder are to be believed, it appears that Mormonism attracted converts during turbulent times and in regions experiencing "social upheaval" or dislocation. Finally, all of these works taken collectively show unmistakenly that, during the fifty-year period from 1830 to 1880, the main source of new Mormon converts shifted from an American rural, small town environment to a European urban setting.[16] Finally, it appears that European Mormon converts who emigrated to the United States during the late nineteenth century came from a lower socioeconomic segment of the population than those who had migrated earlier.

It is difficult to determine the precise relationship between Mormonism's socioeconomic origins and developing Latter-day Saint racial attitudes and practices, particularly as they affected black people. Perhaps some tentative conclusions can be drawn, subject to further investigation. Gordon W. Allport has suggested, without referring directly to the Mormons, that "white people in the lower socio-economic levels are, on the average, more bitterly anti-Negro than white people at the higher levels."[17] Allport and others have suggested that individuals "engaged in farming, or an unskilled occupation," living "on a farm or in a small town" and "fundamentalist" in their religious convictions tend to be the most antiblack.[18] Seymour M. Lipset and Reinhard Bendix suggest that people whose social position changes tend to "conform" to the norms and prejudices of the group or society which they have joined.[19] Thus it is possible that the ever-increasing number of Europeans

who joined the church and migrated to America accepted without question,
and often with enthusiasm, Mormon theories and practices already established (including those adversely affecting black people), as well as the corresponding values of the larger American society. Lipset and Bendix also
suggest that "downward mobile individuals" or groups exhibit a "greater"
degree of ethnic "prejudice" than those moving up or remaining stagnant.[20]
Mormonism as an institution apparently experienced "downward mobility."
After 1855 the church incorporated an ever-increasing number of "lower-
class" Europeans into their midst. Also, the aggregate number of individuals
who joined the church and migrated to Utah declined in the period after
1860. Thus the church suffered a decline in quantity corresponding with
the decline in "quality." In addition, the church itself suffered from the
effects of increased federal antipolygamy pressures after the Civil War.
Such actions ultimately led to the disestablishment of the church as an
organization, and to the imprisonment or exile of church leaders until
polygamy was officially abandoned by the Manifesto of 1890. It is not
so surprising that the Saints exhibited stronger antiblack attitudes and a
greater degree of "prejudice" against nonwhites in general during these
years of social, economic, and political adversity.

NOTES

1. For two accounts dealing with the conflicting socioeconomic interpretations of Joseph Smith and his family see Richard Lloyd Anderson,
"The Reliability of the Early History of Lucy and Joseph Smith," *Dialogue*
4 (Summer 1969): 13-28. Also see his article "Joseph Smith's New York
Reputation Reappraised," *B.Y.U. Studies* 10 (Spring 1970): 283-314.

2. S. George Ellsworth, "A History of Mormon Missions in the United
States and Canada, 1830-1860" (Ph.D. diss., University of California, 1951).

3. Laurence M. Yorgason, "Preview on a Study of the Social and Geographic Origins of Early Mormon Converts, 1830-1845," *B.Y.U. Studies*
10 (Spring 1970): 279-82. Yorgason based the conclusions of this article
on the results of extensive research contained in his "Some Demographic
Aspects of One Hundred Early Mormon Converts, 1830-1837" (M.S. thesis,
Brigham Young University, 1974).

4. Yorgason, "Preview on a Study of the Social and Geographic Origins
of Early Mormon Converts, 1830-1845," p. 282. It is interesting to note
that Yorgason in his thesis, "Some Demographic Aspects," p. 86, has concluded that Mormon leaders "were neither more educated, wealthy, nor

influential in their communities than other converts."

5. Mario S. De Pillis, "The Social Sources of Mormonism," *Church History* 37 (May 1968), p. 77. According to De Pillis, p. 72, Mormonism appealed to the same middle and lower classes i.e., "smaller non-commercial farmers who had suffered dislocation and discontent" that had joined the Hicksite sect of Quakerism that had arisen by 1827.

6. Ibid., p. 76.

7. Ibid., pp. 78-9.

8. P. A. M. Taylor, *Expectations Westward* (Ithaca, New York, 1966); and William Mulder, *Homeward to Zion* (Minneapolis, 1957).

9. Taylor, *Expectations Westward,* p. 33. Also, in contrast to the agrarian thrust of Mormon missionary activities in the United States, the Saints scored their greatest British successes in urban areas.

10. Ibid., p. 158. In his study, Taylor, p. 151, attempts to graph the decline in the "middle-class element" that emigrated from Great Britain to the United States during these later years.

YEARS	PERCENTAGE IN "MIDDLE CLASS"
1840-49	22.20
1850-59	12.96
1860-69	8.39

11. Mulder, *Homeward to Zion,* p. 110.

12. Ibid., p. 111.

13. Ibid., p. 102.

14. Ibid., p. 113. See also pp. 102-3, 114-5, 295, 297.

15. Ibid., p. 121.

16. However, there was one notable exception to this shifting European focus of Mormon missionary activity during this period. The Saints, as noted in Chapter 8, became increasingly involved in the American South after 1865.

17. Gordon W. Allport, *The Nature of Prejudice* (Cambridge, Massachusetts, 1954), p. 80.

18. Harold M. Hodges, Jr., *Social Stratification: Class in America* (Cambridge, Massachusetts, 1964), p. 211; Allport, *Nature of Prejudice,* p. 80. According to both of these men such individuals were also more likely to "have completed less formal schooling.

19. Seymour Martin Lipset and Reinhard Bendix, *Social Mobility in Industrial Society* (Berkeley and Los Angeles, 1962), p. 257.

20. Ibid., p. 71. At the same time, however, Lipset and Bendix are careful to qualify this observation.

Mormon Slaveholders, Black Slaves, Free Blacks, and Census Information on Utah's Black Population, 1830-1980

Although their numbers were small, Mormon slaveholders as well as black slaves and free blacks associated with the Mormon movement had an influence far beyond their numbers in the formation of Mormon racial attitudes and practices. A number of southern slaveholders were attracted to Mormonism despite its northern orientation. The list of Mormon slaveholders included a number of influential Latter-day Saints, namely, David Whitmer, one of the "Three Witnesses" to the *Book of Mormon*; Apostle Charles C. Rich; and William H. Hooper, Utah's Territorial Delegate to Congress (see table 6). Within Nauvoo, the number of blacks living in this Mormon community was relatively small, only about 20 out of a total population of 20,000 (see table 7). But at the same time at least four and possibly as many as eleven of these twenty blacks were associated in one way or another with Joseph Smith (see table 8).

Contact and interaction between the Mormons and black people increased after the Latter-day Saint migration to the Great Basin. Between 110 and 119 slaves and free blacks were brought or migrated to the Great Basin during the first four years of the Mormon settlement in this region. This black migration to Utah, most evident from 1847 to 1850, "peaked" in 1848. The arrival in October 1848 of the Mississippi Company with 34 blacks and the Willard Richards' Division containing 24 blacks represented the largest single influx of blacks into the territory (see table 9). These 110 to 119 blacks were considerably more than the 50 blacks cited by the official United States Census as living in Utah in 1850 (compare table 9 with table

10). It is obvious that the Utah Saints gave the census takers a "low count," for the reasons discussed in Chapter 4. The Saints apparently tried to obscure the continued presence of black slaves in the territory by reporting that the 26 black slaves counted for the 1850 census were "on their way to California" (see table 11). These blacks were part of the Amasa Lyman-Charles C. Rich expedition, which arrived in and colonized San Bernardino in 1851. These blacks belonged to ten Mormon masters, including Apostle Charles C. Rich, and ranged in age from two to fifty years old (see tables 12 and 13). Meanwhile, the blacks who remained behind continued to interact with the Great Basin Mormons and influence the development of Mormon attitudes and practices adversely affecting them, including the legalization of black slavery in Utah in 1852. In addition, Brigham Young, like Joseph Smith, was "closely associated" with a number of these blacks (see table 14). Despite negative Mormon practices and attitudes, Utah's black population continued to grow. The most dramatic periods of growth were the late nineteenth-early twentieth centuries and after World War II (see table 15). This growth had a direct impact on the development of Mormon attitudes and the ways in which the Saints reacted to the burgeoning civil rights movement.

TABLE 6

Latter-day Saints Known to be Slaveholders, 1836-1865

Name of L.D.S. Slaveholder	Years Slaves Held	Migrate to Utah	Number of Slaves Held	State of Pre-Mormon Origins
Unnamed So. convert	1836	No	1	—
David Whitmer[1]		No	1	—
John H. Redd	1840	Yes, 1850	5	Tennessee
Arterbery	1843	No	1	Alabama
James Turnbow		No	1	Alabama
James M. Flake	1844-	Yes, 1848	3	Mississippi
Agnes L. Flake[2]	1844-	Yes, 1848	1	Mississippi
William Crosby	1847	Yes, 1848	6	Mississippi
John H. and George Bankhead[3]	1847	Yes, 1848	12	Mississippi
William H. Lay	1847	Yes, 1848	3	Mississippi
John Brown	1840s-	Yes, 1848	2	Mississippi
Joseph L. Robinson	1847	Yes, 1847	1	—
William Mathews	1847	Yes, 1847	1	So. Carolina
Charles C. Rich	1847	Yes, 1847	6	Kentucky
Abraham O. Smoot	1848-	Yes, 1848	2	Kentucky

Sources: Jack Beller, "Negro Slaves in Utah," *Utah Historical Quarterly* 2 (October 1929); Kate B. Carter, *The Story of the Negro Pioneer* (Salt Lake City, 1965); Ronald G. Coleman, "A History of Blacks in Utah, 1825-1910" (Ph.D. diss., University of Utah, 1980).

[1] David Whitmer apparently did not own any black slaves until after 1838 and his departure from the Latter-day Saint movement.

[2] Agnes L. Flake was the wife of James L. Flake.

[3] Because of the limited information available, it is difficult to "separate" and determine precisely how many slaves were held by each of these two brothers.

TABLE 6—*Continued*

Name of L.D.S. Slaveholder	Years Slaves Held	Migrate to Utah	Number of Slaves Held	State of Pre-Mormon Origins
Robert M. Smith	1848-	Yes, 1848	10	South[4]
Elizabeth C. Crosby	1848	Yes, 1848	3	Mississippi
Francis McKnown	1848	Yes, 1848	2	Mississippi
Thomas B. Graham	1848	Yes, 1848	3	So. Carolina
William H. Hooper[5]	1859	Yes	4	Maryland
Mary Lee Bland Ewell	1849-	Yes, 1849	2	Kentucky
Reuben Perkins	1849-	Yes, 1849	10	No. Carolina
Williams Washington Camp	1850-	Yes, 1850	3[6]	Tennessee
John H. and Elizabeth Redd[7]	1850-	Yes, 1850	1-2	Tennessee
Thomas L. Greer	1855	Yes[8]	2	——
Henry Jolley	1842-	Yes, 1850	1	No. Carolina
William Taylor Dennis	1836-65	Yes, 1855	4	Tennessee

[4] Robert M. Smith's exact southern pre-Mormon origins are difficult to determine. The mystery concerning Smith's background is further complicated by the fact that in some sources he is referred to as "William Smith." See Carter, p. 3; Beller, p. 124.

[5] Three of Hooper's four slaves were held prior to joining the Church. The fourth was acquired in 1859.

[6] This is an approximate total compiled from Carter, p. 41.

[7] There is some confusion as to whether John or his wife Elizabeth owned this black slave or slaves. See Carter, pp. 25-27. This confusion is further complicated by Ronald G. Coleman's contention, p. 37, that Marinda was not owned by John H. Redd but by a "James Reed."

[8] Greer was given two slaves by his father-in-law, Williams Washington Camp, in 1855. The following year, when Greer and his wife were sent on a Mormon mission to Texas, they took their black slaves with them. They remained there for the next 20 years.

TABLE 7

Names of Blacks (Slave and Free) Living in Nauvoo, Illinois, during the Mormon Sojourn, 1839-1846

Name of Black	Years in Nauvoo	Migrate West?
Elijah Abel	1839-1842	Yes, 1853
Jane Manning James	1843-1846	Yes, 1847
Sylvester James	1843-1846	Yes, 1847
Isaac James	1843-1846	Yes, 1847
Eliza Manning	1843-1846	No
Isaac Lewis Manning	1843-1846	No
Lucinda Manning	1843-1846	No
Peter Manning	1843-1846	No
Angeline Manning	1843-1846	No
Anthony Stebbings	1843-1846	No
Sarah Ann Stebbings	1843-1846	No
"Black Jack"	1840s	No
Liz Flake Rowan	1840s	Yes, 1848
Green Flake	1840s	Yes, 1847
Chism	1843	No
Venus Redd	1840-1846	Yes, 1850
Luke Redd	1840-1846	Yes, 1850
Chaney Redd	1840-1846	Yes, 1850
Amy Redd	1840-1846	Yes, 1850
Marinda Redd	1840-1846	Yes, 1850
Sammy Jolley	1842-1846	Yes, 1850
William McCary	1846	No

TABLE 8

Data on Blacks "Closely Associated" with Joseph Smith

Name of Black	Relationship to Joseph Smith	Years
Elijah Abel	"Intimately acquainted" and "lived in Smith's home"	1839-44
Jane Manning James	"Servant" of and lived in home of Smith	e.1840s-44
Isaac Manning	"Servant" or cook for Smith's family	e.1840s-44
Green Flake	"Lived with" Smith family for a number of years	1840s

TABLE 9

Number of Blacks (Slave and Free) Who Apparently Migrated
to Utah during the Period 1847-1850

Year	Slave	Free	Total Blacks
1847	11	17	28
1848	59-68[1]	9	68-77[1]
1849	1	0	1
1850	7	6	13
Totals by			
1850	78-87	32	110-119[2]

Source: Jack Beller, "Negro Slaves in Utah," *Utah Historical Quarterly* 2 (October 1929): 123-26; Kate B. Carter, *The Story of the Negro Pioneer* (Salt Lake City, 1965); Ronald G. Coleman, Utah's Black Pioneers, 1847-1869," *UMOJA: A Scholarly Journal of Black Studies,* n.s., 11 (Summer 1978); and "A History of Blacks in Utah, 1825-1910" (Ph.D. diss., University of Utah, 1980).

[1] There is some confusion as to the precise number of blacks (both slave and free) migrating to Utah in 1848. While the names and status of the 34 blacks migrating with the Mississippi Company (which arrived in Utah in October 1848) are relatively easy to determine, the identity and status of the 24 blacks attached to the third division, which arrived in Utah that same month under the leadership of Willard Richards, are not given in any of the accounts I examined. However, Carter, pp. 18-19, 27-30, and 32-35 outlines the stories of a number of blacks who migrated during 1848 and might or might not have been part of the Willard Richards contingent. Hence the imprecise figures.

[2] The totals for 1850 have been challenged by Ronald G. Coleman, who maintains that 110-119 is too high a figure. He suggests that 75 is a more realistic total, although he fails to present concrete evidence as to how he arrives at this lower figure. See Coleman's "Utah's Black Pioneers," pp. 98, 107, fn. 9 and Coleman's "A History of Blacks in Utah," p. 69, fn. 56. Compare the figures of Coleman and myself with the much lower figures contained in the United States Census totals for 1850 as contained in table 10. These conflicting figures underscore the need for a careful, precise computation of Utah's black population during the pioneer period.

TABLE 10

Number of Blacks (Slave and Free) in Utah according to Official
United States Census Figures, 1850 and 1860

Year	Slave	Free	Total
1850	26[1]	24	50
1860	29	30	59

Source: As indicated in the following: U.S., Bureau of the Census,
The Seventh Census of the United States: 1850 (Washington,
D.C., 1853), p. 993. U.S., Bureau of the Census, *Eighth Census
of the United States Taken in the Year 1860* (Washington, D.C.,
1860-66), p. 135.

[1] In the *Statistical View of the U.S. and Compendium of the Seventh
Census 1850,* p. 31, the 26 slaves were "reported on their way to California." See table 11.

TABLE 11

Names of the Twenty-six Black Slaves "En Route to California"
according to 1850 United States Census Schedules

1. Harriett	10. Ellen	18. Henderson
2. Hark	11. Biddy	19. Mary
3. Charly	12. Hannah	20. Nelson
4. Jane	13. Tennessee	21. Oscar
5. Nelson	14. Fluleman	22. Grief
6. Lawrence	15. George	23. Toby
7. Ann	16. Nancy	24. Vilote
8. Harriett	17. Rose	25. Liz
9. Anna		26. Green

TABLE 12

Names of Black Slaves taken to San Bernardino with the Amasa Lyman and Charles C. Rich Expedition of 1851

Name	Master	Year Arrived in Utah
Hark Lay	William Lay	July 1847
Oscar Crosby	William Crosby	July 1847
6 unnamed black slaves	Charles C. Rich	October 1847
Toby Thomas	Daniel M. Thomas	October 1847
Uncle Phil	William Mathews	1847
Liz Flake Rowan	Agnes L. Flake	October 1848
Grief Crosby	William Crosby	October 1848
2 unnamed black slaves	William McKnown	October 1848
Knelt Lay	William Lay	October 1848
Henderson Lay	William Lay	October 1848
Hannah Smith	Robert M. Smith*	October 1848
Lawrence Smith	Robert M. Smith	October 1848
8 other black slaves	Robert M. Smith	October 1848

Source: The names of slaves and their masters compiled from information in Jack Beller, "Negro Slaves in Utah," *Utah Historical Quarterly* 2 (October 1929); and Kate B. Carter, *The Story of the Negro Pioneer* (Salt Lake City, 1965).

*According to both Beller and Carter, a "William Smith" is listed as a slaveholder, with slaves "Hannah" and "Lawrence." But from a careful examination of these materials it appears that "William" and "Robert M. Smith" were one and the same person.

TABLE 13

Names and Ages of Blacks in San Bernardino, according to the 1852 Census of Los Angeles County

Name of Black	Age
Hannah[1]	30
Toby[1]	50
Lawrence[1]	10
Cato	9
Toby	2
Ann	16
Ellen	18
Ann	6
Biddy	35
Ann	10
Harriet	8
Grief[1]	35
Harriet	30
Tennessee	18
Dick	25
Hark[1]	27
Phillip	26
one child	2
one child	3
one child	6

Source: Census information reprinted in Kate B. Carter, *The Story of the Negro Pioneer* (Salt Lake City, p. 33. Note: No last names are given or any indication of their previous status (slave or free) prior to their arrival in California.

[1] Those blacks whose names correspond to the names on table 12.

TABLE 14

Data on Blacks "Closely Associated" with Brigham Young

Name of Black	Relationship to Brigham Young	Years
Jane Manning James	Lived "in the family of Brigham Young"	1846
Sylvester James	Lived "in the family of Brigham Young"	1846
Isaac James	Coachman for Young	After 1847
Hark Lay	"Associated" with Brigham Young	After 1847
Isaac Graham	Coachman for Young	1848
Thomas Colbourn	Employed by Young	

TABLE 15

Number of Blacks in Utah according to United States Census Figures 1870-1980

Year	Total Black Population	Percentage of Blacks in Total Utah Population
1870	118	0.1
1880	232	0.2
1890	588	0.3
1900	672	0.2
1910	1,144	0.3
1920	1,446	0.3
1930	1,108	0.2
1940	1,235	0.2
1950	2,729	0.3
1960	4,148	0.5
1970	6,617	0.6
1980	7,870	0.5

Official LDS Church Statements on Blacks and the Priesthood and Civil Rights

Although the Latter-day Saint practice of denying blacks their priesthood was long-standing, dating from the mid-1840s, one hundred years passed before Mormon church leaders issued any "official" statement or declaration upholding and justifying this practice. Finally, in 1949, in response to the controversy that black priesthood denial generated, the church issued its first "official" statement affirming this practice (see document 1). Despite the fact that church spokesmen continued to affirm black priesthood denial throughout the 1950s and early 1960s, Mormon leaders in 1963 felt compelled to give tacit approval to the concept of civil rights through an "official statement" (see document 2). In 1969, following a decade of unrest and turbulence during which both the Mormon commitment to civil rights and the church practice of black priesthood denial came under increased criticism, church leaders issued a third "official" document. This document, like the 1949 statement, upheld black priesthood denial, but it also expressed continuing Mormon support for black civil rights, in the spirit of the 1963 statement (see document 3). Finally, nine years later, the controversy surrounding the status of blacks within Mormonism was settled with the abandonment of black priesthood denial in 1978. The "official" 1978 statement affirming this development assured black Mormons the same position of equality enjoyed by all other Mormon males over the age of twelve (see document 4).

DOCUMENT 1

LDS CHURCH FIRST PRESIDENCY STATEMENT
ON THE QUESTION OF BLACKS
WITHIN THE CHURCH, AUGUST 17, 1949

The attitude of the Church with reference to Negroes remains as it has always stood. It is not a matter of the declaration of a policy but of direct commandment from the Lord, on which is founded the doctrine of the Church from the days of its organization, to the effect that Negroes may become members of the Church but that they are not entitled to the priesthood at the present time. The prophets of the Lord have made several statements as to the operation of the principle. President Brigham Young said: "Why are so many of the inhabitants of the earth cursed with a skin of blackness? It comes in consequence of their fathers rejecting the power of the holy priesthood, and the law of God. They will go down to death. And when all the rest of the children have received their blessings in the holy priesthood, then that curse will be removed from the seed of Cain, and they will then come up and possess the priesthood, and receive all the blessings which we are now entitled to."

President Wilford Woodruff made the following statement: "The day will come when all that race will be redeemed and possess all the blessings which we now have."

The position of the Church regarding the Negro may be understood when another doctrine of the Church is kept in mind, namely, that the conduct of spirits in the premortal existence has some determining effect upon the conditions and circumstances under which these spirits take on mortality and that while the details of this principle have not been made known, the mortality is a privilege that is given to those who maintain their first estate; and that the worth of the privilege is so great that spirits are willing to come to earth and take on bodies no matter what the handicap may be as to the kind of bodies they are to secure; and that among the handicaps, failure of the right to enjoy in mortality the blessings of the priesthood is a handicap which spirits are willing to assume in order that they might come to earth. Under this principle there is no injustice whatsoever involved in this deprivation as to the holding of the priesthood by the Negroes.

DOCUMENT 2

POSITION OF THE LDS CHURCH ON
CIVIL RIGHTS, OCTOBER 6, 1963

During recent months, both in Salt Lake City and across the nation, considerable interest has been expressed in the position of The Church of Jesus Christ of Latter-day Saints on the matter of civil rights. We would like it to be known that there is in this Church no doctrine, belief, or practice that is intended to deny the enjoyment of full civil rights by any person regardless of race, color, or creed.

We say again, as we have said many times before, that we believe that all men are the children of the same God, and that it is a moral evil for any person or group of persons to deny any human being the right to gainful employment, to full educational opportunity, and to every privilege of citizenship, just as it is a moral evil to deny him the right to worship according to the dictates of his own conscience.

We have consistently and persistently upheld the Constitution of the United States, and as far as we are concerned, this means upholding the constitutional right of every citizen of the United States. We call upon all men, everywhere, both within and outside the Church, to commit themselves to the establishment of full civil equality for all of God's children. Anything less defeats our high ideals of the brotherhood of man.

DOCUMENT 3

LDS CHURCH FIRST PRESIDENCY STATEMENT
ON POSITION OF BLACKS WITHIN THE
CHURCH AND CIVIL RIGHTS, DECEMBER 15, 1969

Dear Brethren:

In view of confusion that has arisen, it was decided at a meeting of the First Presidency and the Quorum of the Twelve to restate the position of the Church with regard to the Negro both in society and in the Church.

First, may we say that we know something of the sufferings of those who are discriminated against in a denial of their civil rights and Constitutional privileges. Our early history as a church is a tragic story of persecution and oppression. Our people repeatedly were denied the protection of the law. They were driven and plundered, robbed and murdered by mobs, who in many instances were aided and abetted by those sworn to uphold the law. We as a people have experienced the bitter fruits of civil discrimination and mob violence.

We believe that the Constitution of the United States was divinely inspired, that it was produced by "wise men" whom God raised up for this "very purpose," and that the principles embodied in the Constitution are so fundamental and important that, if possible, they should be extended "for the rights and protection" of all mankind.

In revelations received by the first prophet of the Church in this dispensation, Joseph Smith (1805-1844), the Lord made it clear that it is "not right that any man should be in bondage one to another." These words were spoken prior to the Civil War. From these and other revelations have sprung the Church's deep and historic concern with man's free agency and our commitment to the sacred principles of the Constitution.

It follows, therefore, that we believe the Negro, as well as those of other races, should have his full Constitutional privileges as a member of society, and we hope that members of the Church everywhere will do their part as citizens to see that these rights are held inviolate. Each citizen must have equal opportunities and protection under the law with reference to civil rights.

However, matters of faith, conscience, and theology are not within the purview of the civil law. The first amendment to the Constitution specifically provides that "Congress shall make no law respecting an establishment of religion, or prohibiting the free exercise thereof."

The position of The Church of Jesus Christ of Latter-day Saints affecting those of the Negro race who choose to join the Church falls wholly within the category of religion. It has no bearing upon matters of civil rights. In no case or degree does it deny to the Negro his full privileges as a citizen of the nation.

This position has no relevancy whatever to those who do not wish to join the Church. Those individuals, we suppose, do not believe in the divine origin and nature of the Church, nor that we have the priesthood of God. Therefore, if they feel we have no priesthood, they should have no concern with any aspect of our theology on priesthood so long as that theology does not deny any man his Constitutional privileges.

A word of explanation concerning the position of the Church:

The Church of Jesus Christ of Latter-day Saints owes its origin, its existence, and its hope for the future to the principles of continuous revelation. "We believe all that God has revealed, all that He does now reveal, and we believe that He will yet reveal many great and important things pertaining to the Kingdom of God."

From the beginning of this dispensation, Joseph Smith and all succeeding presidents of the Church have taught that Negroes, while spirit children of a common Father, and the progeny of our earthly parents Adam and Eve, were not yet to receive the priesthood, for reasons which we believe are known to God, but which He has not made fully known to man.

Our living prophet, President David O. McKay, has said, "The seeming discrimination by the Church toward the Negro is not something which originated with man; but goes back into the beginning with God . . . ."

"Revelation assures us that this plan antedates man's mortal existence, extending back to man's pre-existent state."

President McKay has also said, "Sometime in God's eternal plan, the Negro will be given the right to hold the priesthood."

Until God reveals His will in this matter, to him whom we sustain as a prophet, we are bound by that same will. Priesthood, when it is conferred on any man, comes as a blessing from God, not of men.

We feel nothing but love, compassion, and the deepest appreciation for the rich talents, endowments, and the earnest strivings of our Negro brothers and sisters. We are eager to share with men of all races the blessings of the Gospel. We have no racially-segregated congregations.

Were we the leaders of an enterprise created by ourselves and operated only according to our own earthly wisdom, it would be a simple thing to act according to popular will. But we believe that this work is directed by God and that the conferring of the priesthood must await His revelation. To do otherwise would be to deny the very premise on which the Church is established.

We recognize that those who do not accept the principle of modern revelation may oppose our point of view. We repeat that such would not wish for membership in the Church, and therefore the question of priesthood should hold no interest for them. Without prejudice they should grant us the privilege afforded under the Constitution to exercise our chosen form of religion just as we must grant all others a similar privilege. They must recognize that the question of bestowing or withholding priesthood in the Church is a matter of religion and not a matter of Constitutional right.

We extend the hand of friendship to men everywhere and the hand of fellowship to all who wish to join the Church and partake of the many rewarding opportunities to be found therein.

We join with those throughout the world who pray that all of the blessings of the Gospel of Jesus Christ may in the due time of the Lord become available to men of faith everywhere. Until that time comes we must trust in God, in His wisdom and in His tender mercy.

Meanwhile we must strive harder to emulate His Son, the Lord Jesus Christ, whose new commandment it was that we should love one another. In developing that love and concern for one another, while awaiting revelations yet to come, let us hope that with respect to these religious differences, we may gain reinforcement for understanding and appreciation for such differences. They challenge our common similarities, as children of one Father, to enlarge the outreachings of our divine souls.

> Faithfully your brethren,
> THE FIRST PRESIDENCY
> By Hugh B. Brown
> N. Eldon Tanner

DOCUMENT 4

LDS CHURCH FIRST PRESIDENCY STATEMENT AFFIRMING THE RIGHT OF THE PRIESTHOOD TO BLACK MORMON MALES, JUNE 8, 1978

The First Presidency of The Church of Jesus Christ of Latter-day Saints today released the following statement:

As we have witnessed the expansion of the work of the Lord over the earth, we have been grateful that people of many nations have responded to the message of the restored gospel, and have joined the church in ever-increasing numbers. This, in turn, has inspired us with a desire to extend to every worthy member of the church all of the privileges and blessings which the gospel affords.

Aware of the promises made by the prophets and presidents of the church who have preceded us that at some time, in God's eternal plan, all of our brethren who are worthy may receive the priesthood, and witnessing the faithfulness of those from whom the priesthood has been withheld, we have pleaded long and earnestly in behalf of these, our faithful brethren, spending many hours in the upper room of the Temple supplicating the Lord for divine guidance.

He has heard our prayers, and by revelation has confirmed that the long-promised day has come when every faithful, worthy man in the church may receive the holy priesthood, with power to exercise its divine authority, and enjoy with his loved ones every blessing that flows therefrom, including the blessings of the temple. Accordingly, all worthy male members of the church may be ordained to the priesthood without regard for race or color. Priesthood leaders are instructed to follow the policy of carefully interviewing all candidates for ordination to either the Aaronic or Melchizedek Priesthood to insure that they meet the established standards for worthiness.

We declare with soberness that the Lord has now made known his will for the blessing of all his children throughout the earth who will hearken to the voice of his authorized servants, and prepare themselves to receive every blessing of the gospel.

Sincerely yours,

Spencer W. Kimball
N. Eldon Tanner
Marion G. Romney

Bibliographic Essay

This essay is selective rather than exhaustive; it calls attention only to those works that were the most useful in this study.

GENERAL SECONDARY WORKS ON MORMONISM

In order to understand the complete Mormon implications of Latter-day Saint attitudes toward slavery, race, and black people, a number of works concerned with the broad sweep as well as particular facets of Mormon history must be examined. The best one-volume overview of the Saints is Leonard J. Arrington and Davis Bitton, *The Mormon Experience* (New York: Alfred A. Knopf, 1979). Also useful are Klaus J. Hansen, *Mormonism and the American Experience* (Chicago: University of Chicago Press, 1981); James B. Allen and Glen Leonard, *The Story of the Latter-day Saints* (Salt Lake City: Deseret Book Co., 1976); Mark P. Leone, *Roots of Modern Mormonism* (Cambridge: Harvard University Press, 1979); and Thomas F. O'Dea, *The Mormons* (Chicago: University of Chicago Press, 1957). A longer general history of the Saints is Brigham H. Roberts, *Comprehensive History of the Church of Jesus Christ of Latter-day Saints,* 6 vols. (Salt Lake City: The Church of Jesus Christ of Latter-day Saints, 1930). This work, despite its narrow, partisan, pro-Mormon thrust, does provide detailed descriptions of essential Mormon trends. Robert's work should be supplemented with a number of other studies concerned with specific aspects of Mormonism. These include: Leonard J. Arrington, *Great Basin Kingdom* (Cambridge: Harvard University Press, 1958); Kimball Young, *Isn't One Wife Enough?*

(New York: Henry Holt, 1954); Klaus J. Hansen, *Quest for Empire* (East
Lansing: Michigan State University Press, 1967); P. A. M. Taylor, *Expecta-
tions Westward* (Edinburgh & London: Oliver & Boyd, 1965); William Mul-
der, *Homeward to Zion* (Minneapolis: University of Minn. Press, 1957);
Robert Bruce Flanders, *Nauvoo: Kingdom on the Mississippi* (Urbana:
University of Ill. Press, 1965); Norman F. Furniss, *The Mormon Conflict,
1850-1859* (New Haven: Yale University Press, 1960); and Gustive O.
Larson, *The Americanization of Utah for Statehood* (San Marino, Calif.:
Huntington Library, 1971). A work which considers the expanding geo-
graphic boundaries of Mormonism during the twentieth century is Spencer
J. Palmer, *The Expanding Church* (Salt Lake City: Deseret Book, 1978).
Two biographies that examine Joseph Smith from somewhat different
vantage points are Fawn M. Brodie, *No Man Knows My History* (New
York: Alfred A. Knopf, 1944); and Donna Hill, *Joseph Smith: The First
Mormon* (Garden City, N.Y.: Doubleday, 1977). Less satisfactory on
Brigham Young are Stanley Hirshson, *Lion of the Lord* (New York:
Alfred A. Knopf, 1970) and Eugene England, *Brother Brigham* (Salt
Lake City: Bookcraft, 1980). Also of interest are two recent biographies,
one on the third president of the Mormon Church, John Taylor, by
Samuel W. Taylor, *The Kingdom or Nothing* (New York: Macmillan, 1977);
and the other on the current Mormon president by Edward L. Kimball and
Andrew E. Kimball, *Spencer W. Kimball* (Salt Lake City: Deseret Book
Co., 1977).

SECONDARY WORKS ON THE INTERACTION BETWEEN BLACKS AND MORMONS AND THE DEVELOPMENT OF MORMON PRACTICES AND ATTITUDES

As noted in the epilogue to this study, several writers have examined
Mormon-black interaction from varied perspectives. The most scholarly
attempt to trace the development of black priesthood denial is Lester E.
Bush, Jr., "Mormonism's Negro Doctrine: An Historical Overview," *Dialogue*
8 (Spring 1973): 11-68. This study is an essential starting point in any effort to deal with Mormon-black relations. See also the comments on Bush's
essay by Gordon C. Thomasson, Hugh Nibley, and Eugene England in the
same issue of *Dialogue*. A second study worthy of note is Stephen G. Taggart, *Mormonism's Negro Policy: Social and Historical Origins* (Salt Lake
City: University of Utah Press, 1970), which argues that black priesthood
denial originated with Joseph Smith during the 1830s as a result of Mormon difficulties in Missouri. Taggart's "Missouri Thesis," however, has
been brought into serious question by Lester Bush in his "A Commentary

on Stephen G. Taggart's *Mormonism's Negro Policy: Social and Historical Origins," Dialogue* 4 (Winter 1969). This commentary actually appeared in late 1970, several months after the publication of Taggart's book. Due to a delay in the publication schedule of *Dialogue,* it appeared with the 1969 date. Also questioning Taggart's "Missouri Thesis" and ascribing the origins of black priesthood denial to the post-Joseph Smith period is Newell G. Bringhurst, "An Ambiguous Decision: The Implementation of Mormon Priesthood Denial for the Black Man—A Re-examination," *Utah Historical Quarterly* 46 (Winter 1978): 45-64. Ronald K. Esplin in "Brigham Young and Priesthood Denial to the Blacks: An Alternative View," *B.Y.U. Studies* 19 (Spring 1979): 394-402, takes issue with this "post-Joseph Smith hypothesis."

A number of writers have examined Mormon-black relations by focusing on black slavery as practiced by the Saints and others in regions where the Saints lived. See James B. Christenson, "Negro Slavery in Utah," *Phylon Quarterly* 13 (October 1957): 298-305; Jan B. Shipps, "Second-Class Saints," *Colorado Quarterly* 11 (1962-63): 183-90; Dennis L. Lythgoe, "Negro Slavery in Utah," *Utah Historical Quarterly* 39 (Winter 1971): 40-54, and "Negro Slavery and Mormon Doctrine," *Western Humanities Review* 21 (1957): 327-38; Fawn M. Brodie, "Can We Manipulate the Past?" *First Annual American West Lecture,* University of Utah, October 3, 1970, (Salt Lake City: University of Utah Press, 1970). For a somewhat different view, see Newell G. Bringhurst, "The Mormons and Black Slavery—A Closer Look," *Pacific Historical Review* (November 1981). An unpublished work worthy of consideration is Naomi Felicia Woodbury, "A Legacy of Intolerance: Nineteenth Century Propaganda and the Mormon Church Today" (M.A. thesis, University of California, Los Angeles, 1966).

The relationship of Utah blacks to the Mormons as they developed their own black community in the Great Basin has been examined by several writers. Henry J. Wolfinger, "A Test of Faith: Jane Elizabeth James and the Origins of the Utah Black Community," in Clark S. Knowton, ed., *Social Accommodation in Utah* (American West Occasional Papers, Salt Lake City, Utah, 1975), provides an excellent introduction to the subject of blacks in the Great Basin and their interaction with the Mormon majority. Ronald G. Coleman has dealt extensively with this same subject in recent years. See his "Blacks in Utah History: An Unknown Legacy," in *The Peoples of Utah* (Salt Lake City: Utah State Historical Society, 1976), ed. Helen Z. Papanikolas; his "Utah's Black Pioneers: 1847-1869," *UMOJA: A Scholarly Journal of Black Studies,* N.S., 11 (Summer 1978): 95-110; and his "The Buffalo Soldiers: Guardians of the Uintah Frontier, 1886-1901," *Utah Historical Quarterly* 47 (Fall 1979): 421-39. Also see his "A History of Blacks in Utah, 1825-1910" (Ph.D. diss., University of Utah, 1980). Michael J.

Clark, like Coleman, has examined the experience of black soldiers along
the Utah-Mormon frontier in his "Improbable Ambassadors: Black Soldiers
at Fort Dougals, 1896-99," *Utah Historical Quarterly* 46 (Summer 1978):
282-301. Several scholars have focused on individual Utah-based blacks in
terms of their interactions with the Mormon Church. See William B. Hartley, "Samuel D. Chambers," *The New Era* (June 1974): 46-50; Linda King
Newell and Valeen Tippetts Avery, "Jane Manning James: Black Saint,
1847 Pioneer," *The Ensign* (August 1979): 26-29; and Newell G. Bringhurst, "Elijah Abel and the Changing Status of Blacks Within Mormonism,"
Dialogue 12 (Summer 1979): 22-36. Also see Kate B. Carter, *The Story of
the Negro Pioneer* (Salt Lake City: Daughters of the Utah Pioneers, 1965),
which despite its less than convincing romanticized account of individual
Utah blacks does contain a great deal of useful statistical and biographical
information. Finally, Joseph Freeman, *In the Lords Due Time* (Salt Lake
City: Bookcraft, 1979) is the vivid account of the "first" black Mormon
to receive the priesthood following the 1978 announcement permitting black
ordination.

A number of writers have also analyzed Mormon-black relations within
the context of the civil rights movement and black protest. For an excellent
analysis that explores the contemporary ambiguities relative to blacks within the church, see Thane Young, "Mixed Messages on the Negro Doctrine:
An Interview with Lester Bush," *Sunstone* 4 (May-June 1979): 8-15. For
two views of Mormon-black relations and the civil rights movement see
Sterling M. McMurrin, "A Note on the 1963 Civil Rights Statement,"
Dialogue 12 (Summer 1979): 60-63; and Margaret J. Maag, "Discrimination
Against the Negro in Utah and Institutional Efforts to Eliminate It" (M.S.
thesis, University of Utah, 1968). Finally Armand L. Mauss has utilized a
sociological-anthropological approach in examining contemporary Mormon-
black relations. See his "Mormonism and Secular Attitudes Toward Negroes,"
Pacific Sociological Review 9 (Fall 1966): 91-99; "Mormonism and the
Negro: Faith, Folklore and Civil Rights," *Dialogue* 4 (Winter 1967): 19-39;
"Moderation in All Things: Political and Social Outlooks of Modern Urban
Mormons," *Dialogue* 7 (Spring 1972): 57-69; and "The Fading of the
Pharaoh's Curse: A Retrospective View of the Portents and Perceptions for
the New Revelation on Priesthood Eligibility," *Dialogue* (forthcoming in late
1981). For two examinations of the international implications of the 1978
repeal of black priesthood denial, particularly in black Africa, see, Spencer
J. Palmer, "Mormons in West Africa: New Terrain for the Sesquicentennial
Church," Annual Religion Faculty Lecture, Brigham Young University,
September 27, 1979, Typescript, Brigham Young University Publications;
and Newell G. Bringhurst, "Mormonism in Black Africa: Changing Attitudes and Practices, 1830-1981," *Sunstone* 6, May-June 1981.

GENERAL WORKS ON RACE AND SLAVERY
IN THE LARGER NON-MORMON ENVIRONMENT
DURING THE NINETEENTH CENTURY

The development of Mormon attitudes toward slavery and black people did not take place in a geographic and social vacuum. The Saints in many ways mirrored and were influenced by the racial practices and attitudes of their non-Mormon environment. Winthrop Jordan, *White Over Black* (Chapel Hill, North Carolina: University of North Carolina Press, 1968); and George M. Fredrickson, *The Black Image in the White Mind* (New York: Harper and Row, 1971), are standard works that explore developing white attitudes towards black people within the United States. Also see Ronald T. Takaki, *Iron Cages* (New York: Alfred A. Knopf, 1979). As a northern-based group moving westward, the Saints were not unique in their racial attitudes and practices. See Leon Litwack, *North of Slavery* (Chicago: University of Chicago Press, 1961); and Eugene Berwanger, *The Frontier Against Slavery* (Urbana, Illinois: University of Illinois Press, 1967). Also see Pierre L. van den Berghe, *Race and Racism* (New York: John Wiley & Sons, 1967); Christine Bolt, *Victorian Attitudes to Race* (Toronto: University of Toronto Press, 1971); David Brion Davis, *The Problem of Slavery in Western Civilization* (Ithaca, New York: Cornell University Press, 1966); Thomas F. Gossett, *Race, The History of an Idea in America* (Dallas, Texas: So. Methodist University Press, 1963); Marvin Harris, *The Rise of Anthropological Theory* (New York: Thomas Y. Crowell Co., 1968); and William Stanton, *The Leopard's Spots: Scientific Attitudes Toward Race in America, 1815-59* (Chicago: University of Chicago Press, 1960).

Mormon attitudes and practices toward slavery and black people can also be better understood by looking at the racial practices and theories of non-Mormon religious groups in both the North and the South. See H. Shelton Smith, *In His Image But . . . :Racism in Southern Religion, 1780-1910* (Durham, North Carolina: Duke University Press, 1972); and Thomas Virgil Peterson, *Ham and Japheth: The Mythic World of Whites in the Ante-bellum South* (Metuchen, New Jersey: Scarecrow Press, 1978). Also see Donald G. Mathews, *Slavery and Methodism* (Princeton, New Jersey: Princeton University Press, 1965); Mason Crum, *The Negro in the Methodist Church* (New York, 1951); Mary B. Putnam, *The Baptists and Slavery 1840-1845* (Ann Arbor, Michigan: George Wahr, 1913); Thomas E. Drake, *Quakers and Slavery in America* (New Haven, Conn.: Yale University Press, 1950); Madeleine Hook Rice, *American Catholic Opinion in the Slavery Controversy* (New York, Columbia University Press, 1944); and Irving Stoddard Kull, "Presbyterian Attitudes Toward Slavery," *Church History* 8 (1938): 101-14.

MORMON SCRIPTURES

Any careful examination of Mormon attitudes toward slavery and black people must start with a thorough reading of Latter-day Saint scriptural writings. The Latter-day Saints accept Joseph Smith's writings— the *Book of Mormon, Doctrine and Covenants,* and the *Pearl of Great Price*—as holy scripture, on a par with the Bible. Although the *Book of Mormon,* published and canonized in 1830, was not directly concerned with blacks, it does provide important insights into initial Latter-day Saint thinking on the questions of race and slavery. The *Doctrine and Covenants,* first published and canonized in 1835 and enlarged in later versions, contains revelations touching on these same issues. More significant is the *Pearl of Great Price,* containing the Books of Moses and Abraham written in the 1830s and early 1840s. Although this work was not published in book form until 1851 and not canonized until 1880, it had a significant impact on emerging Mormon attitudes and practices towards black people. Joseph Smith's *Holy Scriptures,* a revision of the King James version of the Bible written in the early 1830s, was of some influence in the formation of Mormon racial attitudes. This was the case even though this work was never published or canonized by the Church of Jesus Christ of Latter-day Saints.

LATTER-DAY SAINT NEWSPAPERS AND SERIAL PUBLICATIONS

Although the reading of Mormon scriptural writings can provide certain basic insights into the origins of Mormon attitudes toward race and black people, it is necessary to examine various Mormon newspapers and periodicals in order to gain a more complete understanding of the continuing evolution of such attitudes. There were two basic types of periodicals, those "officially" published by the Church itself and less-official newspapers issued by various individuals associated with the Mormons. The "official" periodicals include the *Evening and Morning Star,* published initially at Independence, Missouri, and later at Kirtland, Ohio, from June 1832 through September 1834; the *Latter Day Saints Messenger and Advocate,* published at Kirtland from October 1834 through September 1837; the *Elders Journal,* issued first at Kirtland, Ohio, and then at Far West, Missouri, from October 1837 through August 1838; the *Times and Seasons,* edited at Nauvoo, Illinois, from November 1839 through February 1846; *The Latter-day Saints Millennial Star,* which began publication at Liverpool, England, in May 1840; and the *Deseret News,* issued from Salt Lake City since June 15, 1850. A number of less "official" periodicals also provide valuable information relative to developing Mormon racial attitudes. These include the *Northern Times* (Kirtland, Ohio, 1835-36); *The Wasp* (Nauvoo, Illinois, April 16, 1842-April 19, 1843); *The Nauvoo Neighbor* (May 3, 1843-October 29, 1845); *The Prophet* (New York City, May 18, 1844-May 10, 1845); the *New York Messenger* (July 5, 1845-November 15, 1845); *The Frontier Guardian* (Kanesville, Iowa, February 7, 1849-January 23, 1852); *The Seer* (Washington, D.C., January 1853-August 1854); the *St. Louis Luminary* (November 22, 1854-December 15, 1855); *The Mormon* (New York, February 17, 1855-September 12, 1857); *The Western Standard* (San Francisco, February 23, 1856-November 6, 1857); *The Mountaineer* (Salt Lake City, August 27, 1859-July 6, 1861); the *Daily Telegraph* (Salt Lake City, July 4, 1864-February 8, 1865); and the *Juvenile Instructor* (Salt Lake City, January 1, 1866-). *The Journal of Discourses,* 26 vols. (Liverpool, 1854-1886), containing the sermons of various church leaders, is also an indispensable source for tracing the development of Mormon racial theories and attitudes.

MORMON TRACTS AND PAMPHLETS

A number of church spokesmen also revealed their attitudes toward slavery and black people in various Mormon tracts and pamphlets. Apostle Parley P. Pratt, one of the most prolific of the early church pamphleteers, broached the questions of race and slavery in a number of places. See his *A Voice of Warning and Instruction to All People* (New York: W. Sandford, 1837); *The Millennium and Other Poems* (New York: W. Molineux, 1839); *Late Persecutions of the Church of Latter-day Saints* (New York: J. W. Harrison, 1840); and *Key to the Science of Theology* (Liverpool: F. D. Richards, 1855). Other Mormon pamphleteers were also concerned with race and slavery. See Orson Hyde, *Speech . . . Delivered Before the High Priests Quorum in Nauvoo, April 27, 1845* (Liverpool: James and Woodburn, 1845); John Taylor, *The Government of God* (Liverpool: S. W. Richards, 1852); Orson Spencer, *Patriarchal Order, or Plurality of Wives* (Liverpool: S. W. Richards, 1853); Lorenzo Snow, *The Voice of Joseph* (Liverpool: S. W. Richards, 1852); and Jedediah M. Grant, *Three Letters to the New York Herald* (N.P., 1852).

PUBLISHED DIARIES, JOURNALS, LETTERS, MEMOIRS, AND SOURCE COLLECTIONS

Basic to any research on developing Mormon attitudes toward slavery and black people is Joseph Smith's journal, published as the *History of the Church of Jesus Christ of Latter-day Saints,* ed. B. H. Roberts, 2d ed.,

6 vols. (Salt Lake City: Deseret Book Co., 1978). This is supplemented by a seventh volume, covering the period from Smith's death in 1844 to the Mormon migration west in 1847, taken from the Manuscript History of Brigham Young and other documents 2d ed. (Salt Lake City: Deseret Book Co., 1956).

Among the published journals and diaries that provide additional insights into Mormon thinking on race and slavery are: *A Mormon Chronicle: The Diaries of John D. Lee, 1848-1876,* ed. Robert Glass Cleland and Juanita Brooks, 2 vols. (San Marino, California: Huntington Library, 1955); *Journals of John D. Lee, 1846-47 and 1859,* ed. Charles Kelly (Salt Lake City, 1938); and *On the Mormon Frontier: The Diary of Hosea Stout, 1844-1861,* ed. Juanita Brooks, 2 vols. (Salt Lake City: University of Utah Press, 1964). The following memoirs also contain relevant information: *Autobiography of Pioneer John Brown,* arr. by John Zimmerman Brown (Salt Lake City: Stevens and Wallis, 1941); *Autobiography of Parley Parker Pratt,* ed. Parley P. Pratt, Jr., 6th ed. (Salt Lake City: Deseret Book Co., 1966); and Wilford Woodruff, *Leaves from My Journal* (Salt Lake City: 1882). Also see *Wilford Woodruff: History of His Life and Labors as Recorded in His Daily Journals,* ed. Matthias F. Cowley (Salt Lake City: Deseret News, 1909).

MANUSCRIPTS

The most important collection of Mormon material is located in the Archives of the Church of Jesus Christ of Latter-day Saints in Salt Lake City. Until recently access to the vast number of diaries, journals, letters, and the like contained in this depository was limited. However, within the last 10 or 15 years the church has eased its restrictive policies. Scholars and other individuals involved in serious historical research are allowed to use these materials. Fortunately, I have been able to examine a large number of items in these archives.

These materials provide an essential dimension in tracing the evolution of Mormon racial attitudes. The "Journal History" of the church, a day-by-day compilation of material from diaries, journals, letters, and newspapers, contained a great deal of useful information. I also gained some vital information from the journals, diaries, and correspondence of a number of important churchmen. The papers of Joseph Smith, Brigham Young, John Taylor, Parley and Orson Pratt, George A. Smith, Willard Richards, John M. Bernhisel, and Thomas Kane were particularly useful in providing additional insights into developing Mormon racial attitudes.

CONTEMPORARY ACCOUNTS BY NON-MORMONS

The examination of a number of non-Mormon newspapers and books helped to put my examination of Mormon racial attitudes in an even broader perspective and to bring to light hitherto overlooked information. Such materials must be used with care, however, as non-Mormon observers were sometimes hostile and prone to distort or exaggerate the truth. I used two collections of non-Mormon newspaper clippings. The first was a collection of non-Mormon newspaper clippings in the Latter-day Saints Church Archives. The second was a microfilm copy of "The Mormons and the Far West: Transcripts from American Newspapers," as compiled by Dale L. Morgan. This is located in the Harold B. Lee Library at Brigham Young University, Provo, Utah. I also found a great deal of useful information in the *Congressional Globe,* particularly for the years 1848-50, when the status of Utah and the Mormons was debated within the context of slavery, sectionalism, and the Compromise of 1850. Also of value were *The Valley Tan* and *The Union Vedette,* both non-Mormon newspapers published in Utah during the late 1850s and 1860s. Among the numerous non-Mormon books written about the Saints, the following contained the most useful discussions relative to Mormonism, slavery, and blacks: E. S. Abdy, *Journal of a Residence and Tour in the United States of North America* (London, 1835); William Swartzell, *Mormonism Exposed* (Pittsburgh, Pa.: published by the author, 1840); John Corrill, *Brief History of the Church* (St. Louis: published by the author, 1839); J. W. Gunnison, *The Mormons* (Philadelphia: J. P. Lippincott, 1852); Horace Greeley, *An Overland Journey,* ed. Charles T. Duncan (New York: Alfred A. Knopf, 1964); Richard F. Burton, *The City of the Saints,* ed. Fawn M. Brodie (New York: Alfred A. Knopf, 1963); and Hubert Howe Bancroft, *History of Utah 1840-1886* (San Francisco, 1889).

NON-UTAH OR SCHISMATIC MORMON MATERIALS

Finally, any examination of developing Mormon attitudes toward slavery, race, and blacks has to be considered within the context of Mormonism as a whole. From its beginnings the Church of Latter-day Saints has been plagued with numerous divisions. Such factionalism, which became especially acute after the death of Joseph Smith, had an impact on developing Mormon racial attitudes. Among the schismatic Mormon newspapers examined to gain a better understanding of this development were: *The Latter Day Saint's Messenger and Advocate* (Pittsburgh, October 1844-September 1846), published by Sydney Rigdon; The *Voree Herald* (Voree,

Wisconsin, February 1846-October 1846); *Zion's Revelle* (Voree, November 1846-September 2, 1847); *Gospel Herald* (September 23, 1847-March 9, 1849); and the *Northern Islander* (Saint James, Beaver Island, Michigan, December 12, 1850-June 19, 1856), all published by the followers of James J. Strang. Also *The True Latter Day Saints' Herald* (Cincinnati, Ohio, January 1860-), the official publication of the Reorganized Church of Jesus Christ of Latter Day Saints, also enabled me to place the development of Latter-day Saint racial attitudes in the broader perspective of Mormonism as it existed at that time. Finally, the ways in which the Reorganized Church, the followers of James J. Strang, and those of Charles B. Thompson (another schismatic Mormon leader) dealt with slavery and the status of black people within their respective movements have been examined in two articles that serve as interesting points of comparison with the Utah Mormons. See William D. Russell, "A Priestly Role for a Prophetic Church: The RLDS and Black Americans," *Dialogue* 12 (Summer 1979): 37-49; and Newell G. Bringhurst, "Forgotten Mormon Perspectives: Slavery, Race, and the Black Man as Issues Among Non-Utah Latter-day Saints, 1844-1873," *Michigan History* 61 (Winter 1977): 353-70.

Index

About the Author

NEWELL G. BRINGHURST is Instructor of History and Political
Science at College of the Sequoias, Visalia, California. His articles
have appeared in such journals as *Michigan History, Dialogue:
A Journal of Mormon Thought,* and *Pacific Historical Review.*